LIVING THE BLUES

Canned Heat's Story
Of Music, Drugs, Death, Sex and Survival

by

Fito de la Parra

with

T.W. and Marlane McGarry

*To Roger and Kathleen
Boogie on!
Fito de la Parra*

LIVING THE BLUES
Canned Heat's Story of Music, Drugs, Death, Sex and Survival
by Fito de la Parra
with T.W. and Marlane McGarry

Published by:
CANNED HEAT MUSIC
P.O. Box 52
Nipomo, CA 93444
Website: www.cannedheatmusic.com

ISBN: 0-9676449-0-9
Library of Congress Catalog Card Number: 99-98122

First Edition. All Rights Reserved.

Manufactured in the United States of America
1 2 3 4 5 6 7 8 9 10

Fillmore Posters: Copyright © 2000 BGP

Steve LaVere's Photographs: (Pages 79, 85, 89, 97, 103, 109, 113, 114, 116, 141, 225, 256, 287, 299, 300, 301, 302) Copyright © 1968, 1999 Delta Haze Corporation (unless otherwise noted)

Cover Photography Concept by Walter de Paduwa
Cover Design by Mark Kasserman
Indexing by Gabriele Schwanke
Book and Cover Production by One-On-One Book Production, West Hills, California

TABLE OF CONTENTS

DEDICATION

Dedicated to my son, the loyal fans of Canned Heat,
the young, struggling musicians of the 21st Century,
and with greatful rememberance to
The Owl, The Bear and
The Sunflower

Christians by the grace of God
Gentlemen thanks to our Spanish descent
Noble Lords from our Indian ancestry
Mexican by pride and tradition
And American by destiny

...Thus we are The Mexican-Americans

PREFACE

Afraid to admit you *do* remember the '60s? Or sorry you were born too late to have been there?

If you were part of the kaleidoscopic hippie days, here's everything you hoped your kids would never find out. If you weren't, here's everything your parents will never admit.

This is the true story of Adolfo "Fito" de la Parra, a kid from Mexico City who fought his way into the ranks of top American rock and rollers and barely escaped with his life.

Enter his mind-boggling journey of four decades on the road with boogie-blues music legends Canned Heat, a saga of hit records, world tours, drugs, sex, outrageous behavior and death.

If you were to meet Fito, a man of infinite charm, in a European hotel bar or some backwoods American biker hangout—and that could happen if you got lucky—he might buy you a drink, light up a smoke and tell you how it happened. Through it all, he remembers everything, and the riveting tales flow smoothly. This book is a chance to do that, to sit down with Fito and a beer and listen to how it really was.

It is a story of survival through perseverance as the band reaches the heights of fame in the Woodstock era, and then plunges into decades of death and disaster.

An intense, talented kid, his energy and disciplined determination brought Fito hometown stardom as he grew up in the weirdly wonderful world of Mexico City rock n' roll. But Fito—one of the handful of top-flight rockers with a college degree—dreamed of making it big in the United States, in the homeland of the blues and rock music.

After a brutal apprenticeship in the honky-tonks of Tijuana, he actually smuggles a band of eager Mexican teenagers over the border illegally and delights crowds at a chic Hollywood nightclub, but is caught by the Border Patrol and deported.

Making his way back, his dreams come true when he signs on as drummer for Canned Heat, an L.A. band just about to explode out of Topanga Canyon onto stages all over the world.

v

But Canned Heat, which sold millions of records, was as cursed by bad luck and its own self-destructive manias as it was blessed with musical genius.

Committed from birth to a wildly chaotic lifestyle, Canned Heat took pride in its reputation as the outlaws of the rock world, the hardest living of them all.

Fito's tale is also the story of the band's founders. Alan "Blind Owl" Wilson was one of the strangest characters in the history of rock n' roll, a brilliant nerd, a sensitive genius obsessed with the fate of the earth and obscure recordings by brilliant black bluesmen of the 1930s and 1940s.

Pimply, smelly, forgetful, unfashionably dressed with broken Coke-bottle-lens glasses taped to his nose, he was obsessed with botany and the environment, convinced that man was destroying the earth. He slept outdoors whenever possible, curled up in the weeds outside motels on tour, boiling rice in a pot like a hobo while the others in the band groped groupies in luxury suites.

He was surely one of the few rock stars with a problem getting women. He wrote songs about that, but mostly he wrote about death, about going away ("On The Road Again," "Goin' Up The Country"). Even as the doors of wealth and fame opened to the band members, they spent much of their energy trying to keep him from killing himself.

Bob Hite, the other co-founder and lead singer, was Wilson's polar opposite, a Falstaffian giant of unbounded appetites who everyone called "the Bear." He would eat, drink, screw, play, sing, snort or shoot anything.

He was in the music business so he could party for a living. He enjoyed getting people boogieing so much that he sang for hours, sometimes until most of the audience left out of sheer fatigue and he passed out on the floor.

Several of Canned Heat's best-known songs ("My Crime," "Highway 409") chronicle the band's own arrests or flights from the law. Rights to their hit records are sold for a pittance to provide bail money for the guys after a drug arrest. Reduced to playing in cut-and-shoot backwoods biker bars in the 1980s,

Canned Heat blows one comeback attempt after another, descending into poverty.

The band becomes a front for criminal enterprises from dope smuggling to armed robbery, falling in with remnants of the Manson Family. A Hells Angel runs it for some years, making one of the first rock videos with outlaw motorcyclists writing and producing.

As the years pass, Fito comes into his own, assuming command and clawing his way back to where the band is again putting out CDs regularly, touring Europe several times a year and again playing prestigious venues, both for devoted middle aged fans and younger admirers who have just discovered them.

Canned Heat never disbanded. They play on today.

From Woodstock to the band's resurgence in the '90s, here is the real shit, no punches pulled, not even for me.

As Fito told me the day he was hired, he was "born to play with Canned Heat."

This book tells the story of an unconquerable spirit who never forgot to boogie. Fito will not surrender. Music, Canned Heat, the blues, these are his life.

He *is* "Living the Blues."

Skip Taylor
Manager, Producer, friend

GOIN' UP THE COUNTRY

Fuck Woodstock, leave me alone.

It was the dawn of the Age of Aquarius—literally—and I was damn well not going to get up to greet it. Screw the band's manager trying to pull me out of bed and the cocaine camel he rode in on.

If I weren't too exhausted to think about anything but sleep, I should have been one happy dude. I had made my boyhood dream come true. The little kid from Mexico City who idolized Chuck Berry, Bill Haley and John Lee Hooker, who used to beat out rock rhythms on cookie tins with sticks, had scuffled and pounded his way into a gig as drummer for Canned Heat, one of the legendary bands of rock's golden age. I was a rare non-English foreign recruit in the legion of an American art form that was bursting out with raw, powerful new growth every day. I had rave reviews, roadies, groupies and a rising mountain of dollars and dope.

I was also a 5-foot-7, 135-pound foreigner, who could manage only a little rudimentary English, plunked down in a brotherhood of mad geniuses boogieing down a long dark road to ruin, misery and death.

It was only about 6 A.M., maybe three hours after I went to bed. I was crying from exhaustion, begging.

"Leave me the fuck alone."

With my accent, it came out "dee fawk."

Our manager, Skip Taylor, wrapped his arms around my waist and dug in his heels, trying to break my grip on the bedpost in my room at the Warwick Hotel in New York.

"Please, Skip, please. Don't do this to me. Or fire me. I don't give a shit."

Skip pulled harder.

"Fito, listen to the radio for Christ's sake—there's half a million people out in this fucking field. There are thousands more showing up every hour. We had no idea this thing was going to be this big. There are people dying there. There are babies being born. It's all over every TV station in the country. The band has got to be part of this.

"It's so damn big the cops have closed all the highways. I sent the roadies up with the equipment truck after the gig last night. I've been up all night trying to find a plane or helicopter or something and if you don't get up right now we're screwed."

By now he's bending my thumbs back.

"I don't care what kind of troubles you guys have, you gotta play this one. This is going to be one of the most famous gigs ever."

I'm pulling on my Levis and a T-shirt, my head cracking with fatigue and despair. "Fuck this. I hate it."

Canned Heat's rocket is still rising fast but already there are flames shooting out the sides.

In the previous 34 hours, I played a devastating gig at the Fillmore West in San Francisco where the band's nuclear-pile cast started coming apart, then another at the Fillmore East in New York with a brand new lead guitarist we grabbed from the audience. The guy has an awesome amount of talent, but he has to use it to hide the fact that he has no idea what the rest of us are doing.

Oh, and another gig the same night, in New Jersey or Long Island or someplace on our way in from the airport. I had no idea where we'd been. Or where we were.

I had not been in an actual bed for a long time, until we got to this hotel at 3 A.M. Skip booked on the principle that we could make more money if we worked both sides of the continent and just slept on airplanes, racing in a limo from the airport to the gig and back to the airport.

Up on adrenaline, down on dope. Stewardess, bring me a pillow, slap me awake when you see that other ocean and good night.

Just a little sleep and I could love this life again. Being on the road with a top band, this is the payoff for the years of teen-age gigs in Mexico City rock hangouts and 14-hour nights in border town Mexican honky-tonks. This is the pot of gold I dreamed of as a rock n' roll bracero, following the rhythm and blues harvest, slipping over the border illegally to play with here today-gone tomorrow American bands, living on food my gringa girlfriend stole for me from her college cafeteria.

And it was working. Canned Heat had had three top-selling singles—"Goin' Up The Country" was really big just then—and two of our albums had gone gold, "Boogie With Canned Heat" and "Living The Blues."

So okay, all right. We've got a lot of fans. And I wanted to be a great drummer. And Skip, who's a lot bigger than I am, is half carrying me out the door anyway. I'll play.

Skip has found a couple of small planes for charter at a little country airfield in New Jersey, where our bass guitarist Larry Taylor (no relation to Skip) tries to climb back in the limo, saying he'd quit rather than get in one of those things. Larry doesn't even like flying on big jets. In the back of every traveling rocker's mind are the ghosts of Buddy Holly and Ritchie Valens, who died in a snow covered cornfield in Iowa in 1959 because they had to travel in little planes to keep to their schedule.

After we sort of kidnap Larry and wrestle him aboard one of the planes, we land at another little country airfield at Whitekill, New York, which was as close as you could get to the festival at Max Yasgur's farm. National Guard helicopters were the only way into the festival, and they were full of doctors and nurses, so by 10 A.M. we were stuck at the airfield with other bands and reporters.

I was zonked out on the cement floor of the hangar, trying to get back to sleep with my little gig-bag for a pillow; the little bag I always carry on stage with a clean T-shirt, spare drumsticks, a couple of joints and a towel I wear around my shoulders because the way Canned Heat plays, the drummer's doing sweaty, manual labor.

Skip was giving us a pep talk. "You guys are going to be great today. This is a terrific crowd, you'll see when you get there. This is a Canned Heat event, man. Remember Monterey? Remember Newport? We are the perfect band for these things, these festivals. And this is going to be the biggest."

Under all this optimism, he must be as worried as the rest of us that this is it. That the band is about to simply explode in a puff of smoke.

We went into the Fillmore West in San Francisco two nights earlier on an edgy high. Our "Living the Blues" album had hit Number 14 and we were on the cover of Cashbox. We were headlining over Three Dog Night and Santana.

Sweet victory. We were the same anti-commercial hippies we always were, playing the boogie the way we wanted to play it. Screw the critics. Screw the lightweight pop types. The people are buying it. They're loving it.

Our lead guitarist is Henry Vestine, a long, lean stick of dynamite, tattooed like the outlaw motorcycle gangs he hangs out with. His chest is a billboard. It says "Let the good times roll." Henry is a brilliant guitarist, in many ways a wonderful guy, intelligent, a heavy reader, sort of shy when he's straight.

But he's a Jekyll and Hyde character.

In a business where almost everybody gets a little high on some kind of dope now and then, Henry sets records. He takes anything and everything and he takes a lot of it. This makes him wild or morose or dangerous, no telling what. He sends his head so far away that sometimes his music soars and pounds and howls like he's found a door to whatever they use for hell in some other universe. Too often, he just loses all coordination and skill and goes rambling off to the Doper's Dismal Swamp.

The brilliant Henry got hired into The Mothers of Invention, Frank Zappa's strange but wonderful all-star team. The bad Henry had to quit because Zappa wouldn't tolerate his heavy doping, so now he's with us. Going to excess was not a firing offense in the Canned Heat. It was a given.

Except for Larry Taylor—who is the best bass player in the world. He is a fanatic for order, discipline, predictability, control. He is never satisfied with anything. He's a perfectionist, surrounded by all these party-loving hippies in Canned Heat, where being brilliant was expected, but it took second place to having a good time.

The Bear and Alan Wilson are the founding fathers, the guys who created the band, its core and its star performers. The tormented, introspective Wilson's nickname was "Blind Owl," but we called him Alan. The massive, Falstaffian Bear's real name was Bob Hite but we called him The Bear. They were two white suburban kids who loved black blues and country blues, who collected so many obscure records and listened to them for so many hours that the music just began spilling back out of them like overfilled bathtubs.

Alan gave the band his genius on the harmonica and his strange, questing intellect and encyclopedic knowledge of the blues. The Bear gave the band his own heart, which valued boogie and music and food and love and chaos and sex and drugs and all-night parties. The blues singer's life. There wasn't much room, in Bear's heart or the band's, for good order and discipline. That was driving Larry nuts.

In the dressing room at the Fillmore West, just three nights before Woodstock, Henry was dribbling reds down his throat like peanuts. Before we even got to the stage, he was totally wasted. A little high is one thing but this had the whole band uptight. Me, the new guy, the immigrant with the language problem, I just tried to keep smiling.

Let the old hands, the gringos, deal with this.

By the end of the first set, we had to holler for a roadie to bring Henry a chair. He couldn't even stand. In the "Fried Hockey Boogie" he took off on a solo that rambled on for 25 minutes with no point. In his head he was saying something but whatever it was stayed locked in there with the downers. He forgot what key he was in. It was awful.

The Fillmore crowd thought that was great. To them, dope was a sacrament. They loved Canned Heat because they thought of us as outrageous. They ate it up, the band's mystique of rebelliousness, the idea that we were messing with our perceptions to make brilliant music.

"I love this band," yelled a guy up front. "They play 40-minute songs, and look at this guy, he's so wasted he can't stand up."

Taylor explodes. Out in the audience are some really fine musicians: Paul Butterfield, his guitarist Mike Bloomfield, Harvey Mandel. These are guys we respected and wanted to impress as peers.

"This is terrible," Larry yells at the rest of us on stage. Some of the audience can hear him, but he doesn't care. "I am never playing with that guy again, never. He's out of his mind. We look fucking ridiculous."

We all make stone faces to hide what we're thinking, something I am learning to do often, as we finish the gig. Leaving the ballroom, I even tell a couple of groupies to beat it, get lost. Even me, who likes to take refuge from the band's chaos with a nice, bouncy little girl. I was too upset to fuck. This band was the greatest thing that ever happened to me. We're famous. We're getting rich. And now what? Our bubble pops?

We had a meeting in our hotel, all of us scared for the band's future except Larry. He was still enraged.

"Henry sucks," he said. "If he's in this band, I'm out."

Henry felt guilty, you could tell, but he has this "Yeah, I'm a bad guy, so what?" attitude. He doesn't want to say it was his fault. Henry is the only child of a wealthy family. All his life, he's done anything he wants. So his answer is: "If Larry plays, I don't. Screw this motherfucker. I don't have to put up with him."

Says Skip, the manager, "I don't know who's in the goddam band now and who isn't in the goddam band, but we have another gig at the Fillmore West tomorrow night and I expect every one of you to be on the goddam stage."

That was no solution. Henry walked.

Some other time, that would have been okay. Henry had exceeded the limits of how much you can abuse your fame, your audience, your band. In the decades to come, we got used to it. The brilliant Henry rejoined the band over and over again. Then the spaced-out Henry got fired, or walked out, over and over again.

Except now it meant that when we went on stage at the Fillmore the next night, we were without a lead guitar, which is like trying to get an airplane off the ground without wings.

On stage, we hear someone in the audience say that Mike Bloomfield is there. Immediately, The Bear says, "Let's invite him to play with us. We can jam."

Bob was expert in jam sessions. He knew every song there was and we had such a strong rhythm section that even though Mike had never played with us, he could play around us. Mike was so good The Bear offered him a job after one set. Hell, Mike was as famous as Henry.

"Thanks," he said. "It was great playing with you guys, but I'm burned out on touring. I've been on the road with Butterfield for years now. I have to cool it. I have to get off the road for awhile."

What do we do for a lead guitar in the second set? Somebody says Harvey Mandel is out there too.

"Harvey's really good," Larry says. "Ask him to sit in."

Mandel wasn't as famous as Bloomfield—he got a lot more famous years later when he recorded with the Rolling Stones—but he had played with Charlie Musselwhite, a great blues harmonica player, so he ought to be good with Alan's harmonica work.

Harvey came up and kicked ass. He had a great tone, a virtuoso left hand. Not fast, not a lot of notes, but like Henry, he had a sound of his own. He wasn't just another of the 4,297 guys who tried to sound like Eric Clapton. To the rest of us, who had gotten used to wondering whether the next lead guitar notes were going to come from the brilliant Henry or the wasted Henry, Harvey's control was a relief. We invited him into the band then and there.

Alan was devastated by Henry's leaving. Alan wanted the band to be a family, to be this sort of holy circle together, and it caused him deep pain whenever there was trouble between us. He didn't think

7

anyone should be hurt or pushed out, and for some reason, Henry was especially important to him. Bear used to say "What are you, in love with that guy? Are you a faggot?" But Larry was all jazzed at having a lead guitar who didn't do heavy drugs. I didn't have any power but I was in favor of keeping the band together and playing, and if that meant we had Harvey, fine.

We drove right to the San Francisco airport after hiring Mandel out of the audience, slept on the plane to New York, scrambled in and out of the gig in New Jersey or wherever the hell it was and hit the Fillmore East, where there was another band we didn't know, new guys, I think making their first performance, named Sha Na Na.

Meanwhile, Harvey is learning our numbers and style as we go, learning in front of these huge audiences. With Harvey's talent and a powerful rhythm section, Alan's delicate harmonica notes and graceful rhythm guitar dancing around The Bear's gargantuan showmanship, we were getting away with it.

We were zonked, wasted, uptight, downbeat, ripped, torn and shattered. And we were supposed to be on our way to a festival called Woodstock. Big deal, just another gig, I thought, although we were sure having a hell of a lot of trouble getting to it.

So here we were hanging around the airport in Whitekill, New York for hours, waiting for our turn on the helicopter shuttle that was the only way for musicians to get to the stage, which by now was surrounded by a crowd that reached for miles in all directions, like a fortress of human bodies.

I was trying to sleep on the concrete floor of a hangar. Skip was going crazy, worrying that even if we got in to the festival, we wouldn't have any instruments; from all the radio reports we heard, there was no way they could get through those traffic jams with the equipment truck.

It was after four in the afternoon, six hours after we got to the airport, that a helicopter had some passenger room. A TV crew and some reporters bolted for it, with us chasing them down the runway. They got to the chopper first but The Bear charged aboard after them.

"Where the fuck do you think YOU'RE going?" he asked.

"To report the news," a cameraman said.

"Fuck you, we're going to MAKE the news," Bear roared, hurling the guy through the door.

He glared at the others. "We are the Canned Heat. It is more important that we get there than you, so we're taking this helicopter."

And we did. The Bear was a force of nature, like a tidal wave. Trying to stop him was like trying to stop an armored division. His hobby was breaking down doors. Really. He was always so happy when one of us got locked out of a hotel room on the road, or some dopey stage manager forgot the keys to our dressing room.

"Here, just let me take care of this," he'd growl, and there'd be this big happy flash of white teeth in his thick, black beard.

He didn't kick the door in, with a straight-ahead blow from the sole of his shoe, the way real cops do these days. He'd back up and run at the door, shoulder-first, like the heroes did in 1940s movies, and just crash through. He was always in a good mood after he got to break down a door.

The first sight of Woodstock from the air finally woke me up. A small city of a half million people. Tents and sleeping bags and blankets made little patches of blue and yellow and red on the green grass of the rolling hills for as far as I could see, from horizon to horizon.

I looked at Skip. He and The Bear were taking hits of LSD.

"Okay, man, it's cool," I said. "Dragging me out of that room. Look at the crowd."

I was overwhelmed that we were going to play for so many people.

As the helicopter came in, Skip stuck his brand new camera at arm's length out the door and blindly clicked off one shot. He sold the picture later for the cover of Ravi Shankar's Woodstock album.

"Holy shit," he yelled. "Look."

Down below us, we could see a familiar truck moving slowly through the crowd, casting long shadows in the late afternoon sun. It was our roadies, who had left New York with the equipment at three that morning.

The roadies. The goddam roadies. How the hell did they do that? I read a lot of military history and I always think of the roadies as the infantrymen of rock: the grunts, the beat-up, unsung heroes that you never appreciate until your life depends on them and they come through for you, sort of like Gunga Din in the poem.

When we arrived, the Incredible String Band, the hippie group that played acoustic Medieval or Renaissance type music, was up on the stage. They had a name and all, but the audience could barely hear them. Their type of music was totally out of place. Gentle notes for Robin Hood in some English meadow. They just didn't have the power to turn on all those tripped-out young Americans watching the sun go down on Max's farm.

Skip was delighted with the timing. He had this thing about playing festivals at sunset. "If you start out with the sun going down around you and finish playing in the dark, it does something to the crowd. They think it's magic or something, man."

We did that at Monterey and Newport Beach and he was right. Those festival appearances boosted the band's rep right to the top.

Alan's parents met us behind the stage. They seemed oddly out of place, like running into your grandparents in a hot tub.

But dawdling along behind them, in cutoff denim shorts and a blue T-shirt knotted under her breasts was one of the most beautiful girls I had ever seen. She was just slightly shorter than me, with long dark blonde hair, slightly Slavic cat's-eyes, of a deep blue color. She had the cutest damn legs and the kind of finely chiseled Anglo-Saxon features you see in parts of New England.

She was about 19, a nursing student in Boston. She and her friend Linda, a spectacular-chested brunette who was a friend of Alan's sister Sharon, had set off for Woodstock the day before in a brand-new Mustang that belonged to Linda's mother. Abandoning the car in Bethel because they couldn't get any farther in the traffic jam, they walked five miles into the festival and hooked up with Sharon.

I said hello to Linda, who I had met once before with Sharon Wilson. But no matter how terrific the view of Linda's chest was, I just couldn't take my eyes off her shy friend, whose name was Diane.

The Incredible String Band was limping along toward what passed for a finale in their music. Skip was trying to push us up the steps to the stage, yelling "the sun is setting, you guys, c'mon. This is going to be perfect."

Just looking at this girl made me nervous as hell, but I had to make a try.

"Come on up with us," I said.

She laughed. "Why? What can I do up there? You guys have to play."

In the late afternoon sun, it looked like her head was surrounded by a ball of flames and I hadn't even taken any drugs except one little joint.

"I've got a job for you. Come on."

We were climbing the stairs to the stage. She wasn't coming. Shit.

Alan, right in front of me, said over his shoulder: "Forget it, bandito. Dead end street, man."

"No way, man. I am inspired. She is beautiful."

"She's a virgin. And I bet she stays one. I know her. We used to play in the same sandbox."

"I want to play in HER sandbox," I said.

I liked Alan too much to add what I was thinking: I don't take advice on my love life from the only rock star in the world who is too uncool to get laid anywhere.

In the chaos backstage, we ran into people we knew, Jefferson Airplane, Janis Joplin, Big Brother and the Holding Company. Chip Monck, the emcee, asked Skip when we wanted to go on, since we had just gotten there and the roadies were just opening up the truck.

"We'll go next," Skip said, looking at the sun. We all sort of flinched, except maybe The Bear, because by now the acid was kicking in. Also, he still felt pretty good over throwing all those guys off the helicopter.

"I'll go get our check," Skip said. "I also have to talk to some guy about a contract—film rights and shit. You guys get out there and kick ass."

We had no idea that we were about to play the single most famous gig of our lives, for the biggest paycheck the band had seen up to that point, and right there behind the stage, shouting over the music, our manager was hammering out a contract for our part in one of the most famous, lucrative music movies of all time. Movie rights, something we had no experience with. He wound up making a deal that was followed by all the bands that appeared in the movie and on the sound track album.

And he was on acid.

We were high up above the crowd, on the highest stage I've ever seen, three stories. As we were setting up, a voice said softly behind me: "Okay, so what's my job?"

Fucking great. Diane had gotten up there with us. She and Linda.

"Oh, hey, terrific. Thanks for coming. This is easy but it's important. Here, take my watch and my wallet. And go get anything valuable from the other guys, watches, rings, money, stuff like that,

Our view from the stage: the rain didn't dampen the spirit of Woodstock 1969.

and guard it for us, okay?"

"Okay. But why?"

"You ever seen us play?"

"I've got some of your records."

"We really get it on when we play. We get into the music pretty good. Sometimes watches fly off into the crowd, guys lose their wallets. I break drumsticks if I'm wearing rings."

"You really need me to do this?"

Well, actually a roadie would usually hold our stuff, but it sounded like she wanted to be needed and I was ready to do anything to keep

her around.

"Yeah. We probably can't play if you don't. They'd have to call off this whole incredible scene. All these people would have to go home and it would be all your fault."

She smiled. It was a beautiful smile.

"Okay. Here I go. Little Miss Responsible." She and Linda started collecting stuff from the guys and found a place to stand behind us.

As usual, we had no set planned, nothing coordinated. The Bear simply announced that "We're going to go up the country a little bit now," because "Goin' Up The Country" was number one then in a lot of cities, including New York. It was the perfect song for the moment, just what all these people had done. And in an intuitively brilliant moment, Alan took the mike and, without his harmonica, began playing the opening notes on a guitar, then improvised lyrics to fill in for the flute lines.

I rolled in behind on the drums, Larry slammed into the beat, and we came out tight, Alan sighing out that long, cool, opening line:

I'm going up the country, baby don't you want to go?

Good touch, Alan. A long, slow cheer rolled over the hills, as half a million people came to their feet in joyful celebration.

I'm going to some place where I've never been before.
I'm goin', I'm goin' where the water tastes like wine.
I'm going where the water tastes like wine.
You can jump in the water stay drunk all the time.

The crowd was ours. We could feel it and we punched it, hard. You guys wanna rock? You wanna hear the REAL boogie, the genuine blues? Here it COMES.

Alan knew how to improvise and how to make it happen in spite of us messing up because Harvey didn't know our songs yet. It wasn't Harvey's fault but he had to sort of play outside the music and jump in with a lead guitar solo whenever he thought one would fit.

We were wailing and cooking through a boogie when I noticed a guy's head and shoulders slowly rising over the tall plywood fence that separated us from the crowd.

Suddenly he stood up, and now he was above us, and jumped, swooping down on the stage like Batman. He hurtled into The Bear and they came crashing into my drums.

What the hell? Are we under attack?

A security guard tried to grab the guy, a short, wiry kid about 19, wearing blue love beads. Bear instantly recognized the big, leather vest the kid was carrying. It was Bob's favorite piece of clothing, a primitive-looking piece of thong-stitched rawhide that looked like it should be wrapped around Vulcan in his forge, which was sort of how The Bear saw himself.

He had been moping around ever since he sobered up enough to recall that in a spasm of crazy euphoria brought on by the boogie and beer and pot and pills, he had thrown the vest into the crowd at

Nobody cared if The Bear said "fuck."

a gig we played in some rowdy Texas blues club a month earlier.

"Bear," the kid is screaming. "Bear! I brought your vest back!"

The kid had wound up with it that night in the Texas audience. So when he heard we were going to be at Woodstock, he hitchhiked all the way to New York and wormed his way through that massive crowd and past the security guards to deliver it to him on stage.

The Bear, flying on acid, is still singing. Seeing his funky vest, he is like a little kid reunited with a lost puppy. He pushes the security guard away from the kid, who fishes a cigarette out of the pocket of Bear's yellow T-shirt.

I am banging away on my drums, still trying to figure out what the hell is going on, but the audience has picked up on it. All of a

A fan from Texas gives the Bear a hug after returning missing vest.

sudden, one of them is up here with the musicians, and he's being treated like a royal guest, a long lost pal. They're on their feet, cheering.

The enthusiasm of the crowd washed over us on the stage, waves of grungy, bare-chested, tie-dyed, granny-glassed, weed-ripped, crotch-bursting, rain-soaked, incredulous enthusiasm.

Bear looked over at me. "Man, we could start a revolution right now, this minute, if we wanted to," he said.

This audience, these at least were my people, my adopted tribe, the emerging America of the Woodstock Generation. Canned Heat people. A change from the weird concerts some pinheaded promoters who knew nothing about our music—much less us—had stuck us into as our records started going gold.

Here at Woodstock nobody cared if The Bear said "fuck." We took that stage and we kicked ass. Our heavy music, Bob's energy, that was just what that crowd wanted to hear. We could feel them and they could feel us. The "Fried Hockey Boogie"—our big wall-blaster which we never play the same way twice—we renamed that version "The Woodstock Boogie."

I'll get some argument on this, I expect, but we got a bigger ovation than any band there, at least any band I heard there. "Goin' Up the Country" became the theme song, the Woodstock anthem.

It was an historic performance which was never even used in the film as it was first released, because of goddam record company politics. It WAS in the original director's cut of the film—and it was put back in a special long version released 25 years later. But before the first release, when it was decided that the film was too long, they cut Canned Heat and Jefferson Airplane. We were a United Artists act and the Warner Bros. film people preferred to mangle a Woodstock high point rather than eliminate some performers with Warner record deals. They only played our song "Goin' Up the Country" behind the opening credits.

Okay, we were a little raw, a little unpolished. But that was the spirit of the hour, wasn't it? And the crowd loved us. Our performance, especially "Goin' Up The Country," raw as it was, became the defining moment of the festival—the moment that TV advertisers would pick, decades later, when they wanted to evoke the whole weekend—hell, the whole era—in only a few classic seconds. "Goin' Up The Country" and a mass of American kids in tie-dye and hip huggers says "the 60s" the way Ingrid Bergman, Humphrey Bogart and "As Time Goes By" says "World War Two."

The best part of Woodstock was that Diane was still there, waiting for me back stage when we finished playing.

The worst part was that the Blind Owl had seen too clearly what a challenge she would be.

We had a little time after the show, and we walked around, into the crowd.

It was amazing, the sexual energy, girls walking around with their boobs hanging out, pretending it was just the normal thing for them to do, guys swimming in this muddy little swimming hole with their dicks dangling down, next to them girls washing their hair and soaping their breasts. Couples making love in sleeping bags. One couple was on top of the bag.

An incredible sense of freedom combined with an incredible sense of order. Total liberty with no sense of chaos or danger. A magic combination, gone too soon, a memory that a whole generation chased for decades to come.

Diane and I walked through the crowd and we were infected with all this energy. Diane acted at first as if she didn't really notice the naked guys or the screwing couples, but that didn't last long. We were inflamed. We started kissing, with her back up against the fence near the stage.

I talked her into coming with me backstage again, where the rest of the band was getting something to eat in a food tent the organizers had set up. As we walked in, there was an outburst of voices in Spanish:

"Caray, cabrón, cómo estás?"

"Orale, mano, que onda?"

It was Santana's band, who had gotten there earlier. Santana, a fellow Mexican, his timbale player Chepito Arias, who's from South America someplace, a whole bunch of Latino *cuates*, we had a reunion in Spanish in the middle of this mammoth American festival. It was one of the early signs that rock n' roll was becoming a global language.

While we were eating, Skip (who started out as such a button-down, shorthaired business guy with the William Morris Agency) was taking another step on his colorful road to ruin.

His problem: getting the band out of Woodstock was going to be harder than getting it in. The helicopters were only taking out medical cases and the stage was surrounded by people and cars, shoulder to shoulder, fender to fender, for miles in all directions. It would have been nice to stay and party and all, but we had a gig the next day in Atlantic City.

So how the hell do we get out of here?

Skip reappeared while we were eating.

"C'mon you guys. I've got a car."

"What fuckin' car, man?" The Bear asked. "You gotta get a grip on that acid, man. We came in some kind of airplane, remember?"

"That black limousine there. Get in it."

"Whose is it?"

"Fuck if I know. I swiped it. It was sitting out there with the keys in the ignition so I took it. Now let's get the hell out of here before anyone stops us."

The band thought this was just great. Our manager was becoming one of the guys. The acid has kicked in and he's committing grand theft auto.

I hustled Diane and Linda into the limo too. Somewhere in there, Felix Pappalardi from Mountain had joined us and we started off down the exit road behind the stage, packed solid with parked cars. We rode up to each one in our stolen limo, followed by the roadies in the equipment truck, and called for volunteers.

"Hey man, we're the Canned Heat. We've gotta get outta here. Help us move this car, okay?"

The crowd was glad to give us a hand. One by one, they helped us push cars off the road and onto the grass. Sometimes a big crowd of us actually picked up the cars and moved them. It was a long night—about 8 when we started, and midnight before we got to a clear road.

In Middletown, New York, we stopped at a Holiday Inn, claimed we were another band that had reservations and took their rooms. The hallway was a long, narrow party, filled with musicians spilling over from the festival, passing joints and bottles up and down like a bucket brigade.

Linda went to the bar for some beers. Janis Joplin was hitting the Southern Comfort with her band at one table and Ravi Shankar was at another, drinking tea or whatever sitar players drink. Linda came back with the beers and went off to shower in Alan's room, figuring she'd be safe there. She was right about that too.

Diane was having a great time. I was whispering in her ear that we should go up to my room.

She gave me this long, quiet look.

"We won't do anything I don't want to? You promise?"

"What is it you don't want to do?"

"I'm not sure any more. That's the scary part."

"I promise. Just stay with me."

In my room, I slipped her out of her shorts, jumped out of my clothes and we curled under the covers. I was rubbing against her. I made my move.   "Don't."

I held back. We kissed some more. I had a hard-on that would have gone through a plate of armor.

"Don't. No. Just stop there."

When I started to pull back, she kissed me again. Hard. It was agony.

I got my hand between her legs. She recoiled and curled up in a ball. I pulled back. She locked her mouth on the side of my neck, then swirled her tongue around the inside of my ear.

She was gasping and crying and she had her fingers dug into my back. And every time I tried to get in she would pull back.

We came so close so many times that I could have just taken her if I was a little more forceful. But that has never been my style. I don't like to push my way in. I like women to give themselves to me on their own. It is the greatest compliment a man can get.

We spent all night like that. We kissed until our lips swelled up and our mouths were sore. We threw ourselves into each other, her twisting away at the last moment. By morning I was crazy with exhaustion, from everything that had happened to the band and pushing cars and from lack of sleep, and my balls felt like they had been pounded with hammers.

But it was worth it. I could not forget Diane, and don't think I ever will. I kept in touch from the road. Eventually I did make love to her, but it was not that night. Not at Woodstock.

And by then, I was not the first.

We said good-bye in the hotel lobby and before noon the rest of the band and I were back in another airplane, heads flopped on our shoulders, zonked out cold with fatigue, flying to Atlantic City. Another day, another gig. But I had changed my mind.

Woodstock. It wasn't such a bad idea. Glad I went.

THE EARLY YEARS

"Don't forget. Your body is your limitation.
The answer = Yoga." Love, Noreen

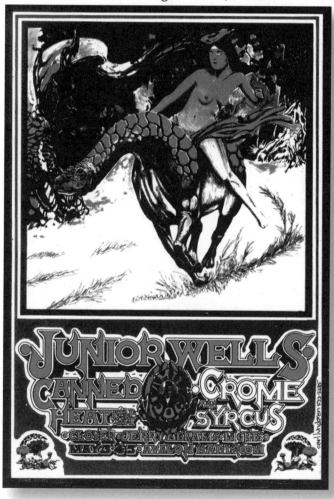

If Noreen Reilly and Alan hadn't turned me on to yoga, I'm sure I wouldn't be alive today. You can't spend your life abusing your body and not expect it to catch up with you.

Noreen was also a wizard at astrology. I gave her all the necessary details: born Adolfo Hector de la Parra Prantl, Mexico City, February 8, 1946, 1:20 in the morning.

A few days later, she handed me astrological charts that turned out to be surprisingly accurate. According to the stars,

- I'm a lover of peace and harmony
- in my quiet way I get what I want and make the other fellow like it
- in youth stubbornness, but with maturity a fixedness of purpose
- my strong point is organization
- I have all the qualities necessary to be a good leader—except the desire to be one
- my father's line shows material achievements
- I'm attracted to 'wimmen' (she used to make fun of my accent) and I'm quite unconventional in regard to sexual matters.

Not bad for someone who had only known me days and the majority of that time was spent tripping on acid.

I was named after my maternal grandfather Adolfo Prantl, a stern, aristocratic Austrian and a very staunch, ultra-conservative Catholic. I must have inherited my sense of order from him and it's one of the reasons I like traveling in Germany. Offenses aren't just prohibited; there are degrees of how forbidden something is: breaking the law may be *verboten* (forbidden) or in some cases *strikt verboten* (strictly forbidden) and if it's really terrible, it's *strengstens verboten* (absolutely forbidden).

Don Porfirio Diaz, the Mexican dictator who coined the phrase: "Poor Mexico, so far away from God and so close to the United States," invited my grandfather to move to Mexico to help organize customs and the import/export laws.

Don Adolfo's mother and his brother Jacob came with him and he waited to marry until his mother died. A handsome aristocrat who walked with a gold-headed antique black cane, he was never seen without a tie on his high-neck shirt, an embodiment of 19th century values. My chief memory of him is sitting in his smoking jacket, reading a book. He was a great architect and some of his buildings have been declared historical. After 100 years and all the earthquakes in Mexico City, the Prantl buildings are still standing.

One sign of affluence Adolfo refused to acquire was an

automobile. The house had a four-car garage, but he didn't believe in them. I guess the environmentalists would have loved my grandfather.

When he was in his forties, he wanted a bride who was untouched by the world and by temptation. What better place to look than a convent. Pilar Baguena was 16 or 17, and had fair skin, brown eyes, and long blonde hair. Her parents, originally from Spain, were both dead and the convent was a safe haven for such a young girl alone. She was a gifted painter and recited poetry. I have some of the letters my grandfather wrote to her; they are very beautiful, very romantic. They really did live happily every after. Relationships like that don't exist any more. In the United States, society is very hung up on age, but in Europe a man twenty years older than a woman is no big deal and in Latin America, it's even less of an issue.

One of the fascinating things about Mexico is the profound European influence and connections, which are very strong to this day. My family was very much a part of that. People who haven't traveled in Latin America tend to think of Mexicans as a mass of poor, uneducated wetbacks.

They don't realize that Mexico City was a thriving, sophisticated city two centuries before the Algonquins sold Manhattan to the Dutch for $24. In 1864, when Austrian-born Maximillian was emperor and French-born Carlota was the empress, they brought over the same architect who designed the famous boulevards of Paris to build Chapultepec Castle and lay out the city's avenues (originally built by the Aztecs) patterning them on those in the French capitol. My great-grand uncle, by the way, donated the *caballito*, the statue of Spanish King Carlos IV on a horse that's one of the main landmarks on the Reforma, the main boulevard of Mexico City.

My father's father was born in Spain and my paternal grandmother, Catalina Luccioto, from Palermo, Sicily, was an opera singer with beautiful green eyes and a heavenly smile. She married Gonzalo de la Parra, a blue-eyed intellectual publisher with the looks of a movie star and the soul of an adventurer. By the time my mother and my father married, his parents Gonzalo and Catalina were already divorced.

Even though my grandfather Gonzalo was very much the free-spirited playboy, while Adolfo was very Catholic and conservative, the two got along well. Both were powerful and wealthy but honest. They neither stole nor killed—rare restraint in an oligarchy.

He was exiled from the country two or three times between the late 1920s and the 1950s for his anti-government rhetoric. He even spent three months hiding in a friend's cellar because the police were hunting for him due to his writings. He also became a well-known adviser to two presidents, a good example of the volatile nature of Mexican political life.

My father was a lot like his father. When he met my mother in church and fell in love with her, he was already married "outside the Church" and had a daughter named Laura. Later he had another daughter out of wedlock, Maria Eugenia, who a few years later would have a big influence on me and my musical upbringing.

For the first eight years of my life I was the only child of my parent's church-sanctified union and my grandparents idolized me. I was a spoiled little kid who went to private school and had all the money in the world because both families were still together, with money and power. Our lifestyle was very much in the tradition of European aristocracy. Grandfather Adolfo's mahogany-shelved library was floor to ceiling with books in three different languages and the centerpiece of the mansion's main salon was a concert-size grand piano where grandmother Pilar would entertain us with the works of Chopin and other classical composers. She was also a talented artist and many of her paintings hang my in house in Nipomo. She was close to 100 when she died in 1993, a remarkable woman.

Unlike car-hating grandfather Adolfo, grandfather Gonzalo would trade in his black Cadillac for a new one each year. In a brief fling with show business, he brought the beautiful Faure sisters from Spain to Mexico to try to turn them into stars. Although the sisters never became great entertainers, they did become famous and the Secretary of the Treasury fell so madly in love with Isabel, he put her face on a five peso bill. Latins really know how to honor women.

Tragically, Gonzalo's death triggered a family feud, which resulted in the beginning of the end of our comfortable life-style and also the end of my family life due to the divorce of my parents. The memory of my father coming to see me at my grandfather's house is still very vivid to me. When I asked him where he had been, all he could do was hold me very, very tightly and cry. And he cried and cried and cried. The strange part was I didn't know why he was crying.

I didn't see my father again for another year. Now, I know it was because of the divorce. He had moved to Tijuana where he was in charge of the local office of the national lottery, a good-paying job. At the time, lotteries were against the law in the United States and Americans would pour into Baja California to buy lottery tickets and otherwise enjoy the openness of a border town.

When I was about six, Pilar bought me my first drum set. I loved playing them but had no idea I was going to become a drummer. I didn't take lessons; I just thumped away. I loved the apparatus. I loved being able to beat on something to make a sound. In fact, I must have been terribly noisy because one day I woke up and the drum set had disappeared. (Most likely Adolfo decided that they were too noisy and hence, *verboten*.) It didn't really matter. I'd had my fun with it and now I had other interests like cowboys and Indians and my toy soldiers.

After my parents divorce, my mother and I had a very stable home with her parents, Adolfo and Pilar, and my Aunt Rosita. By now, my grandfather was in his 80s but my grandmother was still a young woman. My mother was also very young and not at all happy to be a single mother. But for me, it was great. I was eight years old, growing up with three women who showered me with love and affection.

Because of my parents' breakup, my family decided I should become a live-in student at the same all-boys Catholic school I'd been attending. It was very painful, but I was only in third grade, with no choice. I would cry when my mother took me back to the boarding school after the weekend, but she was also burdened with her tragedies: the loss of Gonzalo, the divorce.

Although I hated the Internado Mexico (it was run by the Marist Brothers, great educators like the Jesuits), I developed a strong sense of order and discipline. No detail was too small for the brothers' rules: how to brush your teeth, how to shower with cold water, how to fold clothes, how to make a bed. The one bright spot on my otherwise bleak horizon was being picked for the choir out of the hundreds of kids that tried out.

In retrospect, I think every kid should have a year in boarding school. I think the survival instincts and discipline I learned there saved me from the excesses of the rock n' roll life years later, from the lack of self-discipline that destroyed so many people I knew in that world. God knows, even with the Brothers' training, I developed enough of a taste for some excesses when I grew up.

The Marist Brothers were also skilled at giving young boys a solid academic background. My classical education has stayed with me and enabled me to view the world through more than one prism, something a lot of musicians can't do. And they gave me my passion for history, especially military history—for which I have been frequently cursed by other members of Canned Heat when I've dragged them out of bed during European tours for sightseeing trips to famous battlefields. I once ignored a whole busload of musicians screaming in protest as we made a two-hour detour on the road to Paris to see Verdun, the scene of a famous battle in World War One.

A few years after the divorce, my father decided to move back to Mexico City, marry Maria Eugenia's mother and give the little girl his name. Once I found out he was returning, I started working on my mother to get me out of the boarding school I hated.

I loved my mother and my grandmother (Adolfo had died), but my mother had married again and I wanted to be with my father. He was a very intelligent, cosmopolitan man with a great sense of humor and an aura that I loved. My stepfather Flavio was not a bad man; he treated me well. He was also an excellent guitar player and singer, which would eventually be a musical influence on me, but he didn't have the charisma of my father.

Meanwhile, the death of Adolfo and the division of his estate among my grandmother Pilar, my Aunt Rosita and my mother, caused a marked change in our life style. Overnight I went from an upper class *niño bien* to a middle class kid. But I didn't care. I was reunited with my father.

Even though he never took lessons, my father was very musical and played piano by ear—everything from ragtime to jazz, anything with a great rhythm. I remember him taking me to one of his favorite movies, "Orchestra Wives," featuring the original Glenn Miller Band. In Mexico, it was called *Las Viudas del Jazz,* "The Widows of Jazz," because the wives dress in black and go into mourning when the band breaks up. A few years later, we went to see another favorite, "The Benny Goodman Story." Somehow all those messages started going through my subconscious. I'm sure he never thought I would become a professional musician; he wanted me to become a dentist or a doctor.

My father's wife Alicia accepted me immediately and I became very close to my half sister Maria Eugenia, who was five years older. Because she grew up an American teenager in the California border town of San Ysidro, across from Tijuana, she was plugged into the

26

music scene that was exploding in the United States in the '50s. She also inherited my dad's gift for music.

So here I am, fresh out of boarding school, an 11-year-old with all kinds of weird ideas already boiling in my head as my hormones activate, and I meet this half-sister, a gorgeous 16-year-old. The guilt over my sexual feelings for her and her girl friends made them even more thrilling. She also turned me on in another way. She had hundreds of the latest 45 records—Little Richard, Fats Domino, John Lee Hooker, Big Joe Turner and Bill Haley and the Comets. She was an upper middle class teen-ager from a border town, used to hanging out with Americans and really getting into early rock n' roll.

"Check out this music," she would tell me. "It's great stuff. I know that you like Benny Goodman and all that, but listen to Little Richard, listen to Fats Domino." So I really became introduced to rock and roll and to rhythm and blues by my sister Maria Eugenia.

On my 12th birthday, my father gave me an LP, which I still have, called "Here Is Little Richard". My God, I loved it! He bought me a clarinet, a trumpet and an accordion, but I couldn't really get into them. I did, however, start getting into drums. I got an old banged-up military snare drum like the kind they use for marching bands, along with some cookie tins and cans and assembled my own drum kit. I didn't know how the components were supposed to be set up and I had no technique or formal musical training. I would just lose myself, closing my eyes and playing along with those records in a near-orgasmic state fired by my young imagination.

Years later, I discovered that psychologists call this state of mind "flow." It's a universal sensation. Once identified, you know what it is and seek it again. Playing music on stage, riding a motorcycle or making love. I keep looking for it. Some people look for it on drugs but I know you can't find it that way.

At this point, I had no aspirations to become a musician, but that soon changed. At least once a year, the family went to Acapulco. During one vacation, my American-raised sister pleaded with my dad to let her go out alone with an American guy she'd just met. But in Mexico in those days, nice young ladies, even semi-Americanized ones, were not allowed to date without a chaperone. It was both her good fortune and mine that my parents figured I was old enough to fill that role.

I will never forget that evening. The nightclub (the first I'd ever been in) was absolutely beautiful—outdoors, right by the ocean.

More importantly, for the first time I heard a really great drummer: Richard Lemus. While my sister danced with her boyfriend, I moved to a table right near Lemus and watched every move, thinking "my cookie tins don't sound like that." I spent the evening soaking up everything I could; there was no question that I was bitten by the show-biz bug. I really loved the environment. Everybody clapping. I thought: this guy's a star—look at all these women.

I couldn't possibly foresee all the treachery the music business would hold for me in the future. As Lemus captivated the crowd, I thought "this is great, this is glamorous, this is wonderful, I want to play and be adored just like this guy. I want to be like him; he looks like he's having such a good time."

It was years before I learned that that's part of the job—you have to look like you're having a good time even if your guts are on fire and your soul is sick and you'd rather be dead than on stage. I learned that part too well, later on.

During this period, I was attending an excellent British-run school called Colegio Williams for Boys. It was not religious, but stern, with lots of English-style discipline. I started making friends with kids who liked rock and roll. That was our link, the only thing we really related to. A lot of them had Elvis Presley records, but I was already farther down the road. I was listening to Little Richard, Fats Domino and Big Joe Turner.

One of the guys I started playing with was Javier Flores, *El Zoa*, who had an acoustic guitar. We were among the first garage bands in Mexico City, copying Elvis Presley hits, hanging around just being kids, just making noise. It was all feeling; we had no technique. I hadn't taken any lessons and *El Zoa* knew only a few basic chords.

It wasn't long before we met some other middle class kids in Colonia Narvarte who were also into rock music. Mexico City is divided into neighborhoods called *colonias* and where you live forms your basic identity. This new group of guys had a piano, a couple of electric guitars and a snare drum. A real Slingerland snare drum with a cymbal. Wow! They even put a microphone on the piano, creating sort of a first generation electrified rock band. We were pretty pitiful by comparison. All we had were my marching band drum and Javier's little Mexican acoustic guitar. We used to peek over the fence to watch them rehearse.

One day their drummer wasn't there. "Hey, you, *ojos de gato* (cat eyes), across the fence. We know who you are. We've seen you play

The "original" Sparks in action shortly after Charles Lee's death

with *El Zoa*. Want to sit in with us?"

I was thrilled. They accepted me immediately, replacing their drummer with his fancy snare drum and cymbal with me and my banged up, military snare drum and cookie tins. This became my first band, called the Sparks, with Lalo Toral on guitar, an American kid named Charles Lee on piano, and Ricardo Delgado on guitar and vocals. (Many years later in the 1970s, a band called Sparks became famous worldwide. I doubt they ever knew they had assumed a name that set teeny-bopper hearts to beating wildly in Mexico in the '50s.)

Soon the word was out and people in our neighborhood would pay us to perform at their parties. The other guys didn't share my passion for Fats Domino and Little Richard. They were copying what they heard on Mexican radio, which were actually white covers of the black records I listened to. In those days, much of America was still very segregated and black radio stations played black music for blacks and white stations played white copies for white audiences. They never told their listeners that Elvis Presley was copying Arthur "Big Boy" Crudup with "That's All Right Mama."

Along with the pesos we earned, I enjoyed the recognition. Our rehearsals were more like parties. Every time the band rehearsed, we had 10 to 20 girls sitting around the garage. When we got a job, Lalo and I, along with the rest of the band, had to push his piano down the street to parties, dragging it over pavement, battering it totally out of tune. But we didn't care. We were enjoying ourselves. We bought metallic pants with matching vests and considered ourselves unbelievably cool.

The music was still part of an innocent era in Mexico. In the United States, the beatniks were already bringing a serious touch to the youth movement, such as it was then. Later, it would surface on the streets of countries around the world. But we were still untouched. Rock n' roll was just starting to catch on and all kinds of bands were popping up all over Mexico City.

In 1958, when I was only 12, we got a record contract with RCA Victor covering American hits like "At the Hop" and "Oh, Carol." Unfortunately, Charles Lee, the center of the band, died unexpectedly from an infection just a few months after The Sparks started taking off, so I inherited the band and we went on to record two LPs for Columbia.

When Bill Haley and the Comets came to Mexico, my father immediately bought tickets for the whole family. It was one of the strongest impressions in my life. I was in shock. When I heard that music and felt that beat and saw those American guys rocking and playing the real stuff—so acoustic—so full of tonality and beat—it was absolutely beautiful. I went back to hear them three times. Haley, the grandfather of rock music in America with "Rock Around the Clock," was even bigger in Mexico. So popular in fact, that years later, when his star had faded in the United States, he moved the band to Mexico City where many fans still loved him. He married a Mexican woman, played at one club for many years and went on making records in Mexico after he was all but forgotten in the States.

Before I was 15, great stars like Jerry Lee Lewis came to Mexico, along with other groups that weren't as well known. These people were gods to me. I just idolized them. I remember thinking: "We will turn into salt if we touch them." Even my father was in awe, my sister,

The Sparks fly in this Columbia Records promotion photo before Charles Lee's death.

everybody. We loved the music that America was coming up with. Elvis, of course, was not going to come to Mexico. He was too big.

My father, who was into hot rods and fast cars, made me an offer: If I got A's and B's for six months straight, he would get me an Italian moped, so I could go back and forth to school. It was the start of my love affair with motorcycles that has never ended. I also discovered girls during this period and the connection between the two has never left me.

Across the street from Colegio Williams was Colegio Madrid, an all-girls school, where I saw my first true love, a beautiful blonde named Maria del Carmen, who caused me to blush madly whenever I said hello. For a whole year, I would show off by riding my moped around her, but I never had the courage to ask her to go for a ride.

As I became more serious about my music, my mother began a small business in our colonia selling farm fresh eggs, which she would deliver by car. Our neighborhood was very supportive. They knew I was saving the money for real drums. With their help, plus money from grandmother Pilar, I finally got my first professional set of drums, my first Slingerland kit. *Adios* cookie tins, though I have to admit I got a pretty substantial start with those tin cans and the army drum.

At 16, I met Fernando, who everyone called *El Tarolas* (snare drum in English), but among Mexican musicians it was a nickname for a spastic, odd-duck kind of guy. He was a great pool player, a real ladies man and an adequate piano player who knew all the standards like "Misty" and "Tea for Two," as well as some jazz and a little rock and roll. He had a lot of contacts at coffee houses that were springing up as the beatnik movement spread to Mexico; places full of older guys from the National University wearing beards, playing bongo drums, worshipping Jean Paul Sartre and flirting with communism. Some even smoked pot, but I didn't want to know about it; it just didn't interest me. But I was interested in jazz, which was coming on strong with groups like Art Blakey and the Jazz Messengers, Miles Davis, Dave Brubeck and Dizzy Gillespie.

One afternoon I ran into Fernando in a park across the street from the pool hall which was his base of operations. He was all excited. "Fito, I got you a gig. I want you to come and play in this beatnik joint for me."

"I am too young," I told him. "They won't even let me in because you have to be over 18."

"Don't worry about it. They'll love you. You look good. You have talent. You're great on the drums. You have a thing for jazz. I want somebody who's not just a rock and roller. Come on, Fito, I'll show you a completely different side of music. I'm going to show you how I get a different girl every night and take her home with me and she'll let me do anything I want with her. I'll also show you how you can make a lot of money playing music."

I hadn't really thought about music as a business, as a way to make money, but 50 pesos a day, about four American dollars, was good money for a kid, so the idea was very appealing. Better yet, the gig would give me chance to meet women. I still didn't have a sex life, beyond masturbation. I dated some girls, I kissed them, but that's as far as you could go in those days in Mexico.

Because I was under age, I wore a hat and dark glasses, not only to look like a beatnik, but to hide my face and help me blend into the crowd at the places where we played like *La Faceta* and *El Ego*, which became famous in Mexico City as the first coffee houses catering to intellectuals, rebels, poets, and other members of the avant-garde.

The club owners liked me; I seemed to fit in naturally, but because I was under age, the gigs were the start of a lifelong curse of being exploited when it came to getting paid. I'll never forget one club owner saying point blank, "I'll give you dinner, Fito, and let you drink a beer, but I'm not going to pay you as much as I pay Fernando." I wasn't about to argue. I was in heaven just playing and making what I considered big money for a 16-year-old who still lived at home.

By now, I was attending Colegio Franco Español and working toward a bachelor's degree in psychology, reading Fromm Freud, Sartre and Jung, and I was still planning to go on to the university. But I was having trouble staying awake in class because I was playing almost every night. I was in three different bands: Fernando's beatnik jazz trio, The Sparks in the colonia, and a new group at the school. I was fortunate though. When most students fell asleep in class, the teachers would throw erasers to get their attention, but in my case, some of the teachers would just go, "Shhhh, don't bother him" and let me snooze away.

My father, on the other hand, was starting to put pressure on me. He kept saying, "Don't play so much. Your grades aren't very good." He gave me such mixed signals. If he didn't want me to be a professional musician, why did he take me to see all those wonderful movies? Why did he buy me the instruments? I guess he figured, instead of me joining a gang, music would be a nice hobby.

Fortunately, many of the younger teachers had gotten caught up in the beatnik movement too, including my psychology teacher, my ethics teacher, and my philosophy teacher. They were all becoming regulars at the coffeehouses where I played. They were avant-garde people with a sensitivity towards my music and they knew that's where my energy went. A number of them were homosexuals and they would show up in the cafes with their lovers. (AIDS didn't exist yet.) A couple of them came on to me, but I blew up when one guy put his hands between my legs and that was it. They never pushed it. In some ways, Mexicans are very conservative about that stuff but in other ways they are looser, a little less prejudiced than in the States.

As my recognition grew and I started making more money, I realized that I didn't want to go onto the university. This was reinforced by Luis Maya, my logic teacher, who told me I was already a professional musician. He really appreciated my talent. I told him my father was getting on my case about my poor grades and he said:

"Forget about becoming a psychologist or a doctor because you are already on your way toward becoming a star. You are a *pinche rocanrolero cabrón.*" (Loosely translated, it means a fucking rock and roll sonofabitch, which he meant as compliment.) Forget about going to the university because you're not going to find the same sympathy and support there. You are going to be a drummer and you are going to be a great musician. Don't worry about your grades. I'm going to pass you and you'll get your bachelor's degree."

But not all the teachers were that helpful. My problem with my literature teacher wasn't because she was demanding or cruel or a monster. In fact, she was a good-looking woman with great legs, so when I wasn't fighting to stay awake in class, I'd stare at her legs and daydream. One day, in the middle of a daydream, I was called to the principal's office.

The principal was Señor Carriedo, a very stern, but handsome man of French and Spanish descent. He was sitting at his desk in a hand-tailored English Saville Row suit.

"Please sit down."

I'm thinking, "Shit, this is it. Something terrible is about to happen."

"I understand you have some outstanding talents, Mr. de la Parra."

Did he really say "outstanding talents?"

"I was wondering if you could do us a great favor and perform with your band at the graduation dinner. There are going to be several prominent senators, who are the *padrinos* (sponsors) of the graduation, plus Mayor Uruchurtu. With such illustrious guests, I feel the school should put on a first-class program."

I couldn't believe it. This guy didn't call me in to give me a hard time, he called me in to ask a favor. In the back of my mind I thought: now I've got him. Since I play drums in both school bands, neither group can play without me. And if I'm not there, there won't be any music. Sure, they can hire a marimba band or a conventional businessman's bounce type of band, but the kids don't want to hear that. The kids, the senators, the mayor, everybody wants to hear the now-famous rock and roll band from the Colegio Franco Español— of which I am the drummer. So I'm thinking: Go for it. What the fuck.

I quickly said: "I would be delighted to play for you, but I'd like your help. I'm having a problem with my literature class. I need to pass. I need to get my degree." (Mumbling under my breath the fact that I was unable to take the final.)

"I'm sure something can be arranged," the principal smiled.

It was at that moment I realized for the first time I could use my art as a weapon. Being a musician gave me power. My talents were worth something.

I got an "A" in literature and after the graduation dinner, my logic teacher, the one who called me a fucking rockn'roller, signed my menu "with great pride and joy in his artistic sensitivity" and told the band: "You boys have it made. We make people think. You make people feel. That is much more important."

At that moment, I knew for sure my career was music. It was the point where I broke from the establishment, from my father's expectations, from the pressures of my family to go to the university.

There I was, fresh out of college with a degree in psychology, and the '60s were dawning. From Paris to San Francisco, young people were making their presence felt throughout the world and Mexico was no different. The blooming rock revolution in the United States was spilling over into a thriving rock scene south of the border; underground cafes were springing up even though this was a period when rock n' roll was constantly banned and suppressed by what we called *el déspota gobierno* (the despotic government). To the officials, these clubs were hotbeds of revolution instead of college student hangouts.

From the late '50s up until the late '60s, any minor incident—an accident in the kitchen, a complaint about somebody parking a block away, things unrelated to our youth subculture or our music— would trigger a wave of raids on the coffee houses. Gangs of police would burst through the doors and grab everybody in sight— owners, performers, employees, the audience—throw them into paddy wagons and take them to jail. Some of the plainclothes cops saw me so often they got to know me. Once, they even arrested everyone else in the place but ignored me, leaving me alone with my drums in an empty room as the police wagons pulled away.

The cafes were actually quite innocent and the audiences for the most part were law-abiding kids. Their only sin was to be young and to be there. But the city government was convinced the coffee houses were filled with *viciosos* (drug addicts) and *subversivos* (subversives). Of course that was nonsense. In the early years, pot was occasionally sold on a small scale by individuals but real drug dealing didn't happen until the late '60s. It was a while before Mexican kids got into drugs like their American cousins.

The real *subversivos* had their own hangouts where they could plot in peace; they didn't want musicians around making noise that interfered with their conversation. They also weren't about to pay the kind of prices the music-hungry kids would tolerate for an espresso or lemonade in order to listen to some rock music. The revolutionaries could buy a gun and a stylish set of fatigues for what the cafe owners charged a young couple for an evening's entertainment.

Even dancing was *estrictamente prohibido.* It was really pathetic to play for an audience sitting at tables, doing the jerk or the mashed potato in their chairs, hands waving and necks spasming back and forth, unable to stand and move their feet without being thrown out. Mexicans called this sickening abuse of authority *guaurismo.* Each government official brought in his friends *(guaruras)* and gave them some of his power. Then, they brought in their friends and did the same.

One day a promoter asked The Sparks to join a tour with a big Las Vegas-like variety show that included a comedian, dancing girls, a magician and a band. We jumped at the idea, but El Zoa's parents didn't want him to go. When he showed up to join us, we asked him how he pulled it off. He smiled and said, "I went to the store to buy a loaf of bread and I just didn't go back home."

The performers, all top-flight acts, were on a level with the best rumba and salsa bands around. The tour lasted about a month and we worked six nights a week until 1 A.M. for about 50 dollars a night. Along with improving my musical skills, I learned to live on the road, to get along with other people, to deal with all the problems of a traveling troupe. At that age, you don't feel the strain. You don't get sick. If you do, you get better in a couple of days. You can go without sleep. You're a lot more resilient. Even with the hardships, it put the worm in my head that this was the life I wanted to lead, full of experiences, adventures and danger.

There was a lot of wild sex going on in the troupe, but because we were so young and very naive, the other entertainers ignored us—with one exception. One night while I was on stage, someone stood behind the curtain and started giving my back a massage through the drapery. As I continued to play, the hands dropped down to caress my ass and my legs. I was dying. Between beats, I'm whispering: "Please, cool it. Don't do this to me." It was very embarrassing. To this day, I don't know who it was. I suspected, or maybe hoped, it was one of the pretty dancers I sometimes heard giggling backstage.

On another evening, when I was heading back to my dressing room, I was stopped by a distinguished, good looking older gentleman, who was either an agent or a manager, the type that everybody treated with great respect. Out of the blue, he said: "You are going to make it. I have made stars and I have seen them come and go. You will be a star. I just wanted you to know that." Then, he disappeared. It was amazing. I never thought about stardom or gave it any importance.

By now it was the early '60s, The Beatles had swept away the first generation of American rock stars and I was getting even deeper into music. I was a natural drummer, playing by instinct or copying what I heard on the radio. Now, I wanted to learn the basics like how to read music. I also started to talk to different drummers, some famous and some not, who performed on the same bill with us. Unfortunately, most looked at me as competition rather than as a student, so they weren't anxious to give away any trade secrets.

A notable exception was Vicente Martinez, *El Vitaminas.* A great jazz drummer, he was a short, funny little guy, very dark and Indian looking with greasy hair. He didn't really want to help me either, but I kept pestering him to teach me how to read music and understand some of the basics like the value of notes. Finally, in exasperation, he grabbed a newspaper, held it up and said: "This is a whole." Then he folded it in two and tore it. "These are two halves." Then he took the two halves and ripped them in half, and then again. "These are four quarters and these are eighths." He kept on until the paper was in shreds. Then he lit up a joint and glared at me: "Don't bother me with this shit. Don't worry about it. Just think of it that way."

This was my first and only formal music lesson.

Music was becoming an important part of my life...more than I ever expected. While the original appeal was the glamour and the idea of getting girls, I now realized there was something much more important and difficult about playing an instrument, about expressing emotions through music, about being an artist.

I immersed myself in jazz because that's where the great drummers were: Joe Morello who played with Dave Brubeck, Art Blakey with the Jazz Messengers, Elvin Jones with John Coltrane, and of course, the masters: Gene Krupa and Buddy Rich.

Another tutor was a handsome, fair-haired con artist from Argentina who I knew only by one of his many aliases, "Miguel Casis." He was an ex-con straight out of the movie "The Great Imposter." He was funny and charming and as good looking as he was crooked. He drank a lot, laughed a lot and could convince anybody of anything. He assembled a whole caravan of artists, including me and The Sparks, and decided to go on the road to do "benefits" for the Red Cross. He'd ask the local officials to cover expenses and he'd take care of the publicity that would entice people to donate money. While he told everybody they would make money, we received very little. He kept most of it.

One of his most famous promotions was "the kilometer of pesos," which in those days meant something because one-peso coins were actually made of silver alloys, like old-fashioned American silver dollars, but bigger and heavier. Donors were asked to lay pesos in a line that stretched across the stage of the theater where we played. Of course the "kilometer" never got past about 50 feet because the minute the crowd was out of the theater Miguel pocketed the pesos.

He not only stole from ordinary citizens, but as we wound our way around Mexico, he would organize poker games for provincial bigshots, like the governor of Veracruz, the mayor of Orizaba, and the owner of the Cerveza Moctezuma brewery and he would cheat, using signals and various tricks with his partner, a plump, pig-faced, so-called attorney. Sometimes he stayed up, drinking and gambling and whoring, for three or four days in a row. Then he would collapse for two days, ignoring the phone and knocks on the door as he slept before starting the cycle all over again.

One evening in Tierra Blanca near Veracruz, he came up to us as we were sitting outside the hotel. "Come on, you guys, we're not making any money (a lie, he simply kept it all), but at least we can have a good time. How 'bout a bottle of rum for everybody, all the food you want, and everybody gets laid?"

Of course, we all answered "Yeah, yeah."

Miguel said he'd found a *gordita*, a nice little fat girl.

The guys pepper him with questions. "Is she pretty? Is she nice like the ones you always get?"

"Let's just say she's a gordita and she'll take care of all of you."

She was and she did.

We went to her house where she was waiting in bed with a nice, big smile on her face. She fucked all five of us. One after another. We each were with her maybe four or five minutes, max. He probably recruited her earlier at a local whorehouse. She had a pretty face and a very nice, relaxed manner. God knows what Miguel promised her for screwing the whole band. Whatever it was, I doubt he ever gave it to her.

While I disapproved of the way he cheated people, I did learn from him that there's a certain magic in life, and that it's possible to accomplish the impossible through the power of charisma.

A few weeks after the tour, he was caught by the police in Mexico City and thrown in jail. They found five different passports on him with five different names. He was wanted in several countries in South America and that was the last we heard of him. He was the first, but not the last, guy who came into my life like that—a charming crook who melted away after awhile, without my ever knowing his real name.

Like the music, there were some movies that also changed our lives in the '50s: "Rebel Without a Cause," "Jailhouse Rock" and for me, like a lot of other motorcycle-crazed youth around the world, "The Wild One." I had to have a bike, a real one, not an Italian moped. With a loan from my grandmother Pilar I bought my first true motorcycle, a 1959 Triumph Bonneville, much like the bike Marlon Brando rode in the movie. And just as rock music had become an instant passion for me, I realized that motorcycling was going to be part of my life forever. I was so jazzed I actually slept next to the bike for the first few nights.

This period was one of the best times in my life with my friends, my music and my motorcycle. I joined a popular band called *"Los Juniors"* and two of our records made the Latin American Top Ten Chart. Then I joined *"Los Sinners,"* already famous with several hit records and known as a "quality" band. They also rode motorcycles, so we naturally developed long-lasting friendships based on our love of bikes and rock'n' roll.

The lives of two friends from Los Sinners, Tony de la Barreda and Ramon Rodriguez, would crisscross mine many times in the years ahead, often painfully. But at that time, we were too busy being kid rock musicians to think about the future.

Los Sinners attracted other kids on motorcycles to the coffee houses where we played, turning them into biker hangouts much like the ones I was going to spend a lot of time in, in the years to come. It was all very innocent, no drugs, no crime, and pathetically little sex—just nice kids, hanging out and having a good time.

By now, I was in a top local band, had a motorcycle, had lost my virginity, was a key figure in the biker hangouts and now I was about to score another first that was the start of a lifelong pattern—my first American girlfriend.

In the summer of '63, Kathleen and her friend Carol were Harvard students attending classes at the National University in Mexico City. They were cheerful, intelligent, sexy and they liked motorcycles and rock n' roll. Kathy was tall, blonde, and beautiful with a figure that had my friends rolling their eyes and biting their lips in anguished envy. At 19, she was a little older than me and when it came to love-making, she was a lot freer than Mexican girls. She was my first

Kathy, my first American girlfriend, on my first real motorcycle, a Triumph Bonneville.

serious affair with a first-class woman. I fell madly in love. I would have proposed to her if she had ever come back to Mexico City, but she went on to a very successful political career in the States.

With Kathy gone, my motorcycle turned on me too. Although it was fast and looked cool, the Triumph was a mechanical nightmare, infuriating my family because it leaked oil all over the garage and driveway of our house, and maddening because it regularly broke down. It was my only form of transportation and life turned into a series of missed gigs or late entrances in dirty clothes. My dates often ended with angry, oil-splattered girls snarling at me by the roadside because they would have to take the bus home hours after their parents' curfew. With a river of pesos flowing straight from my wallet into the hands of the local Triumph mechanic, I frequently ended up traveling by bus or taxi, which I couldn't afford now.

Much as I loved the Triumph, it had to go. I took the first offer I got and ran all the way to the local dealer in BMWs, motorcycles famous for reliability and class, to buy a brand new R60. The dream was on again. I could actually wear a tuxedo to the gigs and arrive impeccably dressed. I rode the bike for thousands of miles, day in and day out. It never failed me. It was the start of a life-long affair with boxer-engined BMW cycles.

I was about 18 when I accepted an offer to join one of Latin America's most famous bands, *"Los Hooligans."* They had an impressive career with several gold records and enjoyed wide recognition in Spanish speaking countries, so I was amazed to discover that they were actually bad musicians who played the bouncy, childish crap that came to be called "bubble gum music."

This was my introduction to a cruel truth in the pop music world: sometimes the worst bands are the most successful, while talent, taste and hard work go unrewarded.

Welcome to the music business, Fito.

In 1964, Kathy, who was back at Harvard, sent me a couple of Jimmy Reed records, along with one called "Saturday Night at the Apollo Theater," featuring various black artists. I also got a hold of some James Brown and Ray Charles, which really impressed me. Those early R&B records of my sister's, my growing education in jazz, and the black music Kathy turned me on to brought me to a crisis point.

My changing taste made performing with Los Hooligans intolerable. The money and applause wasn't enough to make up for the infantile, commercial music, the frozen smiles, the silly choreographed steps in our red or blue coats and white patent leather shoes. I could barely go through the motions, not after listening to the records Kathy sent me. She broke my heart because she never came back, but she did leave me that legacy.

One night when I was playing in a cafe called *El Sotano* (the Cellar) with El Tarolas, Javier Batiz showed up and we invited him to sit in. Javier was a singer and guitarist who became a rock star in Mexico for generations; he's one of the best ever, but he just never caught on in the States. He had a raspy blues voice, sang only in English and played guitar like B.B. King, skills forged by long nights playing in Tijuana, where he had to satisfy audiences filled with black American sailors and Marines.

Up there on the border, Javier taught guitar to a young kid nicknamed *El Apache,* because that was the only song he knew at the time. Sitting beside Javier, he learned his first guitar chords. Later on, the kid did okay on his own—not as El Apache but as Carlos Santana.

**A new girl (Sonja my future wife) on a
new bike (my first BMW, an R60)**

Los Holligans (sic) holding one of many gold records from Orfeon

Javier changed the whole scene in Mexico City by doing a lot of Jimmy Reed, B.B. King, and Ray Charles. He taught us that there was something better than bubble gum pop, something beyond what the commercial media was giving us, something with more soul.

While I instinctively liked his music, many of the other musicians didn't get it. They were convinced that Mexico City audiences would rather hear imitations of English pop bands like The Beatles, than the hard-edged black American sounds that came from that crazy *pocho* Javier Batiz.

Sick of the pop scene, I quit Los Hooligans and joined The T.J.s, a hard core rhythm and blues band that backed Javier in Tijuana. But I kept a hand in with Los Sinners, the band I felt most comfortable with. They were just like me: middle-class kids who rode motorcycles, were from the same part of town and had gone to the same schools.

One October night in 1964, at a gig with Los Sinners at a cafe called Milleti, I hit two milestones at once: I met my first wife and went to my first orgy.

Sonja came into the club looking very square in her American-coed outfit, a powder blue skirt and pastel blue sweater plus nylons and white ballet flats. I had just given up hope that Kathy would ever come back and here was another gringa, but a much different one, quiet, straight, a nice Baptist girl from Phoenix with blonde Barbie-doll bangs and an open, clean-cut face. Like Kathy, she was a college student. She went to the University of Redlands in California and was taking language courses at the National University.

I had never met an American girl like her before, so pure, so genteel, so sweet. She fascinated me. At the end of the evening one of the cafe owners invited us to a party, so I talked Sonja and her friends into coming with us.

Suddenly, one of the guys at the party turned to me and whispered in my ear: "You might want to take your gringa friends home pretty soon. See those two chicks over there? They're going to put on a show for all of us. Then they are going to fuck every guy here. If your friends are as innocent as they look, this isn't their scene."

I grabbed Sonja by the hand and headed for my motorcycle. "Time to go home," I said, pretty firmly.

When I kissed her good-bye, she clamped her lips tight. She

didn't know how to kiss. In fact, I learned later that she had never kissed anyone before. Although I liked her a lot, under the circumstances it was not something I wanted to pursue right then.

I wanted to get right back to the party.

It was ironic that at the same time I met this lovely, young saint, I was leaving her to scramble back to an orgy. It was a sign of things to come. An awareness of the darker side of the musician's life was already growing in me.

By the time I got back to the apartment, the two women—both very attractive Latinas—were nude on the carpeted floor. One looked a little reticent, like she had never done this before, but the other was going totally nuts, rubbing and licking her all over. They were surrounded by more than a half dozen men, who were stroking themselves and encouraging them.

The shy one came with a wild scream, then began giggling and laughing: "I'm a bad girl. Oh God, am I ever a bad girl."

Watching them excited me in a way that I had never felt before, and when they finished with each other, they did all of us. It was just like the gordita in Tierra Blanca. We lasted barely two minutes each.

Our quick performance couldn't have been much of a thrill for them after the terrific time they obviously had with each other. But, they appeared to like us, the innocent kids in the band. Since we'd been more than properly taken care of, we headed home to sleep.

We didn't know yet that we were supposed to go on all night.

CARRYING WATER TO THE SEA

Los Sinners at Raul Aston's TV show just before our first U.S. adventure.

In the mid '60s, the other guys in Los Sinners and I began to dream the impossible dream: playing in the United States.

After a gig one night, we were sitting around in a cheap bar, the kind where they have sawdust on the floor, talking about it. In fact, it was all we ever talked about.

The bass player from another band, who was with us that evening, looked at us like we were crazy. "You'd never get a job there. Not even in the worst places. The Americans invented rock n' roll, *idiotas*. It's their music, about their country. There are so many great bands there already. You'd be carrying water to the sea," he sneered.

"Hey, man, there are Chicanos doing it," I pointed out, thinking of Ritchie Valens, Trini Lopez, Cannibal and the Headhunters, ? and the Mysterians. If Chicanos—people who looked like us—can be rock stars in America, why not Mexicans?"

"They are Americans, *pendejo*. They are born there. They grew up listening to that music. They live that life, they go to American high schools. They play football a whole different way. Their girlfriends run around in little short skirts. They have American cars and go to drive-ins and eat hamburgers. Those Chicanos are more American than they are Mexican," he replied.

"The British do it. They didn't grow up on the Mississippi and surf at Malibu and all that," I insisted.

"They have their own sound. And they are like the Americans' smart cousins, part of the family. It's easy for them because the Americans like them. They don't like us. They would just call you a beaner or a greaser. What do you think? You're some kind of gods or something?"

That was the big insult.

Dioses. The gods. That's what other *rocanroleros* in Mexico City called those of us who dreamed of going to the States. They thought of us as arrogant, like climbing Mount Olympus to knock back a few drinks with Zeus and get a date with Venus, as if we could ever be in the same class as the divine ones.

But Los Sinners weren't about to abandon that dream. We thought we sounded just as good as some American bands. We looked good. We could sing in English, at least some of us. We even had Jon Novi, an American, as the musical leader of the band. We called him *El Cachalote* (the whale) because of his size; he was a short-haired, big-nosed guy with glasses, who was well educated

The not so wild ones: Los Sinners and friends arrive at Renato's wedding.

and very knowledgeable about music, but dressed like an accountant from South Dakota.

There was also *El Monstruo* (the monster), the nickname we cruelly hung on lead guitarist Federico Arana because of his acne-pocked face. He was older than the rest of us and a biology teacher by day. He later became a prominent writer on the history of Mexican rock n' roll.

Our lead singer Renato was good-looking and dark-skinned with green-eyes and the girls just idolized him. Girls also flocked to Baltasar, the other singer, although he was so short we nicknamed him *El Enano* (the dwarf).

The other members, Tony de la Barreda and Ramon Rodriguez, were like me, middle-class kids from European-Mexican backgrounds who were heavily into motorcycles. We didn't think Los Sinners would be a good name in America because it sounded so American (which, of course, was the whole point in Mexico). Realizing we couldn't disguise our Mexican origins, we decided we needed a name that said "Mexico" to the gringos. We settled on Los Tequilas.

We worked very hard to prepare for our version of the British rock invasion. We polished the act on several TV programs and even appeared in a couple of Mexican movies. We recorded four tracks of original songs written by Jon and arranged by everybody, paying for and producing the records ourselves in order to have complete control.

Most of the songs were in the British style because most of the guys were hung up on being like the Dave Clark Five, The Beatles or Herman's Hermits. To keep me happy, they included a couple of rhythm and blues songs, because I was always arguing for material that was deeper, more emotional, and more closely tied to the black roots of American rock music. I was determined to play some day in the birthplace of the music I loved.

And, I kept thinking of Sonja, who had gone back to Redlands to finish school. We wrote to each other, sometimes as many as three letters a week. On paper, our romance was flourishing.

By August 1965, the band was in sight of our American goal. Literally in sight. We were playing in a honky-tonk called the Aloha Club in Tijuana, close enough to the United States to see it.

Accustomed to prestige and respect in the small world of Mexico City rock music, we had to fight for a place in the border town where our popularity in the capital was simply dismissed as irrelevant. We had to work harder than we had ever dreamed, and for far tougher audiences than we had ever faced.

TJ was boot camp for Mexican rock musicians. This was where we paid our dues. Whorehouses and honky-tonks ran all night. At the famous Blue Fox, the strippers stripped all the way and just about had sex with drunken sailors right there on the tables. There were great bands and good musicians all over the place and you had to kick ass with audiences full of American sailors and Marines or catch the next bus home. Those tough guys from the San Diego and Long Beach bases were no Mexico City college crowd. They weren't impressed by cheesy covers of American records. They knew the good stuff when they heard it or headed for another bar if they didn't, and the bar owner always noticed if the musicians couldn't hold the crowd.

We got $12 each for playing 12 sets a night from 5 P.M. to 5 A.M., six nights a week, alternating with one other band. We had a couple of stiff drinks as the sun came up, slept 'til 3 in the afternoon in a hotel where mutant cockroaches could eat right through the metal tube to get at the toothpaste, then had a cup of coffee and went back on stage.

Few musicians could survive this grind, but from this crucible came the small group of Mexicans who leaped over the border like me, Santana, and jazz bassist Abraham Laboreal.

The bright spot was that Sonja was close enough to come down on a bus from Redlands on some weekends. Even though she spent many hours with me in bed, she would still go home every Sunday a virgin.

After two months in TJ, we were ready to make our big move. Tony's father was a Mexican Air Force officer who had been part of the Mexican squadron that fought alongside the Americans against the Japanese in World War II. So one day, Tony crossed the border to see one of his father's old American war buddies, a California oilfield worker named Fritz.

Tony came back with a phenomenal gift. Fritz had loaned him a car, a beautiful white Chevy Impala convertible with a red interior. We piled it up with our instruments and told the American border guards we were going to a picnic in San Diego that afternoon.

As we blasted up Interstate 5 to Hollywood, we cranked up the radio and sang Fats Domino's "Ain't That A Shame," leaving San Diego in our rearview mirror. We went straight to the Sunset Strip, the land of our dreams with the famous clubs: The Trip, The Sea Witch, The Whiskey A Go Go, and Gazzari's. The musical and cultural revolution of the '60s was shifting into high gear. We could feel it. We could see it in the hippies on the Strip, a revolutionary energy. And we were there, walking on the golden streets of Mount Olympus; we were going to be part of it.

We managed to wrangle an appointment at the William Morris Agency, one of the best in show business. Jon Novi did the talking, while the rest of us stood behind him, contributing our few words of English like "hello," "yes" and "good-bye."

We were shown into a plush office and asked to play our records for a handsome, button-down, corporate-looking agent named Skip Taylor.

"You guys are great. You remind me of Ramsey Lewis." Our hearts soared.

"But I don't know where I can put you," he continued. "The places I work with will never hire you, a group of underage foreigners with no working papers. Not a chance."

Our English was good enough to understand "not a chance."

"But there's a guy you ought to see named Howard Wolf."

I thought that was the last I'd see of Skip Taylor, but a few months later he became the manager of a brand new band called Canned Heat. (The same would be true of Howard Wolf years later).

Our lives were destined to be closely linked for decades, although it would be three years after I joined Canned Heat before Skip and I remembered that we actually met before the band existed, when a troupe of naive but ambitious Mexican teenagers popped up in his William Morris office.

Before we had a chance to contact Wolf, we got a break. Jon Novi went to see a friend of his father's and came back to our motel with a big smile on his face. "My father's friend has a job for us. Let's get our stuff in the car. We've got a job tonight in Beverly Hills."

We could hardly believe it. Beverly Hills. Palm trees. Movie stars. We were really impressed and a little insecure.

"Don't sweat it," Jon said. "The Americans liked us at the Aloha in TJ; they'll like us in Beverly Hills too."

I suppose it would be a better story if we wound up in the only low-class dive in Beverly Hills, but we didn't. We got out of the Impala at the Daisy, an expensive private club in what looked like some millionaire's mansion. I'm still not sure how it happened, but we landed our first gig in the United States at the pinnacle of chic.

As we came out for our first set, I looked out at the audience and did a double take. Paul Newman and Joanne Woodward were there. Later on, we saw Charlton Heston. It seemed like every woman in the club was gorgeous and dressed in a style I guess could be called rich hippie, all silk and swirls and golden chains.

I mumbled to Jon: "Right man. Just like the Aloha. Lots of whores and Marines here tonight." We all laughed. We were wound up tight, but good tight, as we started to play. We figured we looked sharp as hell in our red silk tuxedos.

They loved us. They applauded like crazy. I was pounding away on The Beachboys' classic "Fun, Fun Fun" and thinking, "We did it. We are fucking here! They were wrong back home. You can join them in the land of the *dioses*. We are good enough. Hell, they absolutely love us."

All we had to do was keep quiet about our lack of working papers and our age. None of us were 18 years old, far too young to be allowed in the club, much less work there.

The exposure at the Daisy not only brought us fans but invitations to play other clubs, good ones like PJ's, of Trini Lopez fame, and the Lazy X, where Ike and Tina Turner and Bobby Bland were also playing. When some of the club owners found out about our age and our lack of working papers, they only gave us half what they would have paid an American band, figuring we couldn't complain. They were right. We couldn't. But we didn't care. It was America, it was magic, it was home to every rocker in the world. We were on our way.

It was not unusual for people to come up and tell us: "You guys sound just like the records." We played Beach Boys, Beatles and Righteous Brothers songs. It was pretty amazing—this Mexican band all dressed up in their corny red silk tuxedos, straight out of the border honky-tonks, sounding like American and English stars.

At the Troubador one night, a bald guy in his 60s, chomping a cigar, stopped us as we were getting ready to leave. In a thick Italian accent, he said his name was Lou Ransella. He seemed to know a lot about us.

"I don't care if you guys don't have work permits. And I don't care if you're minors. You're a great group and I'm going to get you jobs. Don't worry about anything. Just don't get in trouble. Don't say anything to anybody. Otherwise they'll put you in a wagon and send you back and you don't want that. You're going to make it."

We returned the borrowed Impala and Lou bought us a used Ford Falcon wagon. He said we could repay him from the work he got us at a redneck country-rock club, The Farmhouse, in Cathedral City, a small desert town near Palm Springs.

Looking at a map, I realized I'd be playing only 40 miles from the University of Redlands, barely a half hour's drive from Sonja. We were living the American dream: applause, a steady job, a girlfriend I loved and a decent car for only $300.

During our gig at The Farmhouse, Tony fell madly in love with the club's "go-go girl" Karen, "The Sensational Queen of Watusi." She was a gorgeous, statuesque blonde who shook her body to our music for hours every night, driving us and the audience into a frenzy.

At the same time, my relationship with Sonja was heating up. I was falling in love with her and she with me. Actual sex wasn't in the picture yet, but we did everything else that young people did in those times.

I was too young and happy to think that this was too good to last. For two months now, we were living an idyllic existence and we even stopped looking over our shoulders for the Border Patrol. In addition to our steady job at The Farmhouse, Lou Ransella lined up gigs for us in Hollywood and even Nevada, which we were really looking forward to.

The bad luck began when our $300 Falcon blew up on our way to see the new hit movie "Help" with The Beatles. We ended up taking a bus to Indio, a few miles south quite near the border. As we stepped down from the bus at the Indio station, two Border Patrol officers were checking the papers of passengers who looked Mexican. I have blue eyes and fair skin so I just kept walking and they didn't stop me. Novi, of course, was an American. No problem. But our singer *El Chava* was from Tijuana and looked it. They immediately grabbed him and started giving him the third degree.

Watching this unfold killed me. God damn it. We had it all and now it's over.

Novi whispered to me: "I'm going to tell them the truth about everything."

"What the hell for?" I whispered back. "Don't tell them anything."

He was really pissing me off. I was against him copping out because I was convinced they would let us go if we simply stuck with our story: we were a bunch of Chicano kids, Beatles fans, who came down from Palm Springs to see "Help."

But Jon, a straight arrow with strict parents, spilled his guts.

It was my first taste of the American Border Patrol and they were total assholes. To them we weren't harmless kid musicians, we were just one more bunch of damn wetbacks.

They gave us 24 hours to get south of the border, which was just enough time to get our instruments and pick up our pay at The Farmhouse. The owner was nice about it but sorry to see us leave because we had begun attracting regular fans.

Heartbroken, I called Sonja at college. "We got caught, darling, and I have to leave the country right away. I don't know if I can ever come back. They said I might never be allowed to return."

"Fito, wait for me; I'll be right there. Please try to stay until I can get there."

Waiting in the bus depot in Calexico to return to Mexico, we were so depressed we were in a state of shock. Sonja and I just cried in each other's arms.

And here comes the Border Patrol again.

"Take those drums apart."

"Why? We're leaving. We're going home. We're getting out of your country. You got what you wanted. What harm are the drums?"

"There could be drugs in them. So take them apart. Now," he barked.

"Why would I take drugs INTO Mexico?," I asked. "That would be stupid."

"I said take them apart. Now!"

We didn't even use drugs in those days and we looked more like American college kids than dope runners.

It took me close to an hour, my last hour in the States, to disassemble the drums down to the point where he could be sure there wasn't 50 kilos of heroin stashed away somewhere, while everyone else in the station gawked at us. I burned with shame having to do that in front of my straightlaced American girlfriend. Then I had to put the drums back together.

We almost missed the bus. As we ran through the station, I kissed Sonja all the way. My main fear was not being able to come back. I liked the United States, aside from being humiliated by its cops. I wanted to get back to the home of American music. I had met interesting people who were good to us and I had learned a lot about the culture that had fascinated me since those old Benny Goodman movies.

Above all, I wanted to see the woman I loved again. First Kathy, now Sonja. I kept meeting these American angels and losing them.

Four months, two weeks, four days and seven hours after our friends had given us a big farewell party in Mexico City, we tumbled out of a second-class *Estrella de Oro* bus in a station in the same neighborhood. We were grimy and bleary-eyed after a 52-hour run from the border, toting our guitars and drums and the last few bucks we had saved from the invasion of *El Norte,* the foray that was going to make us stars.

Trudging through a cold December rain, we headed right for a coffee house where we could find out what was happening, and maybe line up some gigs.

We ran into Mauricio, a musician I never liked. "The gods return," he said, laughing with disdain.

We sat around staring at the coffees and lemonade.

"Yeah," one of the guys said wearily. *"Los Dioses."*

I saw it differently.

"Fuck that guy. He's wrong. We went to *El Norte* and we played for them and they liked us. The Americans aren't gods. They're people like us and they accepted us. If it was up to the people who heard us play, we'd still be there. Okay, we got kicked out because we had bad luck, but we didn't fail. We showed we could play their music just as well as they do." That was true. But America had seen the last of Los Tequilas. And soon Los Tequilas would see the last of me.

Changing our name back to Los Sinners, we immediately got a gig at the Plein Soleil, the biggest, hippest coffee house in the city. But our disagreements over music became terminal. The other guys wanted to be Herman's Hermits, which to me was the worst of the worst. I hated that shit, but I had to play it with these people because I was only the drummer and singers are more important.

They said it was ridiculous for us to play like Negroes, but it was even more ridiculous for them to try to be pretty English boys. It seemed to me we would be closer to the Negro than to the English, because Mexicans had suffered more, been subjugated, and were not as white. I kept pushing the band into rhythm and blues material. Years later in his book, "Blue Suede Huaraches," The History of Mexican Rock 'n' Roll, Federico Arana *("El Monstruo")* gave me credit for helping change the group into a "heavier" band.

With the members of Los Sinners calling me a deserter and a traitor, I joined Javier Batiz, who was playing the kind of music I liked, also at the Plein Soleil.

One night during a break, this American guy comes up and tells me he's a drummer with a hot new blues band in Los Angeles named Canned Heat. It was the first time I'd heard of them. His name was Frank Cook.

"Hey, you guys are really great. I never expected a Mexican band to play R&B so well. Mind if I sit in?"

Of course I didn't mind. Allowing visitors to sit in with your band is a common gesture of friendship and respect among musicians. I let Frank jam with Javier and the band on a Jimmy Reed song called "Big Boss Man." He was obviously unfamiliar with the tune and didn't do well. Javier—the dean of the Tijuana Graduate School of Rock Music—demanded top quality in his backup and angrily told me to get back on the drums.

Later that night, Frank asked me to help him find some weed, which I did, even though I didn't smoke it then. To be hospitable I showed him and his wife Myrna to a few clubs around town. I told him how much I loved playing in the States and hoped to return. He gave me his number and told me that if I ever got back to Los Angeles, he would help me. I treasured that number. He was my only real professional musician contact in the U.S.

In spite of my untimely deportation from the States and the distance between us, my relationship with Sonja continued to flourish. On December 20, 1966, the straitlaced Sonja and I married

My first R+B gig with American Black Musicians

57

in Mexico City, but the omens for family harmony were not good. Sonja's mother hated Catholics, Mexicans and musicians—in that order. After our honeymoon in Acapulco, Sonja returned to the U.S. to finish her degree and wait for me to join her in California.

Around the same time, Tony married Karen, the Sensational Queen of Watusi and also decided to come to the States with me.

While our U.S. residency papers were being processed, we joined a black group from San Francisco playing in Mexico City. They had a singer named Wally Cox, who sang like James Brown and a saxophone player Snooky Flowers, who later became part of Janis Joplin's Kosmic Blues Band. Their drummer was excellent, but his head was somewhere on the other side of the moon, so they canned him and hired me.

I was back learning rhythm and blues from people who knew the music. We performed in two of Mexico City's best-known nightclubs, *Terraza Casino* and *Los Globos.* Also featured was the legendary Cuban singer Celia Cruz with the original Sonora Matancera. I would lose myself watching them perform. I was barely 20 and felt privileged to be alternating with such superb musicians.

In February 1967, 14 months after being thrown out of the States, I set off with Tony by train for the border to join our new wives in America. Our families were in tears, waving good-bye.

"I know you are never coming back," said my dear grandmother Pilar.

She was right. Oh, I went back often enough, but as an outsider returning for visits, and eventually as an American citizen, a foreigner. That was the last time I experienced the all-embracing warmth of my family's unconditional love as an insider. There in that train station, I yanked out my own roots. From then on, I was going to have to deal with life on my own. I looked forward to the adventures. I didn't know then what a high price I'd pay for them.

When the train arrived in the border town of Mexicali, Sonja was on the platform, looking radiant in a white blouse and pink shorts. As we toted our bags out of the station, she led me up to an old blue Plymouth Valiant.

"How do you like our wedding present from my mom?"

"A car? That's great. And I have my drum kit and $500."

"And we have each other. Welcome to America, Fito."

Javier Batiz and "The Finks"

On TV with Javier and his sister "La Baby"

The civil ceremony with my father, Sonja's mother, and family members.

I got a big long kiss. It was a sweet re-entry to the land of the gods, with all gratitude to my American wife.

Because we didn't have any money, Sonja had to continue to live in the dorm at school, so she asked her best friend's lover, a black philosophy teacher, if I could crash at his house until she graduated.

I bought a drum instruction manual, and while Sonja worked in the college cafeteria, I would spend the day practicing my paradiddles, flams, rata ma cues and other exercises. I still wasn't what you would call a formally trained drummer. I just played the way I felt, but about as close to the instruction book as I could interpret it.

Every evening Sonja would come to my little room. With a big grin, she would show me the food she brought me from the college cafeteria. We lived mostly on milk, tiny boxes of Cheerios and love.

One weekend we called Frank Cook and arranged to see him at his condo in Marina Del Rey. He started telling me again what a great band he was in, this Canned Heat, best in the world. I got interested

**On our wedding day with dear grandmother Pilar's picture
in the background**

After the religious ceremony, with my family

and wanted to see the Topanga Corral where the group was playing, because it had become such a famous spot in the fast-growing hippie scene, which was so closely tied to the music world. It was more than 100 miles of freeway from our place in Redlands to the mouth of Topanga Canyon, and then another 15 minutes on a twisting two-lane road up into the mountains, the lights of the San Fernando Valley twinkling in our rear view mirror, before we found the Corral in a dark hollow.

I was not impressed. It was a filthy, ramshackle wooden barn lost in the sagebrush hills. The floor was covered with sawdust and the place was full of hippies, most of whom looked like clouds of dirty hair held up by skinny, blue denim bellbottoms. I didn't know that this was becoming a center for the whole L.A. hippie music scene, a hangout for the psychedelic elite, the funky frontier. But I had played the Daisy, and PJs, so I damn well knew what American chic looked like. Hell, I had been in the house band at the Farmhouse, which was desert rustic, but it had more class than this.

It looked like Cook's band was going to be as far short of his brags as he was. I didn't expect much from the evening. I was as wrong as I could be. From the first notes of "Got My Mojo Working," I knew that these guys were a whole new world. They had a great bass player—it was Larry Taylor's first night with them—and the combination of musicians that night was dynamic, with a real feel for the blues.

I sat there with Sonja, entranced, envious, trying to keep my hands from drumming obnoxiously on the table. I kept waiting for Frank to ask me to sit in. I had given him a shot with Javier's band in Mexico City. When we do that, the expected thing is to return the courtesy when the other musician shows up in your joint. He knew I knew the songs—this band was playing blues numbers he had heard me play with Javier.

After the set, we joined Frank and his wife at their table. I waited a while, but there was no invitation, just small talk. This was one of the greatest bands I had ever heard and I really wanted to jam with them. Finally, I just came right out and asked. With Sonja prompting me through my still broken English: "Hey, man, you mind if I sit in for a number?"

"No, we don't do that in this country. We couldn't let somebody sit in or jam on a job because it could create problems with the owner," Frank said.

I sat there trying to keep a smile on my face while I felt like I had been slapped. They don't let musicians sit in for a jam in the United States? Hell, this is where that practice was invented. It goes back to the roots of jazz. Did he think we were so stupid in Mexico that we didn't know that? Did he think I had never played in the United States, never talked to American musicians? Was this racism? Or was he just afraid I'd show him up? Maybe take his job? I don't know and I probably never will. But I suppose we're even, Frank and me.

Because later I did take his job.

Not that night, and not because of anything that happened that night. And my knowing Frank had nothing to do with it. It would have happened even if I hadn't gone to the Corral that evening.

By now, Sonja had graduated from college and gotten a job as a teacher, so we rented a house on Woodman Avenue in the San Fernando Valley. Tony was living with The Sensational Queen of Watusi in North Hollywood and we scrounged gigs in beer joints and pool halls with pickup bands of drifter musicians. These guys were always from someplace else, Denver or Tucson or wherever, new to L.A., hoping to make it in the glamorous city where movie stars live. We were all from out of town. Tony and I just came from farther than most. I knew they weren't as experienced or professional as we were, but I told myself it was a new life, a new country and it made sense to start at the bottom again to pay my dues.

There was always the pull of going home. I could be in TJ in two hours, where life was a daily combat zone, but where I had a good reputation in a tough world. Or I could go back to Mexico City where I could be in movies, appear on TV and make records. A whole generation of Mexicans knew my name; I was a home-town star. But I was determined to make it in the U.S., not just playing for beer and change, but I wanted to be a respected musician in the land of rhythm and blues, the cradle of rock n' roll.

It was what my friends and I talked about late into the night over cigarettes and beer, while rain puddled the dark, empty streets outside the all-night cafes in Mexico City. Except for Tony, the others who started out with me were gone now, lapping up teenage adulation or toughing it out in the border honky-tonks. But I was in love with an American girl. And I was going to show her I could take care of her in her own country.

One night in a Long Beach beer joint, I got some encouragement. After a drum solo backing a rhythm and blues group called The Rivingtons, the lead guitar player turned to me and asked: "What the hell is a guy like you doing in a place like this?"

I didn't know enough English yet to recognize the question as an American cliché; something you say to the nicest girl in the whorehouse when you want to cheer her up. But I still think that guitarist meant it as a compliment.

Tony and I decided to team up with two guys from Tennessee named Larry Barnes and his buddy Jerry, along with Dewey, a saxophone player from Dallas. The band was called Larry Barnes and the Creations. Somehow the combination of white southerners and Mexicans came out sounding like a black band. We landed a six-night-a-week gig as the house band at the Tom Cat Club, a big, funky joint at 198th and Hawthorne in Torrance, south of L.A., which generally hired black musicians, even though the audience was mostly Anglo and Latino. Each Thursday was "Celebrity Night," which gave us the opportunity to back some of the greatest rhythm and blues artists of the times: The Coasters, Etta James, Jimmy Reed, Troy Walker, the Platters, the Rivingtons and the Shirelles, to name a few.

No more pretty boy bands. No more arguing for less pop and deeper soul. No more singers who want me to be one of Herman's goddam Hermits. I'm home. I'm in America, playing rhythm and blues with the real article. I'm in the country legally and I'm in the musician's union. By Christmas of 1967, I had a new Pontiac Firebird and I'm in love with my wife. Life is cool. My American dream is coming true.

Like most immigrants' American dreams, they came with a price, a lot of work. I was in three bands at once. Although the Creations were my main gig, I also played in an excellent group called Bluesberry Jam, featuring a black singer named Al Walton and Ted Green, a virtuoso guitar player who went on to become a very famous teacher and jazz guitarist.

One sunny California day, Sonja mentioned that a friend of hers from Phoenix had called. She knew some musicians from Tucson who were new in town and needed a drummer. The group was called The Sot Weed Factor, which struck me as a real hippie kind of name. I was still pretty straight then and didn't have a clue as to what that world was like.

Sonja took me to an address in Hollywood, which turned out to be an old abandoned movie set built for Rudolf Valentino in the '20's. The band had rented it for living quarters. They were young, crazy and the incarnation of the hippie life style. Each band member had a odd-shaped room in a corner of the set. The place was always full of music, beautiful girls and reeked of pot. Between their constant pot smoking and dropping acid regularly, I couldn't understand how they could function, but they did. We recorded a single, "Bald Headed Woman" and "Say It's Not So," for Original Sound, an old Hollywood label. Jeff Addison, the lead guitar player would eventually play a few gigs with Canned Heat years later. We were regulars at The Sea Witch on Sunset Boulevard. Then we started playing as the house band at The Topanga Corral. So there I was, playing in the same place where Canned Heat was becoming a fixture.

Meanwhile, Canned Heat was having a problem with drummer Frank Cook. The other band members wanted someone with more of a rhythm and blues orientation rather than jazz, which Frank was into.

Alan and Bob started Canned Heat in late 1965. Both loved and collected old jazz and country blues records, two of the few things they had in common.

Alan was other-worldly, a fragile poet, a genius, and a shy nerd tortured by the demands for exhibitionism in the entertainment business. He was lovable to those of us who knew him well but very, very weird to most everyone else. His singing voice was high and delicate. He hungered for some kind of solitary, inner peace.

The Bear could not have been more different. He worked in record stores in the San Fernando Valley and West L.A. and was an encyclopedic resource for anyone interested in old blues music. He was large in body and soul, a mountain of appetites. He was Dionysus, the Greek god of wine, sex and theater. He would eat, smoke, drink or fuck anything he could get his arms around. He burned to be on stage because that way he could start a party. He sang for money when he could get it but was perfectly willing to perform all night for free if there was anyone else awake to party with him. His singing voice was like gravel going down a steel chute. He hungered to be loved by everyone, or at least everyone who would have a drink or a joint with him.

Henry was another blues record collector and he introduced Bob to Alan, whose scholarly works on the blues in American music history were published in respected professional journals. As one reference book noted: Alan "was so accomplished a musician by age 20 that he was invited to play at Newport."

The friendship and common musical interests of the three became the nucleus of Canned Heat. At first, Alan and Bob had this idea to form a jug band, an eccentrically American combination that dates back to poor farm boys in the 19th century, making music with the odds and ends found around a barn. Some players blow across the tops of bottles or jugs—bigger ones producing deeper notes—while others scratch washboards with their nails or play an acoustic piano or guitar. Some included kazoos and Jew's harps. The jug band came and went quickly and was replaced by the idea of forming a blues band called Canned Heat.

Taken from a 1929 song by Tommy Johnson, the name refers to a sort of jellied alcohol like Sterno that burns in its own small can when ignited; it's typically used for cooking on camping trips or to warm buffet dishes. During Prohibition, when booze was illegal, many poor southern blacks bought the cheap canned fuel, dumped the jelly into a sock and wrung the liquid alcohol from it. This was mixed with Orange Crush or Coca Cola and the result was a strong potion that could put the drinker away for hours. It was also poisonous. No manufacturer ever put cognac in a fuel can. They used cheap industrial alcohol, which is chemically different from drinking alcohol. Many drinkers died or went blind from it. That was a risk they often knew they were taking, making it the drink of the desperate. If you had to turn to canned heat for relief, you were deep in the blues.

According to Alan, the band held its first rehearsal on November 19, 1965. Two years later, he and Bob were the only original members left. The band went through two other drummers before Cook came in, two other bass players and two other lead guitars before bringing in Vestine, who The Bear knew was playing bar gigs in the San Fernando Valley.

Back in his record clerk days, Bob put together a list of rare records to be auctioned and Henry was one of the buyers. Although Henry's earliest claim to fame was getting bounced from Frank Zappa's famous "Mothers of Invention" for excessive drug use, he actually had acquired music research credentials that put him on common ground with Alan and The Bear. When he was 19, Henry set out on an expedition with acoustic guitar legend/scholar John

Fahey and another young blues fanatic named Bill Barth to track down the legendary singer Skip James, who made a couple of records for Paramount in 1931 and later became a minister before disappearing. They found him in a hospital in Tunica, Mississippi and talked the 62-year-old James back into playing and recording the blues after a 30 year absence. In what was later called "one of the greatest triumphs for classical blues that Newport has ever seen," James appeared at the 1964 Newport Folk Festival, along with blues greats Mississippi John Hurt, Son House, and Robert Pete Williams.

Even with Henry in the band, Canned Heat was having little success. "In Los Angeles at least, there was no interest in blues, and an actual fear of blues music by club owners," Alan later told an interviewer. "We hardly got any work and folded up; one of the most ignominious economic failures of the year in the music business."

The next year, 1967, the band re-formed and attracted John Hartmann and Skip Taylor as managers. As Alan put it (and only Alan, of all the musicians in the world, would phrase it): "They knew enough about music to realize we were playing in an exceedingly specialized area, but they felt the band's personality—The Bear's schtick and all that stuff—would attract enough interest among the record buying public to overcome the relative unpopularity of the blues."

Shortly after Hartmann and Taylor signed on in February, Larry Taylor joined to play bass. When other kids his age were just starting to listen to rock records in the 1950s, Taylor was making them. A Brooklyn-born kid, he was on the road with Jerry Lee Lewis at 16. He performed with Teddy Randazzo, known for writing such best-selling songs as "Going Out of My Head" and "Hurt So Bad." He was a top session player and even made several hits with The Monkees.

By now, the band was getting known, for reasons good and bad. In the spring of 1967, it came out with its first Liberty album called "Canned Heat," which had an orange cover showing the band around a table littered with Sterno cans. It didn't contain any original material, relying on blues classics like Muddy Waters "Rollin' and Tumblin'," Willie Dixon's "Evil Is Going On," Elmore James' "Dust My Broom" and Sonny Boy Williamson's "Help Me." It wasn't a big seller but received rave reviews from authoritative critics like Pete Welding in "Down Beat" magazine.

In June, the band appeared at the Monterey Pop Festival, establishing the group as LA's answer to Paul Butterfield's Blues

Band in Chicago and England's Bluesbreakers, also pioneer white interpreters of black blues. The festival was small by today's standards, only about 35,000 spectators, but it established a new wave of bands as the standard bearers for a cultural revolution. Up there on the same stage with Alan and The Bear were Otis Redding, Janis Joplin, Jimi Hendrix, the Grateful Dead, the Animals and Jefferson Airplane.

"Down Beat" featured Canned Heat on the cover of its festival issue and the band took off. They appeared at the Avalon Ballroom, where owner Chet Helms had a helper, a quiet young Jewish guy who collected tickets and swept the floor. His name was Bill Graham and he went on to found a music empire based on the now-legendary Fillmore Ballrooms in San Francisco and New York, command posts of the '60s rock movement.

Helms booked Canned Heat into The Family Dog, his new place in Denver, setting the stage for a drama that gave the band one of its best known songs, but also saddling it with a financial burden that would have repercussions for decades afterward.

The Denver police hated the idea of a hippie haven in their city and had done all they could to stop the club from opening. Nothing worked. Helms was way too smooth for them and met all legal requirements. When the club finally opened, Helms and his people were subjected to a barrage of harassment and illegal searches. This prompted them to get a restraining order against John Grey, the rabidly anti-drug detective also known as the "Wyatt Earp of the West" for his promise: "I'm going to rid Denver of all long haired people."

It was Canned Heat's bad luck to show up just as the police figured they'd get one of the bands and the bad press and legal troubles would slop over on Helms. On Saturday night October 21, 1967, the police dispatched a stool-pigeon with some weed to Canned Heat's hotel to socialize a little and get the band high. The Bear swore that the band members (knowing the city's reputation) actually didn't have drugs with them that night.

It turned out the stool-pigeon was an old friend of Bob's—Bear grew up in Denver—so he trusted the guy, until he suddenly slid out the door and the cops came barging in to "discover" a lid of grass under the cushion of the chair where the "friend" had been sitting. They arrested everybody on charges of marijuana possession—still a big offense in those days.

Skip, the one guy who did have drugs, wasn't there. He was in his room with a girl, but the cops went to arrest him anyway.

"You with that band?" asked the cop who knocked on the door.

"Uh, yeah," said Skip, who was wrapped in a blanket from the bed. His girl was in a sheet.

Sitting on his nightstand, wrapped in tin foil, was a flat chunk of rich, dark brown Afghani hashish; it looked like a Hershey's bar.

"You're going to have to come with us and the rest of the band," the cop said. As they left, the cop said to the girl: "Sorry to bother you with this ma'am. But you'll have to finish that chocolate bar all alone."

The only real dope in the place—except him—and he missed it.

The band was hauled off to jail after the search. A judge was not available to set bail until Monday, so the boys spent the weekend in the can. Larry—who never got high—was thrown in a tank with 50 drunks and no sleeping facilities. The bust was immortalized in "My Crime," which tells the story best.

I went to Denver late last fall
I went to do my job; I didn't break any law
We worked a hippie place
Like many in our land
They couldn't bust the place, and so they got the band
'Cause the police in Denver
No they don't want long hairs hanging around
And that's the reason why
They want to tear Canned Heat's reputation down.

To a reporter at the time, The Bear said: "To sing the blues, you have to be an outlaw. Blacks are born outlaws, but we white people have to work for that distinction."

Being led away in handcuffs, kicked off the band's image as the bad boys of rock, heavy-duty incorrigibles, which eventually led to our becoming a favorite band of the Hells Angels and other outlaw biker clubs. At the moment, the band was on the downside of the outlaw life. Skip was desperate. He had a band that was far from a sure thing but was suddenly hot. Unless they could follow up, they might get cold just as quickly. Unfortunately, they couldn't play anywhere if they were looking at possible jail time.

In a gin rummy game in Los Angeles with Al Bennett, President

70

of Liberty Records, Skip mentioned that he needed $10,000 right away for legal fees to fight the bust. Bennett, a shrewd businessman, offered him that much for the publishing rights to the band's works and Skip grabbed at it. He had no choice.

Skip hired a brilliant, connected Denver attorney who sprung the band, but at the price of publishing rights that would be worth millions in the years to come. It was the start of a chain of events that created a band that rode a powerful wave of popularity in the rock explosion of the late '60s, but was always just one gig away from being broke. It was only six months later that the "Boogie with Canned Heat" album hit the stores with "On The Road Again," which became a worldwide hit.

To this day, the band has not received a penny of the publishing rights for that song, a song that shows up regularly in TV commercials as a way of instantly creating the aura of the vanished '60s.

This was the band I was so thrilled to get a chance to join. I just didn't know, and wouldn't learn for years, that it was already a band that was crippled financially by the same offstage life that fed its music and its fame.

Shortly after being released on bail pending trial, Skip and John came to the Tomcat Club to hear me play. They'd heard about me from good reviews I got playing with Bluesberry Jam in a concert at UCLA, as well as the guys in Sot Weed Factor, who visited their office looking for a manager.

Boy, had Skip changed. The clean-cut, preppy agent in the corporate suit I met three years ago now had long hair. He was wearing a funky hippie outfit, doing drugs and managing Canned Heat. He'd come a long way from William Morris. On my break, they asked me to sit at their table.

"You do know there's something else happening besides this kind of place?" asked Skip, gesturing at the Tomcat Club. "There's a movement out there. A true musical revolution. Guys like Jimi Hendrix. You want to be part of that don't you? Canned Heat's looking for a new drummer. How would you like to play with Sot Weed Factor or Bluesberry Jam and open for Canned Heat in its next LA appearance? Then Bob, Alan and the guys can hear you play."

They arranged for Bluesberry Jam to open for Canned Heat at a little place on Ventura Boulevard in the Valley called the Magic

Mushroom. We were a little uptight that night because Canned Heat was already THE Los Angeles blues band and people were talking about them with respect.

It was a magical evening. There were drugged-out hippies in paisley and stripes, silk and bellbottoms, chains and headbands, flower wreaths in their hair, dancing and blowing this shiny dust in the air. There was a gang of beautiful women, called Vito's dancers, who showed up as a group at parties and rock shows, 10 to 20 of them, wildly dressed, with Vito leading the pack. Any place they went became a party.

Bluesberry Jam opened and we played a hot set. Can't say as much for Canned Heat, which had just gotten out of that Denver jail. Throughout the years, the band has played brilliantly most of the time, with occasional off nights, when the guys were just terrible. Not just bad, but terrible. Really sucked. Always black or white, never grey, that was the band's character.

Maybe it was destiny that this was one of the rotten nights. And maybe it had something to do with the pressure they were putting on Frank about his drumming. And he didn't even know that I was there auditioning for his job.

When it was Canned Heat's turn, I noticed Frank tried to play the way I played, a strong aggressive rhythm instead of his usual laid-back jazz style. That's the worst thing a musician can do, try to make an instant style change. You might be able to work at it and do it a year later, but nobody can spin on a dime and pick up a new style in a night.

When Sonja and I got home that night, we were both really excited. Around 3:30 in the morning the phone rang. It was either Skip or John, I don't remember which one, but I recall the words:

"The guys really enjoyed your playing. They'd like you to rehearse with them tomorrow, so they can make the final decision on your replacing Frank. OK with you?"

I didn't sleep that night. I lay in bed, holding Sonja, unable to believe my luck. I was getting a shot with the best band in LA, a band with a record contract.

My friends in Mexico sarcastically told me I was trying to be a "god," but I never expected it. I thought I'd come to the States and play funky, black music with people who knew the music well, but I didn't let myself dream of becoming any sort of star. That was too unrealistic. Suddenly, it wasn't so farfetched.

Around three the next afternoon, I showed up at John Hartmann's house in Canoga Park, a ranch with horses stabled outside. (Skip and John were already starting to live the good life.) Under my arm, I'd tucked LPs by Junior Wells and Buddy Guy, two blues masters from Chicago. I always brought records to rehearsals for the other guys to hear, to adapt arrangements from, things like that. I didn't realize the impact this simple act would have. I didn't know that Alan, The Bear and Henry were such avid musicologists and record collectors. I didn't know they were so deep into the same music I had been possessed by since I was a kid drumming on cookie tins in a Mexico City garage.

The Bear told me, a long time later, that as I was setting up my drums, he was thinking: "I've already heard you, I know how you play. But those records under your arm, that's your ticket into this band. A drummer who doesn't come with a jazz attitude or with any other kind of baggage but the blues. That's our drummer, the guy who's going to get us where we want to go."

We played blues standards and I had no trouble fitting in. When we finished, I remember Henry looking at the other guys. He didn't want to make up his mind on the spot. Henry was still a good ol' boy, a Southern racist back then and he thought only a southern white guy could have the right feeling. It took him a decade to lose that crap. But in the minds of Alan and The Bear and Larry, I was in. Skip and John took me by the arm and led me outside. We leaned against a rail by the horse corral.

"The guys want you. What do you think about joining Canned Heat?" Without hesitation, limited English and all, I blurted out what I really felt, a line that became attached to me—my mantra, my battle cry—when the others heard it:

"I was BORN to play with Canned Heat."

THE GOLDEN AGE

December 1, 1967.

A date I'll never forget.

My first gig as a full-fledged member of Canned Heat.

We shared top billing with The Doors at the Long Beach Auditorium.

We were a good fit with The Doors. We were both the vanguard of the L.A. sound, formed in the Topanga-Venice scene, attracting the same kinds of audiences.

The San Francisco groups that got such hot press—the Grateful Dead, Jefferson Airplane, and Country Joe and the Fish—were into the psychedelic sound and Indian music. L.A. bands like Canned Heat and the Doors were more blues oriented.

Even though we did a lot of shows together across the U.S. and Europe, we never really got close to The Doors. The environment was cordial but competitive, though we sometimes spent a few minutes before a performance rapping and sharing a joint. The exception was Alan, who used to hang around sometimes with Jim Morrison—the two creative introverts, both courting death like a dark, elusive sweetheart.

It was a magic time, a honeymoon, when all our heads were in the same place. Although Alan had the most formal musical education, we all contributed to Canned Heat's songs. Each member's ideas were assimilated and used as we saw fit. An idea would very rarely be turned down. Alan would never tell us specifically what to do with our own instruments. We'd experiment, talk about it and then make a decision as a group.

We were adapting existing music, changing it and creating it anew. For all that artists are so individualistic, the art they create is not theirs alone, not totally unique, because every artist has to learn from other artists. Even a painter as individual as Picasso must have seen other paintings that had an effect on him. Only if you were born in a world totally without art could you claim that all your works were created solely by you. Artists take what they receive and give it new form. That's what we were doing. We were messing around with the songs of old country blues artists, changing them into something different and new. When we did, we'd claim them, ethically and legally, as ours. When we didn't, we'd credit the originals.

We deliberately left "blues band" off the name Canned Heat. We didn't want to be labeled as a bunch of white kids copying the old black masters. As Henry put it: "We have to get rid of the coffee

The "classic" Canned Heat line-up.

house mentality." That was where white blues scholars were supposed to be playing—in coffee houses for a handful of the cognoscenti.

From the very beginning, Canned Heat was a band so disorganized that we bordered on anarchy. We hardly ever decided beforehand what we'd play on stage. We'd just tune in to the audience's vibes and then call out song suggestions to each other.

Picture Alan loaded on the stage, his constantly broken glasses sliding down his nose, drooling on his amp, endlessly changing the tuning on his guitars—open tuning for country blues, standard tuning for city blues (electronic tuners hadn't been invented yet)—and The Bear doing his "Jim Morrison imitation," letting the microphone dangle on its cord from his crotch.

If an impatient fan started to yell, Bear would holler back: "We're a blues band, man. This ain't fuckin' Vegas."

We rehearsed, but not a lot, and what rehearsing we did was pretty loose. Spontaneity, unpredictability, a touch of the outlaw—that was the core of our charm. We were just barely organized enough to know it. Our style of music has so much emotion already built into it that we didn't want to rehearse it too much for fear of making it too mechanical, too sterile—the curse of much contemporary Top Ten music.

Our music was never driven by Top Ten goals or a hunger for commercial success that afflicted many other bands. We strove for success with dignity and artistry, doing our own thing—not following a trend. Reconciling our anti-commercial attitude with the demands of the music biz was our managers' challenge. It was more important for us to make a statement, to be different, something special. We wanted our audiences to have a great time and to find our music compelling. We didn't want to be like the Beatles or any of those pop bands, we didn't even like that kind of music.

At the few rehearsals we did have, Bear, Alan and the other guys would be smoking weed. What a bunch of hippies, I thought. Just like the Sot Weed Factor. The Bear would push me to take a drag. "Come on, Fito. What kind of a Mexican are you? Don't you smoke weed?"

"Bob, you know it doesn't have any effect on me."

I didn't have any reaction to the occasional puffs I'd taken just to keep the fat guy happy and because I was still the new kid, a foreigner and wanted to be one of the guys.

**Henry surrounded by a wall of sound—a 1200 watt TNT amp
connected to 8 cabinets with two 15" speakers each.**

The "Classic" Canned Heat lineup—the band members that saw it through its glory days—was now in place. And in spite of our disorganization, or probably because it appealed to our anarchic young audiences, we took off. Although we still played the Topanga Corral now and then, we headed into bigger, richer clubs: The Blue Law, The Cheetah, The Whiskey A Go Go and The Troubadour.

I felt great. I'd been in the States less than a year and I was getting good reviews in the American press, like the January 13, 1968 issue of "The Beat," which called Canned Heat's new drummer "completely fantastic and the equal of any of the best jazz drummers around. Adding more than just a driving beat to Canned Heat's music, De La Parra creates a whole sound of his own.... His solo, which had the audience literally screaming from their seats, was masterful." The critic, Tony Leigh, praised the whole band, saying: "Their sound and their personal magnetism could not possibly be captured on records. They need to be seen and heard in person; there is really nothing like Canned Heat."

There wasn't. One reason was the trend among rock bands then, the race for sheer loudness, ear-bursting volume. We got right out in front on that one. The "arms race" was triggered when we started appearing with Cream and Jimi Hendrix, who were using two modified Marshall amps each, making them very loud.

Henry said he wanted to be able to play loudly enough that he could lean back on the sound waves coming from behind him, and they'd hold him up. An electronics engineer named Frank Cooley, who built custom amplifiers when he wasn't working at a pest control company in Venice, built him a 1200 watt tube amplifier he called the "TNT" and connected it to eight cabinets, each with two 15" speakers. The result was huge, a wall of sound. That meant the rest of us had to get louder too. Larry got two monster TNT amps, sending 600 watts through four cabinets with two 15" speakers each. Alan had 300 watts in two cabinets with two 15" speakers. I had only one or two mikes for the drum set, so to keep up I had to play so hard I sometimes hurt my hands. Alan and The Bear sang louder, with Bob becoming hoarse after many of the shows.

Although a new band called Blue Cheer claimed to be the loudest band in the world, we knew we had them beat after hearing them play. They opened for us at the Fillmore in San Francisco, and when they saw our stage set-up, they knew we were awesome. Canned Heat was definitely the loudest band in the world in 1968-69.

One night an uptight club owner, who was being harassed by neighbors because of the noise, stood by the stage with a decibel meter marked with a red line to indicate the limit the police had imposed on his club. In our first number, we were red lining. He waved frantically at us to hold it down. Henry just grinned and slammed out some truly impressive chords that just about ripped our shirts off. The meter hit the line that equaled the noise made by a jet when it takes off.

Bear laughed. "Pour it on, Fito," he yelled. "C'mon Henry. Boogie time. Kick it loose!" We pegged the meter needle over to the max and held it there until the meter broke.

We were never asked to play there again, but we had a real good time fucking with the man's toy. There was no question that we were leaving the coffee house mentality behind.

The combination of drugs taken by some members of the audience, combined with the brute volume of our sound, was more than some of our fans could take. Some people would deliberately stand directly in front of our speakers or the sound system cabinets. On more than one occasion, we saw people being carried out on stretchers. No joke. It was not unusual to see a fan at the beginning of the show, high, having a great time grooving with the music. After an hour, there he'd be on the stretcher.

One night after a long, brilliant solo by Henry, I turned to Bear: "Look what we did to that guy. He was having a ball and we just flipped him out. He's going to end up in a psychiatric ward."

In the spirit of the times, we enjoyed that. It was a testimony to the power of our music. Take those people and just blow their heads into another dimension.

For the band's second album, "Boogie With Canned Heat," we decided to go with a louder, more rock-oriented sound, something that would catch the spirit of our live shows. We wanted to move beyond the first album, which was mainly a success with the critics. We basically played live. No laying down separate tracks at different times, over and over again.

Skip and John worked to generate a real party atmosphere at the recording session, with flowers, incense, food and drink. Our old ladies, friends and roadies sat on the floor in a circle as we played, passing joints and munchies. It was still the innocent '60s, the "flower power" era and I was out of step. I just didn't get it. I had been drunk in Mexico a few times, but that's as far as I'd gone when it came to altering my consciousness. Grass didn't affect me. I had never taken LSD. I had no personal experience of the whole kaleidoscopic mindset that came with taking psychedelic drugs. I hadn't opened "the doors of perception" yet, as Aldous Huxley would say, even though I was living in hippie command central with my eyes wide open. To me, the hippie girls, with their long, loosely flowing robes and flowers, were funny-looking. I have to confess I preferred sleek, stylish women in suits and tight skirts, hairdos, high heels and nylons. I never really bought into the sandals, tie-dyes, waterfall hair and gypsy skirts. Just not sexy enough.

Everyone at the recording session joined in the spirit as we played. Everything was perfect. No rush, no pressure to make a top 40 hit, no bellyaching about budget problems. It was the only session that captured the feeling of communion that we got listening to records at The Bear's place in Topanga Canyon, the very heart and origin of the band.

No wonder it became our most popular album. It was so different, so refreshing and so beautiful, being able to make something meaningful while having a good time, which the Bear was an expert at. It was his main thing in life. He always said, "If you don't have a good time, it doesn't matter. It doesn't count."

Skip and John decided we should have colorful nicknames. Larry Taylor became "The Mole" because of his teeth and the way he moved when he played. Henry had long blonde hair and a distinctive way of bobbing up and down like a flower in the wind, as he played, so he was "The Sunflower." Alan was called "Blind Owl" because of his eyesight and the glasses he wore, which were always broken and falling off. At 5 feet 9 and almost 300 pounds, Bob was sort of furry and lovable but dangerous, hence the nickname "The Bear," which was originally given to him by singer P.J. Proby, who was also managed by Skip and John. My name stayed the same, because Skip thought it sounded funny enough already. "Fito" is the nickname for Adolfo in Latin America, shortened from the affectionate Adolfito. It's supposed to be pronounced "feet-toe," but in the U.S., everybody pronounces it "Feedo."

Our style of creative anarchy was working. We felt and thought pretty much the same and our musical tastes played off each other.

No leaders, no bosses, no fights. In the turbulent history of the band, it was the golden age.

The glow spilled over to my marriage. Sonja and I were living in the clouds. We were both working. I was in a great band, making a record, making a name for myself. We were expecting a great future.

Even when I learned that Sonja had cracked up my beloved Firebird 400, my first new car, while bringing me the hi-hat cymbals I'd forgotten at home, I was too wrapped up in the session and being a member of Canned Heat to care.

The magic of "Boogie With Canned Heat" was that we barely rehearsed. While the lyrics were arranged on Alan's songs, they were mostly spontaneous when Bear sang. Spontaneity is the fascinating and beautiful thing about playing blues, which makes it the most abstract of all arts. It's not really tangible like a painting or a book or a sculpture that you can revise. With blues, the minute the note is heard, it's gone. It's even more abstract if you're improvising. That's why jazz is such a fabulous forum by contrast to classical music, which is limited to interpreting what the composer put on paper.

During this recording session, we were messing with a song called "The Hunter" by Albert King, a great blues guitar player and singer who was an important influence on us. Bear suggested putting words to it, using a true story about a girl he knew who died from a drug overdose. We made up the lyrics right on the spot, each of us contributing a word here, a line there. "Amphetamine Annie" became a classic, the first anti-drug tune ever recorded. Years later, the U.S. government did a compilation LP of anti-drug songs entitled "Good Vibrations." The most important songs on the album were "Annie" and "The Pusher" by Steppenwolf. Ironically, Canned Heat even received a commendation signed by President Ford.

Another great song on the album was "Marie Leveau," a slow blues instrumental based on the legendary 19th Century voodoo queen from New Orleans whose tombstone appears in the movie "Easy Rider."

Because I had the most experience with rhythm and blues bands, plus playing with groups that included horns, Alan asked me for ideas on the horn parts we added. I would make horn noises with my mouth and he would translate them into written notes. The great New Orleans piano player Mac Rebennack, later known as Dr. John "The Night Tripper," helped with the arrangements on this and "The Owl Song," which he also played piano on.

"World in a Jug" and "Whiskey Headed Woman No. 2" were typical country blues songs, the latter from a 1929 song by Tommy Laclennan. They were the kind of thing the old blues masters performed with only a lone guitar. We wanted to keep the primitive feel, but to appeal to our audience, we added distorted rock guitars and a heavy R&B style rhythm section.

"My Crime," influenced by Chicago blues, grew out of the Denver bust—a charge still hanging over the other band members at the time of the recording. "Turpentine Moan," featuring Sunny Land Slim on piano, and "Evil Woman" were recorded at an earlier session in Chicago before I joined the band, so we replaced Frank Cook's drum tracks with my new overdubbed drums.

"On The Road Again" was based on a traditional Mississippi/Alabama blues tune by Jim Oden, originally performed by Floyd Jones, using a John Lee Hooker's style arrangement. Alan adapted and organized the lyrics, while adding a harmonica along with the hypnotic drone of an Indian tamboura (sort of a one-chord zither) on four tracks. Another Hooker-influenced tune was "The Fried Hockey Boogie." The name was Larry's idea, although it was actually a slip of the tongue. Fried Hockey is a Louisiana term that even Larry couldn't define, but as he jived around with the words, it sounded good so we decided to use it. On the record, Bear explains that we did this song to show people how Canned Heat can really get it on. Everybody had a solo, with Bob improvising lyrics and introductions, playing ringmaster the way he did in our live shows, singing, shouting and rapping between solos. He ended the tune with the phrase that became his and the band's signature: "Don't Forget To Boogie!"

The cover of this album was magnificent, very psychedelic and powerful. Unfortunately, I'm not on it. By the time I joined the band, the artwork was already underway and they didn't want to spend the money or time to redo it. Frank's face stayed on the cover, but my picture and name are properly credited on the back of the album.

We hit the road to promote the album with a real Canned Heat touch. We started in Denver because the rest of the band had to be in court there for the "Denver Bust" trial, which ended with them being put on probation. They flew but I drove with our roadie Bob Gangwer in a VW van plastered with the name Canned Heat in

A salute from the bear in front of the first Canned Heat van.

psychedelic-style stoned-rainbow script. The van was excruciatingly slow climbing the mountain passes, but it was a great experience for me. I saw snow for the first time and in the mountains of Utah and Colorado I fell in love with the natural beauty of my adopted country.

In St. Louis we got our first taste of rock celebrity. An outlaw cycle club called "The Bone Shakers" met us at the airport with a limousine and an escort of 50 dangerous-looking, black leather-clad dudes sporting ZZ Top beards riding Harleys.

Alan, squinting out the window, tried to protect his eyes from the sun with one hand and his ears from the roar with the other.

"Hey, Henry, is this far enough from the coffee house?" he asked.

Henry, who dug motorcycles but didn't actually ride them like I did, was leaning out the window, exchanging friendly one-finger salutes with the escorts.

"Fuck no, man. Not yet. But this is the right fucking direction."

After the show at the Kiel Opera House, we met The Boneshakers in the theater parking lot. The Harleys, with their headlights on, formed a circle and we passed around joints, although Henry decided to try out some new pills.

"Hey Worm," one of the guys shouted. "Do your thing, man."

"You gotta see this," the chief Boneshaker said to Bear. "Worm has a dick so long he can suck himself off."

"Yeah, sure," laughed Bear.

I just stood there, smiling. I figured this was some sort of joke they were playing on the civilians from California.

The other Boneshakers took up the cry. 'C'mon, do it man." "Show 'em, Worm." "Hey man, where else can they see this, just with us, right?"

"Well...okay."

Fumbling in his fly, Worm hauled out this thing that looked like a coiled-up rope, like they have on boats, and uncoiled it with both hands. It sagged between them in loops.

He pulled up the end toward his face and bowed his neck.

It reached.

We stood there, staring. Alan made a funny sound in his throat, like he'd been goosed. "Auto-fellatio," he murmured. Only Alan would think of the precise word at a time like this. Bear let out a long "Woowwww."

Pretty soon Worm looked like he was playing a long, skinny, pink saxophone, just going to town on himself, while some of the Boneshakers gunned their Harley engines to generate more light for the spectacular climax.

In Cleveland, we had co-billing at The Cave with Blood, Sweat and Tears, who were promoting their first album. It was a fantastic night. The place was packed and hot. Between sets, I ducked out in front of the building to cool off and was followed by a tall, slim redhead. She was wearing a sort of Indian buckskin miniskirt with fringe around the bottom and moccasin boots that laced up her calves. Her dark red hair was long and straight. Her T-shirt was wet with perspiration and I could see she had long, muscular arms. Even though I was wearing my wedding band, she started flirting with me.

"Are you really a Mexican?" she asked.

"I sure am." Hell, I still had a pretty thick accent then to prove it.

"I never met a Mexican before."

I could smell the redhead's sweat and perfume. And she was close enough that I could see she was taller than me. A lot taller. I had never made love to any girl that tall. What would that feel like?

I gave her the name of my hotel and the room number.

She was waiting when I got there. After we kissed a little bit, she reached in her bag, pulled out a pipe tobacco can full of weed and papers and rolled a couple of joints. Quickly, expertly.

"Have a toke?"

"Sure."

I took a few hits, just to go along with the ritual as I'd done before with the band, confident nothing would happen.

We both lay back on the bed, taking a few more hits. She snuggled up to me with the lace-up Indian boots still on. One had a little bell on it, a jingle bell.

She wiggled her ankle to make the bell jingle.

Her legs were fascinatingly long. They seemed to go on forever. Like to the end of the world, over the horizon. The bell jingled, only somehow it had become a symphony, with deep layers of joy and sadness mingling in the chimes. Her skin was very soft, like a seal's.

I began to laugh. I looked at the ceiling. I hadn't noticed before how wide it was. How high. As high as the sky. And so white. The ceiling, the walls, everything in the room looked different. I took a swallow of the Coke I had beside the bed. It was the best Coke I ever drank. I sipped at it, savoring the sweetness. At 22, I'd finally discovered what a marijuana high felt like. I'd finally opened my "doors of perception."

"Fito? Have you ever done this before?"

"Oh yeah, a few times. But I never felt like this."

By now she must have been thinking: What am I doing here? I've got to be crazy. Is this really the drummer from that bad-ass druggie band? All he does is stare at the ceiling and mumble how good he feels when he hasn't even touched me! What is he waiting for? What a jerk!

And she was right. I was totally lame.

Without a word, she got up, picked up her purse and left. I was so spaced out I hardly noticed. What I do remember is her skin: I'll never forget it. It was so soft, just like a seal.

I could hear the bell jingling until I faded out. I didn't have a care in the world.

"So how was the first road trip with Canned Heat?" my straight-laced Sonja asked, as we we're having dinner together at home for the first time in three weeks.

87

"A great tour. Really successful. I even got high on grass for the first time."

"Really?"

"Yeah. It finally worked for some reason. Don't know why."

"What did it feel like?"

"It was really strange. But nice strange. It made Coke taste like the greatest thing ever invented."

"Really? Like good?"

"Like really good."

To my surprise she didn't seem shocked. She seemed more intrigued. I was sure as hell not going to mention the disappointed redhead.

When the Bear heard my Cleveland story, he laughed and handed me a fistful of joints.

"C'mon, Fito, now you have to get Sonja to try some. Sex and weed, man. It's like ice cream and chocolate syrup. One of the great combos. You have to try it. Coupla good hits and you'll have the best sex of your life. Sonja'll scream the damn house down. You can't miss this, man."

I still felt guilty about the redhead, even though nothing really happened. But I was raised a Catholic. It's the thought that counts, the priests said, even if you didn't really do it. So by that standard I was guilty. And our whole relationship had cooled lately. Sonja was becoming more of a pal, a great roommate, rather than a hot romance. Maybe the grass would change that.

That night I got my wife high. I corrupted her. But she was already changing, just living with me and hanging out with Canned Heat. She was no wild woman, but she always had a rebel streak and she was learning.

Bear was right. The sex was fantastic again, better than ever. We went into wild giggling fits together as we made love. It was great. Except for the moment that I looked up in the middle of my mild hallucination and momentarily flashed on her mother's stern, Baptist face hovering in the air over us.

With whiskers like a seal.

It was the very next day, while we were rehearsing numbers for "Living The Blues," that Skip and John showed up, looking both confused and wildly happy.

"ON THE ROAD AGAIN"

#56038
Produced by Dallas Smith

La Vere

CANNED HEAT

LIBERTY

KHJ'S BOSS 30 RECORDS IN SOUTHERN CALIFORNIA

PREVIEWED AUGUST 28, 1968

LAST WEEK	THIS WEEK	TITLE	ARTIST	LABEL	WEEKS ON BOSS 30
(5)	1.	ON THE ROAD AGAIN	Canned Heat	Liberty	4
(3)	2.	THE HOUSE THAT JACK BUILT	Aretha Franklin	Atlantic	4
(2)	3.	FOOL ON THE HILL	Sergio Mendes & Brasil '66	A&M	5
(1)	4.	BORN TO BE WILD	Steppenwolf	Dunhill	8
(18)	5.	HARPER VALLEY P.T.A.	Jeannie C. Riley	Plantation	2
(7)	6.	HUSH	Deep Purple	Tetragrammaton	5
(22)	7.	THE WEIGHT	The Band	Capitol	3
(11)	8.	MAGIC BUS	The Who	Decca	4
(20)	9.	I'VE GOTTA GET A MESSAGE TO YOU	The Bee Gees	Atco	4
(12)	10.	WORKING ON A GROOVY THING	Patti Drew	Capitol	3
(4)	11.	PEOPLE GOT TO BE FREE	The Rascals	Atlantic	8
(27)	12.	WHO IS GONNA LOVE ME?	Dionne Warwick	Scepter	2
(15)	13.	I CAN'T STOP DANCING	Archie Bell & The Drells	Atlantic	4
(30)	14.	INDIAN RESERVATION	Don Fardon	Crescendo	2
(19)	15.	SEALED WITH A KISS	Gary Lewis & The Playboys	Liberty	4
(8)	16.	GIVE A DAMN	Spanky & Our Gang	Mercury	4
(28)	17.	LOVE HEALS	Colours	Dot	2
(25)	18.	SLIP AWAY	Clarence Carter	Atlantic	2
(HB)	19.	BABY, COME BACK	The Equals	RCA	1
(6)	20.	BROWN EYED WOMAN	Bill Medley	MGM	7
(16)	21.	LOVE MAKES A WOMAN	Barbara Acklin	Brunswick	6
(HB)	22.	MIDNIGHT CONFESSIONS	The Grassroots	Dunhill	1
(24)	23.	SIX MAN BAND	The Association	Warner Bros.	3
(HB)	24.	FIRE	Arthur Brown	Atlantic	1
(14)	25.	IMPOSSIBLE DREAM	Roger Williams	Kapp	5
(HB)	26.	STREET FIGHTING MAN	The Rolling Stones	London	1
(HB)	27.	HOLD ME TIGHT	Johnny Nash	Jad	1
(HB)	28.	SUZIE Q	Creedence Clearwater	Fantasy	1
(HB)	29.	TO WAIT FOR LOVE	Herb Alpert	A&M	1
(HB)	30.	TIME HAS COME TODAY	Chambers Brothers	Columbia	1

OFFICIAL ISSUE NO. 165

The listing of records herein is the opinion of KHJ based on its survey of record sales, listener requests, and KHJ's judgment of the record's appeal.

"You guys have a hit record!"

We couldn't believe it. Us?

Alan let out a startled "Huuuhhh?"

"Honest, 'On The Road Again' broke in Dallas," yelled Skip. "A disc jockey started playing it on the radio and he got a flood of calls."

"Really?"

"I tell you guys; it's number one in Texas and it's spreading across the country," shouted John.

Eventually, it became number one in most markets and opened the door to the world. It went Top 10 in Germany, Austria, Switzerland, Belgium, Australia, New Zealand, England and France. We had done it. We put a blues song on the charts. Something no other blues band had been able to do.

The hit single propelled "Boogie With Canned Heat" to the top of the album charts. All of a sudden, we were a big band, taking limousines to the gigs, getting invitations to play for $10,000 a night. Hell, $15,000, then $20,000.

At the Newport Pop Festival, we appeared with Sonny & Cher, Country Joe and The Fish, the Chambers Brothers, the Butterfield Blues Band, Steppenwolf, Jefferson Airplane, the Animals, the Byrds and the Grateful Dead.

"The biggest hit" in that lineup was us, the Los Angeles Times critic reported. Too bad a typo turned us into "Canned Meat" in one reference. But never mind.

A pre-Woodstock "make love not war" state of mind was already taking over the country's youth as the Viet Nam war loomed over them. And me.

When I got my green card in 1967 I was told that I had to register for the draft within three months. Any young immigrant like myself was a prime candidate to be drafted and sent to the slaughter. As with other American wars, like Korea and World War II, Mexicans fought and died valiantly alongside American citizens. Mexican-Americans have the highest percentage of decorations for valor given to any ethnic group in the American Armed Forces. As my buddy John Quain said of the Mexican troops: "Send them macho fuckers over there to kick ass."

But I was not a macho fucker. I was a drummer, not a fighter. I thought: "They have plenty of 6 foot, 200 pound Anglo-Saxons ready to kill for their country. They don't want to bother with me, a little guy with flat feet who probably couldn't understand many of the commands." More important, I'd just joined the best blues/rock band in the world, the only chance I was ever going to get to make my lifelong dreams come true.

I didn't register, thinking that they wouldn't come after me because I was married. It was single men without college deferments who were prime meat for that mincing machine in southeast Asia.

I was wrong. Returning to the U.S. from a show in Canada, an American immigration official asked to see our IDs, since many deserters and draft-dodgers were fleeing north of the border. When I pulled out my green card, he nailed me.

"You've been in this country a year. Why haven't you registered?"

"Uhh...well...sorry, officer, I'll do it when I get back to L.A."

Two weeks after registering, I got a notice for my physical.

"Ohh shit, Fito, nooooo," was Skip's reaction. We were in the very nice office he had just rented on Hollywood Boulevard on the strength of our new success.

"We have a tour of Australia nailed down. I even think I have a tour of Europe lined up. Europe, Fito—London. Paris. Germany. The Europeans have never seen anything like this band. This will put us over the top. And we already know how the band plays with other drummers. Not so fucking hot. We need you."

"What the hell can I do? This is the goddam government. Your goddamn government. They're going to come get me, Skip. I can go to Viet Nam or go back to Mexico and never return here. What choice do I have?"

"There's gotta be a choice, Fito. We'll find a way."

It turned out there was an alternative.

He was about 70 years old, with a long white beard and hearing aids in both ears. A fragile body housing an agile mind. He was an attorney who had been fighting draft boards since World War II and had just helped two members of The Beach Boys avoid Vietnam. His office was in downtown L.A. in a decrepit old building on Spring Street. His name was J. B. Tietz.

On June 5, 1968, we were playing in a Harlem blues club for an all-black crowd when an angry looking man jumped on stage and yelled: "Stop playing, stop playing right now!" For a second I wondered if we were being attacked for playing in a black club.

Then someone shouted: "Robert Kennedy has just been shot!" We felt terrible, as bad as anyone in the audience, but the club owner hustled us out of there as quickly as he could. "Some of the brothers are angry, man," he said. "They could be looking for white people to get back at. And you guys may be the only white people for miles, so put it on the road, okay? Get in these taxis and sit down low 'til you get back downtown."

Fleeing Harlem because of a crazy murder a continent away, I thought: "This is the dark side of America. This is where the pain in the blues of the black experience is still alive, in the distrust and fear. It's not all history and it's not all good. When will it end and only the music remain?"

With money rolling in, Bear, Skip, John and Gary Essert, a new business partner, moved into a beautiful mansion in the Hollywood Hills overlooking Sunset Boulevard, a block from the famous Whiskey A Go Go.

"Elvis used to live here," Bear told people. There were a lot of them to tell because Bob turned the place into a non-stop party, one of the great circuses of the '60s. There was a steady stream of fans, wandering hippies, outlaw bikers, chicks, music lovers and occasional drug dealers. I'd go over there and have no idea who most of the people were. They'd be sprawled on the floor, making love in the bedrooms, dancing beside the pool, toking up in the kitchen.

Bear was in heaven. His main delight was still to play his records for visitors, but now he had a bigger audience and a pair of gigantic studio monitor speakers to blast out the music. His fantastic record collection overwhelmed the living and dining rooms. Everywhere you looked there were old 78s and 45s, piled around shoe boxes full of marijuana and bowls crusted with dried chili.

The house had a crystal blue swimming pool surrounded by a small garden with beautiful trees. There was even a room with a window so you could watch people as they swam.

I dropped by one afternoon and couldn't help noticing a guy in a leather vest and blue velvet jeans sitting in one of the trees, playing harmonica.

I was getting used to the Bear's guests, but this was new.

"Who's the dude in the tree?" I asked Skip.

"Hey, be nice to him," Skip said. "That's John Mayall."

"Mayall? The Brit with the Bluesbreakers? He's here?"

"Hell man," Bear said. "He LIVES in that fucking garden. Other people around here got statues in their gardens, we have a live limey muscian playing in our fucking trees. Gives the place some real class."

Mayall, a highly respected musician and the first European to form a viable white blues band, did indeed live in the house for awhile. Just listen to the song "Living With the Bear" on his "Blues from Laurel Canyon" album. We became friends. And though he eventually moved out of Bear's house, he kept his ties to Canned Heat, touring with us for years and at one time or another hiring ex-Cannel Heat members Larry Taylor, Harvey Mandel and Walter Trout.

In San Francisco, the Fillmore had become the center not only of the rock music scene but of the whole swirling '60s social revolution. Bands like Santana and the Grateful Dead turned it into a command post for the youth rebellion. Skip, John and Gary decided that Los Angeles should have a club like that, a big place where people could get high and listen to the best music while they came together to push for social and political change.

They leased a big, beautiful building in Hollywood on Sunset Boulevard, a couple of blocks east of Vine, that was originally the Moulin Rouge. After installing a light show and a spectacular sound system, they renamed the club The Kaleidoscope. Canned Heat was basically the house band, playing with groups like Jefferson Airplane, the Grateful Dead, the Doors, Buffalo Springfield and Sly and the Family Stone.

These were the best of times. We were free of responsibilities, enjoying our hit record, our best selling album and being spoiled to death by the record company. Henry and Bob were taking more dope—Henry's popping uppers and downers had him on a roller coaster—and Alan was a tortured Hamlet with a guitar, but what the hell, it was the '60s and we were a rock band, not Trappist monks.

Whenever we had any kind of problem, whether it had to do with family, finances, legal, whatever, Skip would say: "Don't worry about anything. We'll take care of it. You just worry about making good music. We'll take care of everything else."

We were young and naive and we believed our managers

completely. Maybe their intentions were pure. But we paid dearly for that trust in the years that followed.

"You guys better come up with something new. You can't let this thing disappear. You're a big band. Now, you have to keep being a big band," said Skip, as we started on our third album "Living the Blues." "You better come up with great stuff, new stuff. You can't let this thing slide away."

Well, it wasn't Bear's nature to worry about the next hour, and the rest of us figured we always had Alan's amazing ability to take some old blues classic, add a couple of licks and change the lyrics into something as simple as "Goin' Up the Country," which was inspired by "Bulldoze Blues" written by Texas bluesman Henry Thomas. We knew it was a hit as we joined Alan writing it in our heads, humming and jamming. We didn't know it would go on to become the Woodstock Festival theme and one of those rare classics that can evoke an era with just a few bars.

Comfortable that "Goin' Up the Country" would be a commercial success, we felt free to make the rest of the album a major creative effort, stretching our limits and ignoring commercialism. It became a total, pure Canned Heat experience, a double album for the price of one, including our versions of "Walking By Myself," originally done by Chicago blues master Jimmy Rogers, and "One Kind Favor" by Blind Lemon Jefferson.

Another tune was "Parthenogenesis," the term for a cell or egg splitting and reproducing itself, without sperm or an outside influence. It was the perfect song for the spaced-out '60s, for carrying listeners stoned on grass or tripping on LSD into another dimension.

In fact, our hard-core fans still ask for it, which is difficult to believe, because it's impossible to perform live. It was strictly a creation of studio electronics with every member doing a multi-track performance with himself. Four Alans played harmonica simultaneously; Henry played on top of three Henrys; I overdubbed three times. We had John Fahey on guitar and Bear's garden gnome, John Mayall, on piano.

A cult classic from this album is "The Refried Boogie," the longest song ever recorded at the time, an insane 41 minutes. This was the complete opposite of "Parthenogenesis." It's an actual live performance with no overdubs, no gimmicks. What you hear on the record is what you would have heard if you were there in The

Pop Festival Draws 80,000

A crowd of about 50,000 fans sweltered in the sun for nine hours to hear a succession of rock groups that played from morning to evening at the First Newport Pop Festival held on a recent weekend at Costa Mesa, Calif The group above, called "Canned Meat," was the biggest hit.

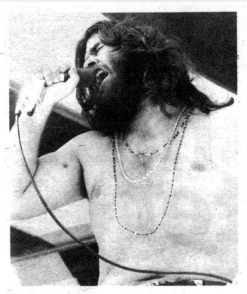

Bob "Beas" Hite, alias The Fat Boy, made a big hit with his shoutin' blues, swaying his head and shirtless torso to the beat of the music.

An example of how the press can fuck up. Note- "Canned Meat" and Bob "Beas" Hite.

Kaleidoscope that night, with all kinds of improvisation, a long drum solo and a long bass solo, two long guitar solos and Bob singing and doing his ringmaster trip in the middle. A Mexican version was edited into a 45 and released as a single called "Boogie Refrito," which became a classic south of the border.

Crossing the Hudson River from New York to New Jersey in a limo one afternoon, Skip suddenly shouted to the driver to stop.

"Look at those woods over there. We could take pictures there for the new album. Everybody into the woods."

Alan loved that but he kept trying to go off and look for moss and stuff until Skip told me it was my job to keep him with us.

It wasn't easy. Everyone was loaded. Bear, always the instigator, yelled: "Let's take our clothes off. Skip, take a picture of us naked!" So we did.

Not typical record album art but typical of us and typical of the imagination John and Skip brought to managing the band. They had vision, great imagination and real showmanship.

John, in particular, was a great cheerleader. He'd come to our shows and whip up enthusiasm in the audience by clapping the hardest, shouting the loudest and boogieing the wildest. He often brought his little brother Phil with him, who later became famous on "Saturday Night Live," as well as other film and TV roles until his wife blew him away thirty years later.

One of the best examples of their creativity was a gig they promoted at the Shrine Auditorium in Los Angeles on New Year's Eve 1968, the apogee of flower power and psychedelia. The poster advertised "8 PM to exhaustion" and the bill also included Poco and Little Richard.

Skip and John mixed up two large jugs of orange juice laced with LSD and put one on each side of the stage with paper cups so the audience could ring in a spaced-out new year.

Rushing backstage, they whipped out a couple of table cloths.

"Come on, Bear, get your naked butt over here," yelled Skip.

They frantically tried to construct a diaper to wrap around the Bear.

"Why do I have to wear this, man?"

"For the elephant."

I was a little stoned, but not so stoned that this made sense.

photo Steve Lavere

The Bear, atop a flourescent purple pachyderm, kicks off New Year's eve, 1969 at LA's Shrine Auditorium

"What elephant?" I asked.

"The one outside that window," Skip said.

"Oh yeah, sure, man, like there's really an elephant..."

I looked out the window.

"Jesus Christ. Larry, Henry. Check it out."

"What?"

"The elephant. Like, there is really an elephant out there."

"Far out," murmured Henry, slumped in a chair, totally unimpressed.

"It's purple."

He got up then to see it.

Our managers had rented some poor elephant and spent the afternoon spraying it with fluorescent paint so it would "glow" under the black lights.

At midnight, Bear made a regal entrance to the auditorium, like some psychedelic version of an Indian maharajah, riding atop the glowing elephant. He wore a table cloth big enough to serve as a diaper so he could be the spirit of the infant New Year, his belly quivering as the elephant swayed from side to side.

A few fans, deep into acid trips, ran screaming from the building. The rest dug it.

A tour to promote our record took us to Houston where a record collector friend of the Bear's casually said that Albert Collins, the legendary black blues guitarist, was playing in a little joint called The Ponderosa Club in the city's black neighborhood. The club had fewer than 10 tables and only two were occupied, one by a couple, the other by a girl sitting next to Albert caressing his crotch as he played. When we walked in, Albert was cooking with "Sno-Cone" and he followed up with the gritty slow blues "Dyin' With the Flu."

"Hey, this is great. Two of our favorites," said Bob, as he stuffed a couple of ribs in his mouth and plopped down at one of the tiny tables.

We all admired Collins and followed his recording career, especially Henry, whose style of lead guitar was very clearly influenced by Albert. It was a pleasure to hear him live. We were fascinated with his unorthodox style, his D minor tuning with a capo in the middle of the guitar and the way he used his thumb and right hand.

Alan, for once allowing his admiration for Albert as a living legend to overshadow his shyness, walked over between sets to introduce us.

"Hello, Albert."

The girl began a slow rhythmic stroking, her nails clicking along Albert's zipper.

"Um, We're.... We're... " Alan couldn't take his eyes off her hand. She smiled wickedly up at him. He turned red and sputtered to a halt.

Bear took over. "Albert, we've got a band and we love your work. We've listened to you for years, man. We do some of your songs. Fucking great to meet you, man."

"You boys have a band? What's your band?"

"Canned Heat."

"You guys are the Canned Heat? God damn. I been listening to you too. You guys cook."

He pushed the girl's hand away. "Honey, get these boys a drink."

"Albert," I said, jumping in. I was starting to speak up as my English steadily improved. "A guy like you, you shouldn't be in a place like this. You should be out in LA where the bread is."

"You think that?"

The crotch-stroker returned.

"Honey, get another round for my business advisers here."

Accepting us, of all people, as business advisers might rank as a dumb thing to do, but this turned out to be a real success story. Albert headed west where we helped him get an agent and introduced him to the executives at United Artists, who signed him to a recording contract. He developed a hell of a career, becoming well-known in blues circles throughout the world.

As the years went by, we continued our relationship. In 1993, when we were leaving an outdoor festival in Europe, I spotted his tent behind the stage, so I jumped out of the limo to say hello. He was as friendly and nice as ever, but he didn't look very good. I thought it's just being on the road. But I was wrong. He was dying. He passed away a week after that, leaving another void in my life, like everybody whose music has moved me. With his death a bit of me died too.

A couple of nights later, I was standing in our hotel corridor, totally pissed off, when Bear came by. "What are you swearing at?"

"I lost my fucking room key."

Bear's grin almost split his head.

"Oh yeeahhhh. Ain't that a shame."

With a maniacal grin, he backed against the opposite wall and ran at the door, shoulder first, like a cop in an old-fashioned movie. All 300 plus pounds of Bear hit that door full tilt. The lock snapped, the jam pulled halfway out of the frame, the frame pulled loose from the wall. Bear surveyed this with the expression of an artisan who has completed a masterwork. Then, he rubbed his shoulder and burst out laughing.

"There. That's good. You can get in now."

Without realizing it, I had given Bear an excuse for one of his favorite recreations: smashing doors. Bear loved to smash doors. He broke doors in hotels, motels, recording studios, dressing rooms, friend's houses, our houses and once Skip had to stop him just as he backed up to charge the door of a restaurant in Chicago that had a big "Closed" sign on it. Bear regarded locked doors as an affront to the universe. I guess he was just such an open guy he figured everything else should be open too. If a lock so much as slightly resisted turning, Bear launched. All the rest of us in the band learned never to mention a problem with a lock, but we still left a trail of battered doors behind that you could have found us by.

Back in LA, when we showed up for a gig at The Kaleidoscope, we were surprised to see that Randy, the spectacular blond amazon who usually worked the ticket booth, had been replaced by some stranger. As we approached the door, we were stopped by several hostile-looking Latin dudes in expensive suits and ties.

One guy stepped forward. "Who are you guys?"

"We're Canned Heat; the band playing here tonight," Bear said respectfully.

"No you're not," he said, as two more Central Casting thugs stepped up beside him.

Quietly, we turned and left.

When I asked Skip what had happened to the club, he just said "Don't ask; it's better for you if you don't know."

We never really learned the details of what happened, but it became clear that money had been borrowed from the mob and somewhere along the line, the mob took over the club. That was the end of the dream of duplicating Bill Graham's success with the Fillmore.

In the beginning of 1969, everybody was taking a lot of LSD, but how much LSD can you take and manage a business? Especially one that was making more than half a million dollars a year. An enterprise such as our band required a lot of care—financially and spiritually. Eventually, arguments between our two managers became so disruptive that they split, with John leaving Skip to manage the band. The next day, when I stopped by the Elvis house in Hollywood to hang out, it hit me. John was no longer a part of the family. The magical combination suffered its first crack.

My personal life also suffered its first crack. The U.S. military establishment was mounting another offensive, this time against me.

Towards the end of 1968, I gave J.B. Tietz, the ancient but brilliant attorney handling my case, $5,000 to file my conscientious objector plea. When he contacted me a few months later, saying he needed more money, I was in that strange world of musicians. Famous and rich on paper, but without a penny in my pocket.

As I pulled up to his shabby downtown office, he was looking out the window and saw me arrive in my brand new Jaguar XKE. When the conversation turned to money, I told him about my financial situation. With a smile, he said: "Well, you do have that beautiful roadster you arrived in. Is it a stick-shift?"

"Yes," I said agreeably.

"Excellent. My doctor recommended that I move my limbs more, so a stick-shift would be just fine."

As much as I loved my car, the most important thing in my life was not to let the U.S. government send me off to be riddled with bullets for a cause I knew nothing about.

I handed over the car keys.

By now, my dear wife Sonja had become a good pal, a buddy....but the romance was dying. She was comforting, but not exciting, especially compared to the wild women I met on the road. There was just no comparison between a night with my sweet, gentle, good-girl wife and the hellions who'd wait for me outside a stage door in black leather shorts and high heeled boots with a purse full of joints and tell me exactly what they wanted to do my body before I knew their names.

AIDS didn't exist. We couldn't even spell herpes. Most women were on the pill. And I used rubbers anyway. Sex had no consequences beyond the night. My standards for exciting sex got higher by the week as experiences multiplied. Sonja just wasn't part of that and never could have been.

We were very young and our relationship lacked experience—not love. Plus, I didn't know yet what was important in life. Drumming with Canned Heat, life on the road, that was my existence. I had become my job and lost myself, something that happens to a lot of people, regardless of age or profession.

"She's the best woman you'll ever have," said my father, who loved and admired her. He was also concerned about the fleeting nature of fame and insisted I send him some of my earnings to invest for me safely outside the U.S. "Anybody can make money, but not everybody can save it," he liked to say.

Sonja filed for divorce under California's community property law, which was ironic. When we married in Mexico, she had a choice. The law there provides for either community property or individual property marriages. She chose the latter, under pressure from her mother, who obviously figured she had to protect the family fortune from the penniless Mexican drummer. It never occurred to my mother-in-law that I was the one who would end up with money.

My attorney claimed that the Mexican law we were married under could shield me from having to give Sonja anything at all, but I didn't want to fight her in court. It was bad enough to be in a legal battle with the U.S. Government. More importantly, I still loved her in a way and would be forever grateful that she helped me come to the United States, the land of my dreams, and that she put her heart into building a life for us here.

So we sat at our kitchen table one night and calmly, sadly, agreed there was no future in our marriage. To hell with the lawyers, I thought, let's just make an agreement between us. On a simple dime-store stationery pad, we wrote down who would get what. Sonja got our lovely Laurel Canyon house, our savings and I would make monthly alimony payments. I would keep the money my father had in Mexico—he refused to give it to me, in any case—my drums, my records and my Triumph Bonneville motorcycle.

I stayed in the Laurel Canyon house and paid rent to Sonja, who moved to New Mexico to start a new life. The first night alone, I lay there in the darkness, realizing just how painful the loss was going to be. What have we done?

The pain brought to mind a line from the epic Spanish poem "El Cid" that I learned in school in Mexico City a lifetime ago:

"Es como la uña que se separa de la carne."

"It is like the fingernail that separates from the flesh."

One of the last pictures of Sonja and me before our divorce and the start of the "long slide"

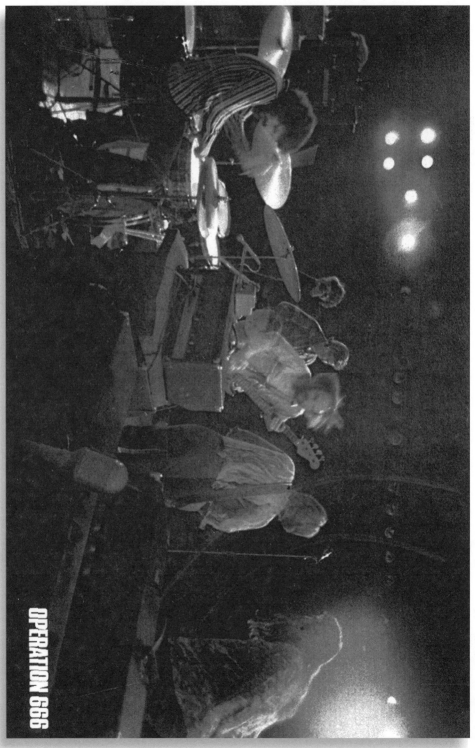

The "Future Blues" band at the Olympia in Paris. From Left to right- Me, Alan, Larry, Harvey and Bob.

OPERATION 666

START OF THE LONG SLIDE

Me in the 60's

Canned Heat was acing its implausible, contradictory mission: to make a mountain of cash on hit records while remaining a non-commercial band and non-commercial guys, bad-ass outlaws, bearers of the country blues torch, no compromises. Not purist nerds, but totally whacked-out hippies who could serve up the blues with the spirit Alan, Bear and Henry had acquired in all their years of marinating themselves in unknown recordings by toothless black guys who died in alleys of booze and razors. Long-haired hard guys who deep down sort of envied those blues legends dying in their poor, back alleys. Volcanic thinkers who could dip the blues in a powerful frosting of rock n' roll and bring boogie to the people.

Unlike many bands, Canned Heat was not a one-hit wonder with the proverbial 15 minutes of fame. We were one of America's Top 10 bands in 1968-69 and in a league with the best British bands, Cream and Led Zeppelin. We

SKIP TAYLOR PRODUCTIONS INC.
9118 SUNSET BOULEVARD • LOS ANGELES 90069 • (213) 273-5410

L to R- Larry "The Mole" Taylor, Henry "Sunflower" Vestine, Bob "The Bear" Hite, Alan "Blind Owl" Wilson, Adolfo "Fito" de la Parra

IN ASSOCIATION WITH KRLA

CANNED HEAT
STEVE MILLER
BLUES BAND
KALEIDOSCOPE

SAT., JULY 12 8:00 P.M.
ANAHEIM CONVENTION
CENTER

TICKETS: $5.50, $4.50, $3.50
ON SALE AT ANAHEIM CONVENTION CENTER
BOX OFFICE, MUSIC CITY STORES, MUTUAL
TICKET AGENCIES, COMPUTICKET OUTLETS,
UNITED CALIFORNIA BANK — ORANGE COUNTY.

IN ASSOCIATION WITH KRLA

CANNED HEAT

BLUES GUITARIST

B. B. KING

—GUEST STAR—

"FATS" DOMINO

FRI., JULY 11 8:30 P.M.

HOLLYWOOD BOWL

BOXES: $7.50 & 6.50; RESERVED SEATS: $5.50, 4.50, 3.50, 2.50
ON SALE AT BOWL BOX OFFICE, MUSIC CITY STORES, MUTUAL
TICKET AGENCIES, SIGHT & SOUND STORES, AUTO CLUBS OF
SO. CAL., COMPUTICKET OUTLETS, BULLOCKS STORES. SEND
MAIL ORDERS TO HOLLYWOOD BOWL, HOLLYWOOD 28, WITH
SELF-ADDRESSED STAMPED ENVELOPE.

BILL GRAHAM PRESENTS IN NEW YORK

FILLMORE EAST

BYRD

BILL GRAHAM PRESENTS IN NEW YORK

CANNED HEAT
THREE DOG NIGHT
SANTANA

JOSHUA LIGHT SHOW

Extra Added Attraction:
SHA-NA-NA
(Late Shows Only)

FILLMORE EAST
August 1-2, 1969

BILL GRAHAM PRESENTS IN NEW YORK

CANNED HEAT
ALLMAN BROTHERS

DREAMS

TOE FAT
(Late Shows Only)

JOE'S LIGHTS

FILLMORE EAST
December 11-12, 1970

BILL GRAHAM PRESENTS IN NEW YORK

CANNED HEAT
THE PENTANGLE

RHINOCEROS

JOSHUA LIGHT SHOW

FILLMORE EAST
February 7-8, 1969

Canned Heat Press Kit designed by Gary Essert in form of a 78 rpm record jacket.

The killer rhythm section with me and Larry "the Mole" Taylor

were headlining over Santana and the Allman Brothers at the Fillmore East and B.B. King and Fats Domino at the Hollywood Bowl. Creedence Clearwater Revival was our opening act at the Swing Auditorium in San Bernardino.

One of my fondest memories was our performance at the Masonic Temple in Cleveland. We were on a double bill with Cream and I got into a drum duel with Ginger Baker. The local paper's reviewer not only said I had outplayed the fabulous Baker but that "De la Parra brought down the house with his slowly accelerated paradiddle that had old-timers reminiscing about Gene Krupa's riffs and Benny Goodman's Carnegie Hall concert of 1938." It wasn't just a matter of being better than Ginger Baker that night; I was really honored that my playing was reminiscent of Gene Krupa, my idol. It was one of the best ego strokes I've ever had.

When we hit the charts, it brought out promoters who thought they had the music business all figured out—just clump together the bands or singers who were in the top 10 or the top 40 last week. Now a lot of these guys grew up with Jimmy Dorsey or Dinah Shore and didn't have a clue when it came to the mysterious, obnoxious kids who buy tickets to see Jimi Hendrix, Janis Joplin and Canned Heat. But they could read a Cashbox sales chart, so they'd call the agents and put together a show.

Which is why our traveling circus of foul-mouthed boogie-blasters, our brains fizzing on dope 24 hours a day, sometimes wound up on the same bill with people whose music we sneered at, bubble-gum rockers like Bobby Sherman, the 1910 Fruitgum Company, and Paul Revere and the Raiders.

The Monkees, for Christ's sake. (Larry had actually played on a Monkees' record, so we'd give him a ration of shit when we wanted to pull his chain.)

To the promoters, we were all just names on a list.

Promoters think like: "They want $10,000? Okay, give them the ten grand and block out 20 minutes in the arena show."

They must have regretted not learning more about us.

First, we never did 20-minute sets. This is the band that recorded "Refried Boogie," at 41 minutes, the longest number ever released. This is the band that later would fight with horrified theater owners over not leaving the stage, that would play until the audience left in

Fito de la Parra, der Mexikaner

Fito "The Mexican"

Steve LaVeer

"The flying Bear on stage...high energy boogie"

A typical C.H. gig in the late '60's

Any questions as to why Henry was called the "Sun Flower"?

Alan, John & Bob outside the Kaleidoscope in 1968

a stupor, that would play until Bear actually collapsed and spent the night in a coma on the floor. Twenty minutes. Fat fucking chance, bubble gum people.

The Doors, Santana, Jefferson Airplane, Sly and the Family Stone, with them we pulled in the same kind of fans.

But teenybopper shows attracted just the opposite—little girls, 12 and 13 years old, colt-legged bump-tits in plaid shorts, cute as baby bunnies, a whole different species from our older crowds at the Fillmore and the Avalon in San Francisco, who wanted raw sensation, who wanted to be get-down bad, who wanted to wring the juice from their adrenal glands and drink it hot.

There was the time we appeared in Chattanooga, Tennessee, with Bobby Sherman. Our dressing room was on the second floor of the theater, overlooking an alley packed with little teeny-boppers, screaming "Bobby Sherman, Bobby Sherman." Every time any of us walked past the window, there was shrieking and crying like the old days with Elvis.

We were passing a few joints, pissed off that nobody is screaming "Henry" or "Owl," when suddenly Henry has this wonderful idea. He writes a note on a little piece of paper: "I want to come on your tits."

Then he signs it "Bobby Sherman" and throws it out the window.

My God, the screaming when they see the paper fly out. So we all start writing notes.

"Learn to give good head. Ask your mother."

"Backstage passes for the girl with the biggest tits."

"Special classes in how to lose your virginity—come to my room after the show."

Of course, we all signed Bobby Sherman's name.

The girls in the alley went into shock, except a few sort of smiled and looked up. We figured we should go back in a few years and look for them. We never heard what that dork Sherman thought, but we were falling down laughing.

At another bubble gum show in Portland, the vibes went bad the minute the stage manager told us we had only 20 minutes on stage. He added that one of the other acts was complaining about the strong marijuana smell from our dressing room, as Sonny and Cher did a little earlier when we were taping Hugh Hefner's "Playboy after Dark" TV show in L.A.

By the time we went on stage, we were wasted, pissed off, and worse yet, Skip wasn't there to head off The Bear, who grabs the mike and unloads:

"These guys only want us to play a twenty minute set, but we are the Canned Heat and we are going to fucking get it on. We don't give a shit about some fucking rule, we are going to play the boogie, and we're all going to get down and we will get you boogieing and fucking in the aisles and if they don't like it, fuck them."

There must have been some baby hippies there because a few of them actually clapped. No booing, because these kids took a look at Bear and Henry—the thundering giant and the tattooed madman—and they were damned well afraid of us. But in the audience were parents with their 11-year-old daughters and groups of little kids with their school teachers.

Worse yet, the whole concert was going out live on the radio.

The promoter was furious. To top it off, Larry did a disgusting thing during one number, picking his nose and trying to throw the snot on the floor. It stuck to his fingers and he's shaking this big, gooey hunk off his hand on the nice shiny clean arena floor while all the bubble gummies try not to throw up.

Parents and teachers wrote to the governor, to all the record companies, to Liberty and United Artists, to the radio stations and Sears and K-Mart and all the other stores, so that we didn't sell a record there for the next 10 years. The band was formally charged with public obscenity and had to go back to Portland to stand trial.

But we didn't give a shit. We were rock stars. We were omnipotent. If Oregon didn't want us, fuck them. Lenny Bruce had just died. Bear figured he was like Lenny, breaking new ground so artists could say "fuck" on stage. That might have been a brave fight but then he did what the lawyers told him to do to fight the charges. He just denied he said it, which was pretty stupid, given that thousands of people heard him. I got away free, pointing out that as a drummer, I had no mike and thus could not have said diddly.

That was just business as usual, because the band was in constant trouble with the law anyway, turning our escapades into songs like "My Crime," and "Highway 409."

The craziness started to spill over into my personal life. While I hadn't taken LSD yet, I did experiment with peyote and the famous psychedelic mushrooms of Mexico. It was in the middle of a mushroom trip that I decided to buy a new car. By now, Sonja had most of my assets and my attorney had my Jaguar, but with my mind bouncing around on wonderfully colored clouds created by the psychedelic mushrooms, I opened the mail to find a $5,000 check. Damn it, screw them all, it's time to get my life going again. I'm supposed to be some sort of a rock star. I'm paying the damn price for it, doing the damn work, time to have some of the fun. Within minutes, I got Tony (who had moved in with me when his marriage to the Sensational Queen of Watusi dissolved) to give me a ride to the bank and on to Pasadena.

It was a blinding hot day when I walked into the British car dealership, my hair and beard a bushy black tangle, my mind racing through other dimensions; I was wearing Levis and high, multi-colored checkered leather boots.

"May I help you, sir?" sniffed the salesman, as he gave me the once over. He had an upper-crust English accent and what appeared to be a Saville Row suit. I might have been a spaced-out Mexican blues musician but I had been to London and performed at the Albert Hall.

"I want a car."

"What price range were you thinking of, sir?"

He was very polite but the clear inference was "glassy-eyed hippies should be in the used-car lot down the street, looking at clapped-out VW vans with a lot of swirly painting on the sides."

"I want that one right there, the convertible."

"Sir, that's an Aston Martin DB4."

"The one James Bond drove in 'Goldfinger,' right?"

"Yes, sir. That model at least."

"How much?"

"Rather a lot, sir."

"This much?"

I handed him an envelope stuffed with bills. He spread them over a nearby desk. His expression changed completely. He became warm and friendly, my best buddy.

"That's almost enough, sir."

"How 'bout this?" I gave him a second envelope.

"A bit too much, sir. Here." He handed back about half the bills then quickly did the necessary paperwork.

"The keys are in the ignition, sir."

I drove off into the sunset in 007's car. The skyline looked spectacular, like a watercolor painting of the mouth of hell. I'll never know whether it really looked that good, but as I wound out that engine, with the double overhead cams and triple carbs, I felt great.

In mid-1969, we finished the album "Hallelujah," one of our finest projects and the last to feature the "Classic" Canned Heat line-up. It represented a new stage of maturity in the way we were creating music. For starters, we were more businesslike at the sessions, despite the great pressure to keep on top, to come up with another "On The Road Again" or "Goin' Up the Country." We held onto the character, the musical standard, that was so basic to the band's identity. We insisted on recording innovative approaches to blues music and experimented with odd-measure blues progressions. The album went to number 30 on the charts anyway.

We enjoyed the musical challenge required by these kinds of songs. The black masters of country blues would usually play alone with a guitar or maybe accompanied by one harmonica player. They would freely change the structure of the bars, adding more magic and spontaneity. When you have a rhythm section and three other musicians trying to repeat this approach, it requires much more concentration until you get used to playing those odd forms.

In "Hallelujah," Alan would just wail. He loved to mess with the structure of the songs, especially the ones he sang. "Do Not Enter" was 13 and a half bars and "Change My Ways" was 15 bars, a challenging change from the traditional 12-bar progression that dominates blues and rock music.

It got to a point where we didn't want to do any more standard blues. We started experimenting with free musical forms, inspired by avant-guarde jazz players, especially saxophone player Albert Ayler, who later on would feature Henry on some of his records, which were recorded under the prestigious, now defunct, jazz label Impulse.

We also did a song that was very appropriate for the times. The inspiration came from an old blues tune by Bukka T. White named "Sic 'Em Dogs." At my suggestion, we called it "Sic 'Em Pigs" to appeal to the '60s revolutionary feelings. It became quite an underground cult classic; 30 years later we still get a lot of requests for it even if it was never a hit single or intended to be.

Toward the end of the song, against a backdrop of oinks, snorts and squeals, Henry raps:

Are you looking for a way to serve God and country?
Your chance has come.
We are now recruiting trainees for the Los Angeles County
Sheriff's Department.
If you're big, strong and stupid, we want you.
Please call 626-9511.
Remedial courses are available for the culturally deprived.

We used the real phone number for the Sheriff's Department.

Some of our songs reflected the spirit of the times: Drugs, Vietnam, cops hassling students, but many others had one meaning on the surface and another for ourselves.

Some were cries from Alan's unhappy soul, rebelling against his family as in "Get Off My Back" and "Do Not Enter," or trying to come to terms with his inadequacy with women, like "Change My Ways."

Well I need some woman to stand by, to stand by for me
Well I need some woman to stand by, to stand by for me
And I'm so so tired sleeping by, sleeping by myself.

I've been alone so long got to change, got to change my ways
I've been alone so long got to change, got to change my ways
I want to love some woman better than I,
better than I love myself.

I went down to the ocean sat down by, sat down by the sea
I went down to the ocean sat down by, sat down by the sea
But the waves and the water would not give, would not
give me peace.

By contrast, the Bear's songs like "Canned Heat," "Same All Over," "I'm Her Man," and "Big Fat" were rollicking and full of life, optimistic and right for a good time—just like he was. "Down in the Gutter, But Free" was a slow blues jam in which we all switched instruments and had a great time with Bob just rapping about being free and in the gutter.

"Huautla" is an instrumental I wrote, reminiscent of a song I did with Los Sinners. The title is the name of a town on a cloud-wrapped mountain peak in the state of Oaxaca in southwestern Mexico. It was famous as the home of a woman called *"La Sabina,"* one of the most respected psychedelic gurus of the late '60s. Famous people like John Lennon and George Harrison made pilgrimages to Huautla to join Sabina and the Indians who lived there in a unique ritual of specially prepared food laced with the best psychedelic mushrooms available.

It seems really bizarre now, but Skip talked me into listing "V. Wolf," his wife Venita, as the writer. As a result, I don't show up on the album credits as the author.

"Hey, Fito, we have all these obligations, all these debts to Al Bennett because of the Denver bust. He might try to claim your royalties as part of that deal, you never know. This way, when the checks come to my wife, she can sign them over to you. This is the safest way to handle it; otherwise, you might never see a dime from your work."

Still the young innocent, I took his advice. Sure enough, when Skip got divorced, I never saw a dime from the song.

The Bear fell for the same line. He let Skip give the writing credit for "I'm Her Man" to Skip's daughter, A. Leigh. It would have been a hell of a piece of work if little Amy had actually written that worldly-wise blues number, considering that she was only two years old at the time. Like me with Venita, Bear never found little Amy slipping him checks under the table. For what it's worth, neither song ever made any money.

A number of friends also joined us on the album, including Paul Butterfield's piano player Mark Naftalin, percussionist Mike Pacheco, blues pianist Ernest Lane and guitar players Elliot Ingber and Javier Batiz.

One of the album's songs starkly forecast our approaching trouble. "Time Was" sounds to an outsider like a song about a broken romance, but it was really Alan's lament for the tensions brewing among us, the animosities eating at what had begun as a band of brothers. There were especially bad feelings growing between Larry and Henry over Henry's dope intake.

Time was when we got along,
Time was when we got along,
It's too bad that the feelin's gone.
Times was when we could agree.
Times was when we could agree.
That time's gone now you find fault with me.

Henry was pissed off, Larry was pissed off, The Bear was high and couldn't control it and Alan was depressed to death. With all that, I was getting pretty pissed off myself. I could see that each member's self-destructive streak was setting the band up for a crash. I can even pinpoint the moment I realized it. We were in a dressing room at a small club in Ventura called The Backdoor when I asked Bob what the set list was for the night. He was so preoccupied passing joints and jiving around that he didn't answer. I asked Henry.

He said: "Fuck it. Who cares?"

Withdrawing to a corner, I sat there watching. For the first time, I could clearly see them self-destruct. My stomach tightened with nausea and fear. I had fought my way up, all the way from garage bands and Mexican honky-tonks, pushed my way over the border, cut off my roots, begun life over again in a new nation and another language, scrapped my marriage, all for this band.

This was the biggest break I, or any of these guys, was ever going to get. Did these guys think we'd be famous and loved forever, no matter how stupid we acted? The arrogance brought on by success and the ever growing dope intake was clouding their senses.

By this time, I had been in the band for two years and had more than paid my dues. Yet, somehow I was still the little Mexican drummer, sitting in the back of the bus. For all that my playing was fundamental to the band's sound—everyone agreed that Canned Heat didn't jell until I joined—my face can't be seen on the inside cover of "Hallelujah," it's barely visible on "Living the Blues" and is not there at all on "Boogie with Canned Heat." My musical ideas, were taken seriously and almost always used. But when the press asked for interviews, they only wanted to talk to Bob, Alan or Henry, even though my English was improving. Although I had hit records and TV and movie deals in Mexico before Canned Heat even existed, and had more time as a professional musician with the exception of Larry, I was completely ignored by the media. At this point, I figured I deserved at least an occasional pat on the back and some time in the spotlight, but I didn't get it.

We were at the top, but success was bringing out our worst tendencies. Especially drug use. We could afford all we wanted.

Unlike, say, a bank clerk or a high school teacher, we had jobs where it was simply assumed we were on drugs and where that was regarded as the appropriate thing to do.

Henry and Bear were driven by a belief in the words of the English poet William Blake: "The routes of excess are the palace of wisdom." Henry's attitude: "I'll get as high as I want. You guys can't tell me anything. I'm gonna play great no matter what. I'm heavy and I'm gonna show all these lightweight motherfuckers what drug taking is all about." He would counteract one drug with another. If he was too tired or too slow from taking tranquilizers, he would pop a couple of uppers to "get in the middle." Then, he'd take sleeping pills to come down again in a never-ending circle.

I took drugs too and we experimented as a group, getting as loaded on speed as we could. We'd play fantastic sets, pushing the threshold of normalcy to the max to see where it would take us musically. When it worked, we sounded great. We confirmed it by recording performances and by watching the audience reaction. But that was not the rule, it was the exception. Sometimes drugs work and you do play brilliantly, but only about one time out of a hundred. Searching for that magic high, you screw up the other 99 times, and make mincemeat of your brains as well.

Skip was no guiding hand. He was taking as many drugs as we were. He had moved from a corporate world to an anything-goes world of musicians. He had become the Executive Hippie, a long-haired wheeler-dealer, a guy in a beard who did deals and grass. Worse yet, he had discovered the drug of the executive class: cocaine.

Even The Bear, who was usually warm and lovable, could turn into a mean, ugly asshole when he was hung over or on downers, which was becoming far too often. Burned in my memory is the night I first met his dark side. We were having dinner at a hotel in Rotterdam, Holland with Carlos Santana, one of the greats. Carlos and I were talking about James Brown and his funk music.

Bob, like a lot of white blues purists, regarded funk music as far inferior to the blues. He suddenly blurted out: "Brown's music sucks. All funk music sucks. He's a fucking nigger playing stupid nigger music."

I was stunned. First of all, Bear had devoted his life to the black man's music—researching it, resurrecting it, reshaping it and talking about it day in and day out with knowledge and passion. He loved the music and many of the musicians, helping them when he could. And he had profited mightily from their music. Next, even if he had a well of racism hidden deep in his heart, he sure as hell should have kept his mouth shut in front of Carlos, who had many blacks in his band.

Carlos was equally shocked.

"Fuck you," I shouted at Bob. It was the first time I had ever spoken up to him. "That's a goddam rotten thing to say. You should apologize to Carlos."

"Fuck you, Fito. You like all that nigger music and all those niggers playing that shit."

He lumbered away, leaving me to apologize to Carlos as best I could.

"I'm really sorry, Carlos. Bob can be an asshole sometimes when he's coming down." I hope that, coming from a fellow Mexican, he could feel how ashamed I was.

Stupid outbursts like that were creating a bad reputation for us among our peers and others in the music industry. The band's bad-ass outlaw character, so loved by the fans, had a price, feeding the tensions that were eating Canned Heat from the inside. It was just those inner sicknesses that Alan sang about and that drove Larry to that confrontation with Henry at the Fillmore West three days before Woodstock,

But I cared. And I'm sure Skip cared too. This was my band, the band I knew was my home. This was the music I loved and the spirit I grooved with. I wanted to succeed, on our terms, and I was ready to devote my life to it. Alan was a tortured nerd of a genius but he was our genius. Bear was one of a kind ringmaster whose heart, hidden evils and all, was bigger than his brain.

Henry and Larry were exceptional talented musicians. Together we made music that no one else could match. Alan and the Bear had made their dream of taking the black country blues into a new age. I had found mine playing with a band like this in a land I had come to love.

I didn't know it was going to be my role to guard the Canned Heat flame, to keep it burning far into the future. I sure didn't know what that would cost. But knowing wouldn't have made a difference. Pissed off, worried about the band's future, I soldiered on, as obsessed in my ways as the others were in theirs.

My long battle with the draft continued. I got caught in an east coast snowstorm, which prevented me from reporting in person for my physical. J.B. Tietz got me an extension and when I finally appeared in August, five months later, I followed the old wizard's instructions. And I also followed the Bear's.

During a chili-eating, record-listening, pot-smoking session at Bob's house a few days before my physical, he and his buddies barraged me with advice, knowing how worried I was.

"Hey, Fito, you gotta show up really loaded and they'll let you go," Bear said, passing a joint.

"Tell 'em you're a faggot. A couple of my friends did that, and they got away with it, after signing a document saying they were homos."

"Just tell them to fuck off. Do something crazy, like take a shit right there on the table."

"When they send you to the Army shrink, act stupid. Tell 'em you're addicted or crazy."

On the day of my appointment, I did what Bear told me to do and got totally wasted on grass, which was a terrible mistake because it only made me more paranoid. I showed up at the induction center, a tall building in downtown L.A. and as I approached the guarded gates, it hit me that you stop being a human being the minute you cross through those doors. You become part of the military, an inhuman machine. You become just another number, marching in lock step with the other numbers.

In the end, I was classified 1A, which meant "do not pass go; go directly to Vietnam." It was time to take the oath of induction but Tietz had instructed me to refuse.

"No matter what they threaten you with, don't take the oath," he said. "After the oath, your ass is theirs. They can do what they want to you. Until then, you're a civilian and they have to deal with you in the civilian system. Of course, you also have to realize that one of these days, the FBI will show up and you'll be arrested and prosecuted."

His instructions left me determined, but hurt. I didn't want to deny America, to refuse America. I loved this country and if some other country attacked it, I would happily give my life to defend it. But I didn't love the war in Vietnam. Maybe some Army brass wanted this Mexican with the long hair and the beard to die for America. I didn't want to die for America, I wanted to live for it.

"Form a line," said a sergeant in razor-sharp khakis. "You will now take the oath."

As Tietz had instructed, I stepped out of the line as a sign of refusal.

An officer stepped briskly up to me.

"Are you aware that you're committing a federal offense? And if convicted, it will mean five years in jail?"

"Yes," I replied.

"Do you still refuse to take the oath of induction?"

"Yes."

A couple of mean-looking MPs grabbed me by the arm and took me to an office on the second floor. They knocked on the door and without waiting for an answer hauled me into a room where a captain sat behind a desk. The captain repeated the whole ritual, including the threats of prison.

Again, I had to step forward and say "no."

The same MPs took me up to the third floor into a bigger, more elegant office where a general, who looked liked Orson Wells with a hangover, was sitting behind a big desk.

"You are to take the oath...," he began. It was the same speech the sergeant and the captain had given, word for word. "If you refuse, take a step forward."

I stepped forward a third time. I couldn't help it. I used the line that was on everyone's lips:

"Hell no, I won't go."

The general glared at me.

"You're making a very big mistake, son. Get out of here, but don't think for a second this is the end of it."

I walked out of the building, past the long lines of young men filing from one test station to another, depressed by what I had done and what I had to look forward to. I knew the general was right. This wasn't the end, but the beginning. Now the nightmare of fighting and dealing with the court system was about to begin, casting a cloud of depression and worry over what should have been the best time of my life.

Tietz had told me what would happen next. One of these days, the FBI would show up and I would be arrested and prosecuted.

As shattered as we were by Henry's quitting before Woodstock, it had a bright side. The cumulative dope intake went down. Not that Harvey Mandel didn't get high, it just wasn't to the degree that Henry did. He mostly smoked weed. The change affected the rest of us. Even Bob started to "moderate" his consumption, which in his case meant fewer pills and "only" ten or so joints a day.

With Harvey in the group, we entered a good year of peace and positive energy and began work on the album "Future Blues." In one of our traditional sessions, sitting around in Bob's living room listening to records, he had an inspiration.

"Hey, check out this song. It's written by the same guy who wrote 'Kansas City'." He put on Wilbert Harrison's "Let's Work Together." When it finished, he said, "I think it's a hit." We all agreed.

Skip made the suggestion that we wait a few months to see if Wilbert made the charts. If he didn't, we should give it a try.

So we waited. The Bear had a thing about taking numbers from live black musicians. He thought we shouldn't cover their work if there was a chance they could get a hit. If they didn't, if the song languished among blues collectors, then he thought we could carry it to a bigger audience and at least get the composer the writer's royalties. Most of these guys rarely got anything for their creations. Bear wanted them to get their due, one of the reasons I was so surprised by his strange "nigger" outburst in front of Carlos.

A few months later, we recorded it, playing only one or two takes. That was it. There was nothing else to do with it. It was one of the greatest songs we recorded. Listening to "Let's Work Together," you appreciate the guitars, the sound of the drums, the sound of the drive, the cymbals, the bass. Everything came together perfectly. If we'd stayed there 12 hours working on it, it wouldn't have been as good. The magic was the fact that we just laid it down and didn't mess with it. It became a gigantic record, Top Ten worldwide.

In a sense it was an answer to Alan's mournful "Time Was," with its message of sad disintegration. Here was The Bear, roaring an exhortation to work together to make things better.

Together we'll stand - divided we'll fall
Come on now people let's get on the ball and work together
Come on come on - let's work together, now people
Because together we will stand, every boy, girl,
woman and man.

Before when things go wrong - as they sometimes will
When the road you travel it's been all up hill
Let's work together, come on, come on, let's work together
You know together we will stand, every boy, girl,
woman and man.

It was the perfect vehicle for Bob, summoning the world to get together and make someone happy. It was his greatest and only hit. The song also enhanced Canned Heat's dual character, a band with two lead singers with very different styles and voices.

The Bear's singing was good but raw. He was a blues shouter who had never taken a voice lesson. But he was a natural performer, a perfect front man with a magic touch for reaching people, for getting them excited, for turning a night with Canned Heat into an experience you'd remember the rest of your life.

His personality and lifestyle were captured perfectly by a magazine reporter, who experienced a night with Bob, his records and his friends:

Bear, a huge mountain of hair, smiles and Levis, is all over the stage...shouting out how glad he is to be home.... 'It sure is good to be home back here in L.A. There's nothing like a gram of hash on the 4th of July to make you feel good'.

A week before the group left, I went over to the Bear's house. It was supposed to be an interview. I walked into an enormous Hollywood Hills decorator art house full of people sitting, lying about and standing around Bear, who was playing old 45s and older still 78 rpm blues records.

He slapped a beer into my hand.

Record after record was sifted out and put on the turntable with accompanying rap as to how and when it all came about. Facts on records so obscure and good as to make the evening go flying by till there were six beer cans in front of me and I found myself in the midst of a party. Somehow I wrote down that Canned Heat would be doing tons of major European TV shows, getting billed over the Doors in many of the major European cities....

I can't remember much else. I woke up the next day on a couch in the living room in time to see Bear climb out the front door mumbling about passports and a drummer lost in Mexico.

Even at the peak of our fame, we never stopped playing in nightclubs—or outright dives and gin mills—because they kept us in close touch with our audiences and we were able to get off musically in that kind of environment. They were much better than the large arenas where you can't hear properly and oppressive security establishes a wall between you and the people, rather than creating communion. No wonder the Beatles broke up for that reason. Besides, it was nice to have the money, even though the clubs didn't pay a lot compared to what we could make in an auditorium or arena.

When I try to reconstruct where the money from all these gigs was going, it's still a mystery to me. Since I thought of myself as a rookie, a drummer and a Mexican, I wasn't about to complain when I was pulling down over $50,000 a year, at a time when you could buy a pretty nice house in Laurel Canyon for less than that. Larry and I talked about the way the band's finances were handled—with no control or sense of proportion, as if this river of money would flow eternally. Skip always had us traveling first class, using limousines for everything, staying in the most expensive hotels. The constant partying added up, with all the expenses, coming out of Canned Heat's account. Skip was getting a 15% commission from the gross earnings (not the net, the profits the rest of us split) plus a 10% "administration fee" on checks coming from royalties, for merely writing a few checks a month, something I always thought should have been covered by his manager's fee. It was too loose and it got even looser as time went on.

And like most Hollywood managers, Skip was also handling other groups as a way to cover his bases for the future. He tried to repeat our success with South Wind, Rockin' Foo and Tarantula. They were good bands, they just didn't have the magic of Canned Heat. Years after they had faded, Canned Heat was still playing on. Maybe not with the headlines the Grateful Dead got due to sharper marketing and stricter controls, but in many ways we were just like the Dead. We never surrendered. We just kept going, boogieing over the horizon for decades to come.

Some macho Mexican *rocanrolero* stud. I had failed to get laid at Woodstock. Worse yet, the same thing happened to me a few weeks earlier when we met the famous Plaster Casters, the two girls who made a collection of plaster replicas of rock stars' cocks.

They were trying to get everybody who was anybody. They really got a lot of us, too. They had a hell of a collection, from things that look like little shrunken toadstools to long, skinny wands.

By then, the girls were famous. Every rock musician in the country had heard of them. They would show up at your hotel toting a little bag of equipment. All they had to do was tell somebody on the house telephone "The Plaster Casters are here" and doors opened, right away. Their procedure was for one of the girls to give you a blowjob, while the other one mixed up some kind of casting medium, sort of like a tube of wet Jell-O. When you were at maximum size and firmness (you hoped, because all the other guys are standing around watching and waiting their turn) you plunged your pride and joy into the mixture, which hardened around it. It was sort of like fucking a wall of mud, some of the guys said. As soon as the stuff hardened, you could pull out.

Even if you were some kind of weirdo who really enjoyed mud fucking, you still had to pull out anyway, because moving would spoil the cast. When it was good and hard, it could be filled with wet plaster, which would solidify into a duplicate of your magnificent flagpole.

At the time, this wasn't considered all that strange. A LITTLE strange maybe, but compared to everything else that was going on, not all that crazy, when you consider honor students were getting loaded on drugs, black power rebels carrying shotguns were taking over college campuses, and suburban mommies and daddies were jumping into fuck-piles on the wall-to-wall carpet at neighborhood swing parties.

So why not collect rock stars pricks? The Smithsonian will want those things in a few years to display with the original album cover art.

It happened in Chicago, when we were playing The Electric Theater, which was to become Aaron Russo's Kinetic Playground. We had an excellent night on stage, all of us cooking just great, and we went back to our hotel, a very nice one.

In the hallway, I meet this gorgeous, brown-eyed girl with a thin face and jet-black hair combed short like a man's. She was dressed in tight black silk pants that outlined her spectacular figure.

"Help me," she said.

"What's wrong?"

131

"I took some acid. I think I'm going crazy."

She started to shake. She was really blasting.

"Please stay with me," she whispered. "I'm peaking and I don't even know where I am."

I knew what LSD does. I've only taken it about five times in my whole life. It's too strong, too chemical for me. I knew she shouldn't be alone.

She said her name was Alice.

We ended up in my room, where I talked to her, reassured her, and gave her some orange juice I ordered from room service because it tastes very good while on acid.

As she sat on the bed, hallucinating and looking so beautiful, I had to restrain myself. She was too flipped out to try getting her under the sheets. I guess that's part of an old-fashioned code I acquired someplace in my Mexican past: a gentleman does not screw women who are too far gone on drugs to know what they're agreeing to.

The phone rang. It was one of the guys in the band.

"You better come down, man. The Plaster Casters are here. They just did Harvey's dick. This is far out."

"Fuck off. I'm not falling for that one."

A girl's voice came over the phone.

"Come on, Feet-o. We need to have you in the collection too. We'll take good care of you. You'll love it."

I said, "I'm sorry, I'm with a girl that is loaded on acid and I have to stay with her."

So I missed my chance with the great Plaster Casters. They never came back to us and all those people who go to the Smithsonian for the great 50-year "Sixties Retrospective" in 2018 will see what the Bear's dick looked like, and Harvey's and Larry's. From what I heard, they will see that Harvey's was the biggest, but they'll just have to go home wondering about mine.

That night, I didn't go to bed with beautiful Alice, who came down off her trip, took a little nap and left. Twenty-eight years later, I caught up with Alice again. She confessed that she had deliberately planned to meet me at my hotel that evening, dropping the acid there and hanging around near my room till I showed up.

But all I knew then was that I couldn't let her freak out all alone in the corridor. It was a perfect example of my co-dependent personality. We didn't use that term back then. Although I never

Harvey Mandel "The Snake"

made use of my college degree in psychology, I tried to read enough to keep current in the field. I know now what a case I am. I suffer from rescue fantasies, suffering along with the sufferers, trying to keep the wounded and the cripples from going down for the last time.

I had no idea that my biggest co-dependency was going to be Canned Heat itself.

I might have held back with Alice but I made up for it a short time later, kicking off a distinctive chapter in my sex life.

As Harvey and I were leaving an outdoor festival in New England after a performance, I spotted an absolutely dynamite-looking redhead walking beside our van toward the exit. She had on little denim cutoffs and wore black cowboy boots on her long, long legs. I rolled down the window.

"Hey, wanna party with us? We've got some pretty good weed."

She turned and obviously recognized us. She had light green eyes and porcelain skin, one of the most beautiful creatures I'd ever seen.

"We're going to have a real good time," I said. "You could be having a good time with us."

She jumped into the van. Harvey and I made room for her between us. Harvey lit a joint and passed it to her. I took a couple of hits. As the weed took hold, I was fascinated by her thighs—so silky smooth, slim, so muscular. I found myself caressing one. She took a long drag on the joint and buried her face in my shoulder. After a few minutes, I looked over and noticed Harvey was caressing her other leg.

In my room, we lit up another joint and opened a bottle of wine. She was standing by the bed, taking a long drink from the bottle when Harvey came up behind her and slipped his arms underneath her arms and cupped her breasts in his hands. I handed her the joint.

"Hey, guys, guys, hold on a minute. Gimme just a second. No really, wait just a second, Harvey. Which one of you guys am I with? Sorry, but I'm a little confused. I mean, do I choose?"

Harvey and I both said it together. "Nope."

"I don't choose? You mean... um... both of you?"

I slipped my arm around her waist and kissed her, whispering: "We said you'd have a good time with us. We didn't say with one of us."

Harvey had begun unbuttoning her blouse. By now she was kissing me back. Harvey pulled her backwards onto the bed and I stretched out beside her.

"This is going to be a very special night. You'll always remember us. And we'll always remember you as the most beautiful girl we've ever been with."

I was working away at the top of her shorts and got them unzipped.

"Isn't this a little...," she started to say.

I slipped in my hand just as Harvey got hold of her bare nipple.

"Ohhhh," she sighed. " Ohh. Wowwww."

She started to giggle.

"Okay, okay," she said. "But let me get these damn boots off."

Oddly enough, an early childhood memory popped into my head as she took off her bra, something I once overheard my grandmother say, when she probably thought I was too little to understand. "She has a wonderful bosom—breasts that could fit into champagne glasses."

Ana's breasts were a perfect champagne glass fit.

She giggled again as I slipped off her panties.

"Okay you guys, this is going to be something special all right. Only how do we do this?"

"We'll figure it out as we go," I said.

What we figured out was something we had seen in a porn movie a short while before. We penetrated her at the same time. First one of us was in her ass, while the other one was in her pussy and then we reversed it. She was having the time of her life, screaming with ecstasy. She had ball-bearing hips that swiveled fluidly in any direction and she could wrap those long legs around us like an octopus.

The evening was so memorable, we decided the occasion deserved a name, so we called it "The Double-Wang Mambo."

We had such a good time that for several months after that, Harvey and I just about always did threesomes. We didn't pick up a girl unless she liked both of us, and both of us liked her. It worked out well, because we tended to like the same women. In fact, I had an affair that went on for years with his ex-wife, who lived with me for awhile.

Although we tried and tried, we never got the double-wang mambo to work again. We could never get both of us inside at the same time. The minute the girl would move toward one of us, the other guy would fall out. It was just too hard to do. Making porn movies must be tougher to do in real life than it looks on the screen. I know the double wang mambo can be done if circumstances are just right. Maybe it had something to do with the length of Ana's legs and that incredible hip movement of hers.

Interestingly, there was no competition or jealousy between Harvey and me. We just joked with each other in cornpone accents about being "deviated preverts" and had a real good time. For the era, it wasn't even that unusual. Just about everybody went a little nuts sexually in the late '60s and early '70s. We were maybe just a little farther out than most.

Again, we went on the road non-stop. It was crazy. It reminded me of the classic World War II movie "Twelve O'clock High" when Gregory Peck's commander orders him: "I want you to fly those boys until they can't take it any more. And then, I want you to fly them some more."

Our agents and manager worked us to exhaustion. For someone like Larry, who had been on the road since his early teens, it was too much. Weary after a show in Atlanta, Larry started complaining about everything.

"Fito's time is dragging, Alan doesn't have any soul and Bob can't sing worth shit. Fuck it, you guys, this is the last time I'm going to do this. I'm giving notice, when this tour is over I'm quitting."

We were so drained ourselves, we just accepted his rage with hardly any reaction, except for Bear. Faced with the loss of the best blues bass player in the world, he yelled: "Damn it, Larry, you just don't know how to have a good time!"

To give Larry his due, it was his pursuit of perfection, his dissatisfaction with Frank Cook, that got me into Canned Heat. And he was right about Frank not being a strong enough drummer and right about Henry Vestine being addicted and crazy.

But there was no reason to blame Canned Heat this time. This time it had to be him. You just don't walk out of a band making $10,000 a night, one of the top bands in the world with a string of hit records, unless you're hopelessly exhausted.

Harvey followed Larry out the door. For all that we liked and respected Harvey, it was Henry who was the quintessential Canned Heat lead guitar, especially in Alan's mind. Harvey felt that vibe. Without Larry as an ally to back him up, he didn't want to fight

Larry "The Mole" Taylor

Henry's ghost anymore.

They weren't out of work long. They went right into John Mayall's band, which by then was known as the training ground that got Mick Taylor into the Rolling Stones.

With Larry gone, we decided to give Henry another chance, hoping the drug problems of the past were history. Actually, Henry, since leaving us, had acquired a whole new drug habit. In Canned Heat, he was smoking a lot of pot and dropping a lot of pills. Out of the band, he began hanging out with a group of outlaw bikers and shooting speed—big time. He was consuming quantities of drugs I couldn't imagine anybody else surviving; but he did. Henry's body was something of a miracle. I never understood how he survived the huge doses of so many kinds of drugs.

Henry wasn't, by any stretch, an outlaw biker type. He didn't even know how to ride, back then. He was an upper-middle class kid who came from a very refined family. His father was a physicist who developed the formula for determining the exit window for Space Shuttle flights, the man after whom the Vestine Crater on the dark side of the moon is named. But Henry was always trying to get street tough, to "live the life," so being a cycle mechanic fit the role. His garage and driveway were filled with a half dozen clapped out Harleys, an old Lincoln, the hulk of an ancient Studebaker that looked like a submarine and a Maserati so rare, there were only three like it in the world, one of them belonging to the Shah of Iran. His upper-class neighbors were stunned. Not only was the driveway full of broken-down bikes, it was full of loaded, dangerous bikers.

And not only was Henry stoned, but he bought a parrot, got it addicted to speed by dosing its water and taught it a huge vocabulary of dirty words. It talked up a storm after a good hit, squawking and swearing from its cage on the patio, while the bikers napped against the wall of the house and Henry ripped apart their Harleys in a speed frenzy, breaking more stuff than he fixed.

The same day Larry and Harvey left, we had a band meeting and decided to call Henry back. He returned, establishing a pattern of leaving and rejoining that continued for more than a quarter of a century. He came back with a real "fuck-you" attitude towards the rest of us. We had turned our backs on him and he wasn't about to forget it. And he brought back all his drug problems and added to ours. In no time, he had Bear shooting speed, too. I even snorted it a few times myself, though I prided myself on never shooting

138

anything. I thought that was crazy.

Henry and the Bear had a lot in common, including the fact that they both came from nice families in comfortable circumstances and were constantly trying to "get down," to show the world they were street-tough dudes. They were blown away by a movie called "The Cool World" about New York junkies and street people. For weeks, everything was judged by whether it was "in" the Cool World or "outside" the Cool World. They started talking be-bop, trying to sound black. To convince themselves they were heavy-duty, "get-down bad," they started taking heroin. It was worse than if Henry had never left.

By this time, I was a key member of the band, so the other guys asked me if I had any ideas for a new bass player. It had been four years since we were two insecure Mexican kids, pushing our way over the border to join *los dioses*, but I hadn't forgotten Tony de la Barreda. Although he wasn't great like Larry—very few people are— he was a good bass player, he was my friend and he had a good stage presence. All Tony needed was to hang around us to get infected with our love for this kind of music. I figured, if he took it seriously, he'd do a good job.

Tony had been playing with Sam and The Goodtimers, an outstanding black R&B band that recorded most of the great Ike and Tina Turner songs. They used to play on the Sunset Strip at The Soul'd Out Club, notorious for its rowdy party atmosphere.

In the '60s and early '70s, The Strip was lined with clubs, great places for young musicians to learn, jam, and get exposure. Another talented musician I met at the club was the great piano player Ronnie Barron, who had just arrived from Louisiana and who would play with Dr. John and Paul Butterfield and eventually with Canned Heat.

When I called Tony, I asked: "Do you want to be a rock star?"

"Hey, man, what's happening?"

"Larry quit and I get to choose the new guy. I want you."

"Count me in," said Tony.

After a few rehearsals, we were cooking again. Henry's initial anger had mellowed and the band felt like a brotherhood again, with our old creativity revived.

Our new songs not only had an odd-measure blues approach, but this time we were really into playing "free form" music, expressing emotion without restriction, breaking the beat, playing in another key, mixing noise with notes, and trying to homogenize all this into musical pieces.

(When my father heard us during our first Mexican tour in 1969 he liked us very much, because his roots in swing music responded to our beat. But once he was exposed to our "free" approach, he called us locos, madmen.)

We had an informal, demo-like recording session where we tried these tunes, but they were never properly mixed and the production was never finalized. Some were eventually released in 1995 in a triple collector CD from EMI entitled "Uncanned," which also included some yet to be released Canned Heat material EMI held in its vaults for over 25 years. I suppose it's no surprise that I haven't received a penny.

One night in Miami, Jim Morrison joined us on stage, then hung around afterward sitting at a table with Alan, talking quietly. Two very tormented souls. It was the last time they saw each other and the last time I saw Jim.

When we returned to LA, the band got together to rehearse for a gig at the Veterans Auditorium. As the clock ticked away, Bear got increasingly agitated: "Where the hell is Alan? You'd think after three days in the fuckin' woods, the least he could do would be to show up on time."

Moments later, Skip appeared in the doorway, his jaw tight. "Alan just tried to kill himself. He drove his van off the road. He's in a psychiatric hospital."

We bolted out the door and piled into a van to go to the hospital. Somewhere behind us, as we drove away from the rehearsal hall, we left our golden era, and set off down a very long, hard road.

LAST NIGHT I LOST THE BEST FRIEND

Topanga Canyon is a winding, narrow pass on the northwestern rim of Los Angeles, running 14 miles through the Santa Monica Mountains from the squared-off tract houses on the sun-baked floor of the San Fernando Valley to the Pacific Coast beaches that outsiders think of as L.A.

It is close enough to the city's corruption for residents to join in the dance, rural enough that they can raise horses and listen to the coyotes howl at night. Legend has it that Old West outlaws hid out there, the first of generations of Topanga dwellers to build a little fortress against the civilization they rejected, fed on and could not leave. Stashed back in the tall, dense brush, which explodes in devastating fires in late summer, are little frontier cabins and rambling old ranch houses and slapped-together shacks. Scattered hidden estates provide refuge for odd religions and nonsked lifestyles.

In the '60s, this place was hippie central for Southern California. With the Haight-Ashbury, it was the capitol of the hip and the mellow and the cool worldwide. Some even said the first hippies were a Topanga creation, the ultimate expression of the earth-child Topanga mindset, who spun off colonies up in San Francisco, where they got better press because the Bay Area has a sense of community while nobody in Los Angeles cares what happens a few miles away.

Just off a narrow side road near the northern end of the canyon, stands a one-story house, once condemned by the city as a place unfit for human habitation, surrounded by hillocks of sun-dried mud and weeds. This was once the Bear's house. Some of his museum-class collection of blues records still wash out of the mud when heavy rains regularly flood the site, the reason the house was condemned.

This house was the crucible where Canned Heat took shape. The band grew out of the record-listening parties the Bear gave, which went on from the afternoon of one day to sunrise the next. Guys hanging out, loafing on the floor, smoking joints, killing some beers and the Bear and Alan playing disc jockey: "Listen to this, this is outta sight..."

Alan, Henry, and the Bear had incredible knowledge of blues music. If you named a song, say "Three Hours Past Midnight" by Johnny Guitar Watson, they would tell you who recorded it, what month and year, what label it was on, who was in the studio that night, who played on it without credit and what became of the musicians afterward. It was like they had been there, at every blues recording gig ever, going back to all-night together sessions in some Memphis garage in the '30s.

These all-night blues-and-pot parties in the house, where the Bear lived with a woman who entertained his friends with stories from her career as a hooker, became a sort of soul school and initiation rite for members of the band. Flowing back and forth between the house and the Topanga Corral—the grungy roadhouse nearby where Canned Heat became the house band, and the place where Spirit, Neil Young, Linda Ronstadt and the Stone Ponies, among others, made their bones—the party sessions forged a sense of brotherhood in the blues, a feeling for its black roots.

To the outside world, when our records began selling heavily, Alan's cool, blade-thin tenor on "Goin' Up The Country" and "On The Road Again" was Canned Heat's voice. But in the band, Bear was the father figure. Not a boss exactly, in such an anarchic group, but he was the central figure, the commanding presence, the well of spirit.

Alan and the Bear reminded me a lot of Laurel and Hardy. The skinny guy, stumbling bewildered through the unforgiving world, lost in some cloud, and the bluff, growlly fat guy, trying to love him and save him by whacking him on the head.

It was at the house in Topanga Canyon that the band gave Alan a van, which had been specially equipped for camping with a bed and a small stove. Alan was in love with trees. Plants and trees and the earth. He always tried to sleep outside. Even when we were on tour, if the weather was warm enough, and there was a park or a vacant lot or a freeway strip or something nearby, he would leave the hotel at night and go curl up on the ground out there in a blanket or a sleeping bag. If he had to stay in the room, he'd throw a blanket on the floor and sleep there. He said his yoga studies had taught him that it was better for you to sleep on the hardest surface you could find.

Sometimes we would be partying in a suite or something, smoking joints, turning up the music, telling jokes with outlaw bikers and fooling around with the girls you meet on the road, and Alan would be out in the weeds behind the parking lot, cooking brown rice on his little alcohol camping stove, laying out in the bushes in the dark in his sleeping bag, looking at the stars.

He was the first environmentalist I ever knew, and cared about the earth deeply before it was fashionable. He eventually became a sort of a martyr to his passion for nature.

So after "Living The Blues" became a hit, we gave Alan this van. And we are all standing outside the house in Topanga and Bear is saying "Well, okay, Alan, you can bug out for the woods now. Say hello to the other owls, and the squirrels and shit. Good-bye."

But Alan didn't go anywhere.

"I don't know how to drive."

The Bear was astonished. Always before, when the band went anywhere, somebody else drove, never Alan. But we didn't know that he didn't know how.

"You don't know how to drive? Aren't you an American? How did you grow up? God, you're such a pain in the ass. We give you this great van so you can go sleep in the redwoods and talk to the birds and stuff and you don't even fucking know how to drive. Well, I better show you."

So there was Alan, trying to drive up and down Topanga Canyon, screwing up like Stan Laurel always did, and there was Bear sitting beside him like Hardy, shouting "You cannot shift like that. No, no, put in the clutch! God, you'll never make it out of the city."

That was enough motivation. To get to the trees, he learned to drive. After that, when we weren't playing, Alan would be in his van, parked under a tree someplace in Yosemite or Big Sur.

He was never anyone's idea of a typical rock star. He was a nerd. A brilliant nerd, an unusual nerd, and a lovable and tragic nerd if you got to know him. But a nerd.

It wasn't only the thick glasses. It was just that a lot of the time he'd break the arms off and then try to balance them on his nose. Or tape them on. Without the glasses, Alan literally could not recognize the people he played with at two feet, that's how blind the "Blind Owl" was.

He also had these strange problems with organization. He constantly lost stuff. He didn't know things most people learned before kindergarten. Like, he didn't know how to hang up his pants when he took them off. He always just sort of rolled them up like you would a beach towel and put the bundle on the floor.

He was really funky. He never grasped the whole idea of personal hygiene. I didn't know how funky until I went on the road with him for the first time. I had just been hired. The band had to go back to Denver to try to deal with the drug charges that we sang about in "My Crime" and play a gig while we were there. When we got to the

hotel, Bear just handed me a key and said "Here's your room."

I was the rookie and they were treating me like the rookie, giving me the short end of the stick—rooming with Alan.

I didn't know it then but nobody else in the band would room with Alan if they could get out of it. Hey, we are rockers on the road. After we play to make the people happy, it's time to make ourselves happy. It's the '60s and musicians meet very interesting girls who will do all sorts of things even if you don't buy them dinner and take them to a movie. Or even ask them their names.

But nobody could get laid if they had to share a room with Alan.

First of all, he smelled bad. Really bad. So the room would stink. You finally get some girl up to your room, and you can't kiss her because she's gagging too hard to open her mouth.

Some of that was because Alan usually slept out in the weeds and some of it was because he was just a child of the earth. We would tell him, "Wash for Christ's sake, and comb your hair and get some hipper clothes and keep them clean." God knows, he tried to please us. He did whatever we told him. But it was no use. He didn't understand what we were talking about. He was just not of this world.

Skip used to show up at gigs with all new clothes he'd bought for Alan, who would put everything on, including new underwear. Then he would put his three-inch thick wallet in his left front pocket of the new pants and stuff newly-collected leaves in the other. By the end of the set, it looked like he'd slept in the new outfit for three days. It was just part of Alan's persona.

That night in Denver, Alan tried to get drunk after the show and threw up all night. He did drink and he did take drugs, but he had strange ways of screwing that up too. I was trying to get to sleep and there was Alan, sleeping on the floor and vomiting on it at the same time.

After that, I almost never shared a room with Alan, much as I liked him.

Socially, he had nothing happening. He was not ugly, but he repelled most women, which took some doing for a singer with a top rock band in the '60s. But the uncool way he dressed, the thick glasses taped to his nose, all the pimples he had, he always looked even nerdier than he was.

But he wanted to be touched, to be loved, to be loved physically and the lack of love in his life was one of the things that tormented him, that brought that profitable melancholy to his songs but that screwed up his life. It broke my heart. We tried to fix him up, we tried to tell him how to act with women, because his loneliness was literally killing him. But it never worked for him.

One reason he was ill at ease around women was because he had sexual problems. He had a hard time getting an erection or keeping one. When he did manage to get it up, he came right away, often before he could get it in.

He told me things like that when we got to know each other better as my English improved. He was the only one in the band who was interested in the fact that I had a college degree, interested enough to figure out that I was not some dimbulb comic-book Mexican mascot, but that I simply had trouble expressing myself at first because I still spoke English so poorly.

Sometimes I wonder if things could have been different. What if

Dino Lappas of Liberty asked us during the "Boogie sessions" to keep Alan away from the mixing board-"We spent several hours cleaning greasy hairs out of the electronics".

the band had hired some hooker, or found some crazed female fan, secretly paid her to pretend she was madly in love with Alan, take care of him, make him feel like a man? Would that have prevented what followed?

Alan was very serious about Hatha yoga and turned me on to it. He thought it gave him power and control, things he had a big shortage of. He would go into one of his yogi owl numbers at the damndest times.

Like, when we had to go back to Portland to fight the obscenity charges brought after The Bear's outburst of "fucks" before the teeny-boppers. Alan had to give a deposition. He was sure he could bring yoga power down on the prosecutor with proper breathing techniques, so he would breathe in hard while answering each question.

"Are you in this band?"

Sucking in his breath: "Yes."

"Were you on the stage with Bob Hite on the night in question?"

Big suck: "Yes."

"Did you hear Hite say 'fuck' on stage?"

Whooooosh: "No."

The other guys in the band are laughing behind their hands. Even the district attorney obviously didn't know whether to worry about these dangerous lunatics he was questioning or just give up and giggle with the rest of us.

One night right after we finished a gig in Tampa, Florida, we were in somebody's room at the Holiday Inn when this girl knocks on the door. She was gorgeous, maybe 18 or 19, long blonde hair, big white teeth, long, suntanned legs in a little white skirt, like a tennis skirt. She had this pink-cheeked, childish face, like you see on high school cheerleaders in little towns in the Midwest.

"Hi, y'all," she said. She had this thick southern drawl.

"I'm the Canned Heat Mama and I wanna fuck y'all."

For whatever reason, this southern angel had decided she wanted to be our official main groupie and she was ready to get on with it, right then and there.

It was a little odd, but at that point the band had never fucked any groupies together, a common thing for touring bands to do. We had picked up girls and gone off with them individually, and sometimes maybe two of us rooming together shared a girl, but we had never done any all-on-one numbers. We were still just getting to know each other, not really a tight unit yet.

The Bear, he was always trying to get us to do things together. He wanted us to be more than just a bunch of musicians, he wanted us to be a family, to be brothers of the road. But Henry was kind of reserved, Larry was even more reserved, Alan was downright introverted and I was a foreigner. To Bear, the angel of Tampa was an opportunity to promote some togetherness, and he's roaring encouragement at us:

"All right you guys, we have us a really beautiful mama here, let's show her one hell of a good time. Boy, I love this life. Let the good times roll."

Meanwhile, the official Canned Heat Mama-to-be is taking off her clothes, hanging them up real neatly on hangers like her mother taught her, and telling us how wonderful our music is and how much happiness we are bringing to the people with our art, and how she certainly hopes she can return to us some of the joy we have given her and so many others. It was a hell of an impressive speech. I was struck by her easy manner, very confident, with old-fashioned courtesy.

Then she steps real daintily out of her underpants, folds them up and puts them in the bedside drawer with the Gideon Bible. When she has nothing on but her little white socks, she stretches out on the bed, on this pink flowered bedspread and smiles sweetly up at us.

"Okay, now which of y'all is going to be first?"

We are all standing around in our shorts, drinking beers, passing a joint and making these nervous noises. "Uhhhh, heh....uhhh, heh heh heh."
Nobody is up for this.

The Bear is sort of growling at us, "Well come on, you guys. For God's sake you don't see pussy like this every day, let's get it on." I think he is worried that the band will lose its reputation as bad-ass outlaws if it ever gets out that we had this golden vision offer herself to us but she left untouched. However, we can see he is not ready to do anything himself yet either.

Well, I am still the rookie. But I had actually done this sort of thing before, when Miguel Casis got the "Gordita" for the band in Mexico. And I am a Mexican and one of the few good things *Norteamericanos* think about us is that we are eternally horny little bastards. My people's honor is at stake here. So, what with patriotism and playing with myself a little, I am on top of Miss America, pumping away and thinking "*Viva Mexico* and thank you God."

Larry confessed later that watching her with me turned him on. So by the time I was through, he was ready, and all the other guys were getting into it. I had triggered what we later called "a feeding frenzy."

The Canned Heat Mama is having a hell of a time, laughing and whooping and breathing hard like she is playing a really good game of volleyball on the beach.

149

I go into the bathroom to clean up and there is Alan, standing on his head, doing deep yoga breathing.

By then I was used to Alan being a little weird, but this was a new world record.

"Alan, man, what the fuck are you doing? You for sure don't want to miss that scene out there, man. She's fantastic."

Bear yells out: "Leave him alone, Fito. He read in some yoga book that hanging upside-down gives you a hard-on."

I left him there.

The now-official Canned Heat Mama, after about an hour of squealing and thrashing on the bed with the rest of us, thanked us politely, ("Y'all are just ever so nice and I had a really good time"), and bounced out into the night with our best known singer still trying to find strength through yoga in the bathroom.

Alan Christie Wilson was born on the 4th of July 1943 in Arlington, Massachusetts. His father always wanted him to be a bricklayer. Once we were in a limo outside his parents' house, while he made a quick visit, and he pointed to the street running uphill from the house, and said "God knows how many times I came running down that street, running away from the other guys, chasing me and yelling at me and beating me up."

He was that kind of kid, the real bright but strange one that the other guys beat up.

It was the same street where as a little kid he would walk with his fingers in his ears on cold, snowy winter days, bawling his little eyes out. "I can't stand it," he told people. "The trees are hurting. I hear them crying."

He was hearing the branches creak in the cold, under the weight of the snow, a sound that little kids who grow up in cold climates hear so often they tune it out. Only Alan took it personally, already gripped by his obsession that nature was suffering.

His family wrote him a whole series of letters when the band got successful and he was living mostly at the Bear's place in Topanga Canyon. Long afterward, the Bear found them in the house. They had never been opened. At one point he wrote his father a long letter, sort of divorcing his family. He just didn't want to know them anymore, at least then.

Over time, the rift healed a little. The Wilsons always had the band over to their house when we were in Boston, a hell of a sharp change of pace from our usual life on the road—Sunday dinners with a nice, straight, good old folks American family, things like that.

Maybe it evened out in the end. If his family was an irritant to Alan, because they were clearly not the people he would have invented for a family if he could have done that, then Alan with his strangeness and inconsolable pain was surely not the ideal son.

Flying with Alan was a trip in more ways than one. First, we had to find him to get him on the plane, because a lot of times there are marshes or fields or vacant lands near airports. They would be calling our flight, an airplane would be warming up to carry us to some other city where we were going to make thousands of dollars playing a gig, and all of a sudden Skip or the Bear would realize that Alan was gone.

Usually he was either sitting in his cross-legged yoga position in some remote corner of the airport, studying his books and wrapping his hair around his fingers, or else he had gone off to the boondocks to study the plants and animals there.

Skip and Bear and the roadies would go running across the airport to the nearest field or marsh or whatever and haul him back, sometimes with big chunks of wet mud on his clothes from laying on the ground so he could get close enough to see some plant.

When we found him, we had to watch while he turned in his ticket or his boarding pass to the attendants. We could never teach him about taking care of papers. The only way he knew to save them was to wad them up in a ball and stuff them in his pockets with the leaves and rocks and soil samples he collected. Skip or Bear would hustle him up to the gate, in his muddy nerd clothes, and he would turn in this wrinkled, dirty ball of paper that looked like it had been a year underground in a garbage dump.

The attendant would usually hold the ticket as far away from herself as she could. Of course, the rest of us were all bearded and wearing funky hippie/musician clothes, like big purple and yellow tie-dye shirts, and maybe the Bear and Henry were loaded on something and acting crazy and loud, so we were probably not any airline crew's favorite passengers, although it was not until later that one crew actually landed the plane and had most of the band arrested.

On a European tour, in Sweden or some uptight Scandinavian country like that, we had to haul Alan out of a swamp near the airport. He wanted to stay because he was sure he had found some kind of rare oak tree or something. He got on the plane carrying bunches of leaves and twigs, very muddy, smelling very bad. We spent the whole trip with the other passengers glaring at him and muttering about us.

This was after Alan had decided to learn the names, in Latin and English, of all the plants and trees in the world. I could not test him, but I'm pretty sure he actually did that. He would carry these enormous botany books with him on tour, gigantic tomes the size of big dictionaries. While the rest of us were partying and getting wasted and looking for girls, he would be in the woods or someplace, collecting leaves and things to put in the books on the pages that discussed that specific plant or tree so that he could study the actual sample alongside the scientific definition.

When we landed in New York on our way home from Europe, the customs people see this bunch of hippie rock musicians coming in and decided that if anybody has dope on them, we're the ones. So they start searching all our bags and the poor guy they assigned to Alan shakes his books and out fall all these leaves and pine cones and dried moss and wet roots from swamps in Sweden. The inspector was pretty sure this was some new kind of dope, but he couldn't figure out what it was, and whether Alan was smoking it or injecting it or what.

Alan by now was sitting on the floor doing yoga, but every now and then he would get up and try to help the guy by showing him that right there in the book it had the whole scientific description of the rare Swedish swamp oak or whatever the hell leaf the guy was trying to identify.

They eventually had to let us go, but I bet that customs inspector is still trying to find out what kind of psychedelic drug there is in Swedish oak trees.

It was funny as hell, and we would all be breaking up when he did things like that, but sometimes it was too much even for us. The Bear or someone would take him aside and sort of plead with him: "Alan, for God's sake, enough with the weirdness. At least try to be a LITTLE less weird in public, man. Have mercy on the rest of us."

A couple of times, I wondered whether there was some girl nerd at UCLA or some other college who spent all her time in the library, memorizing the names of plants, or sitting out in the woods by herself, talking to the birds and the stars.

There probably was. If we had just gone and found her she would have been the girl of Alan's dreams, his salvation, somebody who was like him. She would have loved him because she understood him, instead of the stupid groupies he could sometimes get to spend a night with him, which just made him more depressed.

But we were young and we were starting to make big chunks of money. We all had our own problems and so none of us ever really went looking for Alan's earth-child soulmate. And the girls you meet on the road, like the Plaster Casters and the Canned Heat Mama, are not much like that.

Alan brought that scientific mind even to his music. His playing seemed cold to some, but to me it was precise, exact. Like Alan's mind. Nobody in the world could do what he could with a harmonica. Ask any great blues musician like John Lee Hooker, Paul Butterfield, Charlie Musselwhite, Kim Wilson—they all recognize Alan Wilson as a uniquely talented performer. The simple blues harmonica he used, not the more sophisticated chromatic scale version, is a very limited instrument, with only one scale, one chord. But Alan got more notes out of that thing than anyone else.

Rare for a blues man, Alan was a school-taught musicologist, who had studied in Massachusetts, where he grew up. Alan was so fascinated by the blues, by the music's early black roots, that he would spend hours listening to scratchy old 78s, trying to write down and explain lyrics that had never been preserved in any other form, working his way through difficult southern black accents and 1920s black slang and all the rich metaphors of the music. He was devoted to forging keys that would make the blues safe for white people, that would give them—and a lot of blacks too—the knowledge to appreciate and savor this raw art that he loved.

It was this academic background that got him to California, when he was hired as a musicologist by John Fahey, an acoustic guitar legend and esoteric folk music producer, to help Fahey write the biography of Charlie Patton, one of the first recorded blues singers, the father of us all.

On stage, Alan would have stood out in any band, but especially so in the Canned Heat. He looked distant and emotionless while he played, a rigid robot, which was all the more striking because around him the rest of the band would be getting carried away, their bodies shaking to the beat, making music-fuck faces, grimacing with effort or throwing their heads back in satisfaction.

Larry bobs back and forth from the waist like a spastic stork, lost in his own world. Henry swivels and waves his head on his neck, as if he's playing every note with his whole body and I tighten into the drums, punching out a beat.

Bear rolls around the stage, his vast belly quivering as he stomps and roars, like a demonic Santa, the microphone shoved inside his mouth, sliding off his tongue, trying so hard to transport the people, to make them LET GO, that he rips loose his own weak mooring to reality.

But Alan stood up straight and still and sang in his high, clear voice like his mind wasn't even on stage, like it wasn't even in his body any more. Which, now that I think of it, it probably wasn't. He looked soft, almost feminine sometimes, a half-blind version of that famous picture of Billy the Kid, the bandit who looked like a nerd even if he was a stone killer. Alan was like that, all chubby-cheeked and squinty-eyed, sort of like a squirrel that's been struck by lightning and is trying to figure out where he is.

The first time I saw Canned Heat play, I didn't much like Alan because he seemed so cold, so strange. I had no idea what a genius he was. He just seemed to me like this girlish hippie, who wasn't loud enough for this kind of music, who wasn't projecting to the people.

But then I saw that fat guy screaming "got my mojo working" and I heard Henry and Larry's guitars, and I was just blown apart. Like a lot of others, I realized that Alan's cold head trip was making a band like this something completely new, taking it somewhere nobody else had gone before. He was taking this music, so full of joy and pain that blood runs out the edges, and putting a clear, cool frame around it. He was clarifying all this gutsy reality with a bit of abstraction.

Some of our most famous songs grew out of Alan's knowledge of old blues music, black music that is a wonderful legacy of America that most Americans don't even know—hell, that even most young black Americans have lost touch with now, a great tragedy.

"On the Road Again," which was number one all over the world, was based on a traditional Mississippi blues tune. The original, long ago, was done by Floyd Jones. But our song, the one that became famous, was based more on a number by John Lee Hooker, the legendary Mississippi blues man. He was not only a huge influence on our music, but wound up playing with us on one of our best albums and in some great lives shows. He kept in touch with the band and sometimes sat in with us.

After our first few hits, we were under a lot of pressure to come up with something new. "Your are a hit band, now you have to STAY a hit band," Skip would say.

We went back to the band's roots—hanging out at Bear's place in Topanga Canyon, smoking joints, listening to the old black blues masters, listening for that something that made us feel good, or sad, or wonderful or wistful. Very collaborative, everybody joining in with ideas. We figured what did it for us would do it for the people when we gave it the Canned Heat touch.

In February 1969, we were rehearsing at a little old hall called the Veterans Auditorium on La Brea between Hollywood and Sunset Boulevards when Alan came in, all flushed and out of breath the way he usually was, carrying a big Indian-weave bag full of books.

"I have a song I think is good," he said. "It comes from an old Texas country blues song called 'Bull Doze Blues' by Henry Thomas, the one man band."

I didn't know who Henry Thomas was but Vestine and the Bear knew right away. They knew all those old blues guys.

Alan starts going da, da, da, da, the little flute lick that opens it, and sings "I'm going, I'm going down south."

"I'm going to change the lyrics to 'Goin' Up The Country,' and we can rearrange it right now."

We started to rehearse the song—just Alan, Larry and me, just a trio, very simple, very primitive, which was the sound we really wanted.

There was Alan, shifting it around as we played. "Goin' up the country, baby, don't you wanna go...". This was when Alan's genius would just pop out. He could compose right there, his mind running faster than any of us could keep up with, changing the song in his head over and over, playing bits of it here and some of it there, until it was a new song, something that was really his. And all the while he was doing that, he was taking us along, helping us follow him.

The second time we played it, at the end, we all just stared at each other grinning.

"That's a hit record," Larry said. "This is going to be a fucking monster."

We just knew it, that early, this was going to be a great one.

And it was. It broke in city after city and hit a peak on the East Coast just in time for Woodstock. The crowd there knew it so well that when Alan took that mike and began putting words to the opening flute lick, they just exploded. Both the music and the words—we all HAD gone up the country that day—were perfect for the moment. That's how it became the Woodstock anthem.

Once we had "Goin' Up The Country" as a single, the rest of the album was no problem. We knew we were going to do blues, that we were going to stretch out and push our imagination to the limits, knowing that single would get us commercial acceptance. The record company, our management, it was all going full blast.

Life couldn't have been sweeter. We had no idea how ironic it was when we came up with the title for the album. Inspired by a tattoo of Henry's, we decided to call it "Living The Blues."

We couldn't know then that we'd earn that album title, over and over again.

But to Alan, the point of Canned Heat was not to get him fame or groupies or sex or dope or even money. He used his paychecks as bookmarks in his botany textbooks, like he did the leaves and roots. He just stuffed them in the books, uncashed.

To him, the purpose of the band was to use the power of the blues (with its roots in black tragedy and sorrow) and the boogie (which took people out of themselves and made them happy) to protest against the destruction of the earth.

Alan became increasingly convinced that mankind had irretrievably poisoned the earth. Later there would be "green" political parties and environmental movements for that. But Alan felt alone in this. He didn't know anybody like himself and he worried.

He worried about it so much he sort of drove himself over the edge. He was convinced it was too late, that mankind was too addicted to machines and destruction to save anything. He didn't want to live to see what the future would be like, because he was sure it would be too awful to live in.

He was not just some pretty boy, some Elvis Presley, writing about trying to get the girl next door into bed. He was not just some Jim Morrison, picking at the scabs on his own psyche.

Listen today to "Poor Moon," the 1970 tune that was inspired by the first moon landing. In the song, Alan sees even the moon being ruined by man and technology.

Poor moon, I think you see the cloud we made
that covers up L.A.
I wonder if you'll hide behind
a shroud like that someday.

He wrote that because he was devastated by a news story that the Pentagon was thinking of using the moon as a dumping ground for radioactive waste. He was terrified by the supersonic plane everyone thought was going to be the next big thing for air travel, because he was sure it would destroy the protective layer of the stratosphere. He was obsessed by that plane.

Canned Heat has never gotten the credit it deserved for being the first band to focus on the sad state of the environment. Our reputation suffered because of Alan's militancy. It was his idea to put the American flag upside down on the cover of "Future Blues" with the band members, dressed as astronauts on the moon, raising the American flag like the famous World War 11 photo of the Marines on Mount Suribachi on Iwo Jima. In the background, a polluted Earth is surrounded by a cloud.

With the Vietnam War in full swing, that was too controversial a statement for many record sellers. Environmentalism, a movement that had not yet jelled, was lumped in with "hippie commie pinko traitors." Many stores—sales giants like Sears and K-Mart—refused to carry it.

The "Future Blues" LP also featured Bob on our Cajun rendition of "Sugar Bee" with Alan playing harmonica in place of the accordion on the original Eddie Shuler version. We also did a version of Arthur 'Big Boy' Crudup's "That's All Right, Mama," which unlike Elvis's, was more country blues oriented, like the original. The other two songs that feature Bear are "So Sad" (the world is in a tangle) and "Future Blues." Both deal with our concern about the environment.

"London Blues" was another odd-measure slow blues based on one of Alan's many failures with women. His treatment by a London groupie so depressed him he wrote about it in the album. She was not very pretty, a brunette with short, straight hair who was plain enough that the rest of us figured Alan might have a chance with her. She teased him, flirting with him and leading him to believe they were going to have a big romance. Alan had a crush on her like a 13-year-old boy discovering the girl next door.

"We're going out tonight, Fito," he told me, as we went back to our hotel in a taxi. "Help me with this. She's coming over and I'm taking her to dinner at the hotel. It's going to be just the two of us. I've been looking for a girl like this. I don't want to screw it up. I want her to have a really good time, and when she comes back to my room, we'll both have a great time. I don't want to just write the songs, I want to be IN one."

I helped Alan get dressed. We had a barber come up to his room. We had an optometrist down the street make up a pair of glasses that I wouldn't let him wear until he got in the elevator to meet her, knowing he'd break them otherwise. We had the hotel valet clean his one decent pair of bellbottoms. He bought a pair of boots. I knotted a silk scarf around his neck under an open collar silk shirt. Very Carnaby Street. He actually looked like Swinging London for a brief shining moment.

We went down to the bar to wait for her. She came in wearing one of those long Afghan sheepskin coats, covered with embroidery, also very fashionable, grabbed Alan's arm and put her face up close to his.

"Aaaaalan. You look absolutely beautiful."

A flashbulb would have caught a cool couple, the English beauty and the American bluesman, quintessential '60s hip.

Alan was even smiling.

"Are we having dinner here?"

"Uh, yes. Yes, we are. You know Fito? He was just leaving. He has a date. I have a table for us."

"You wouldn't mind if some friends, join us would you? These are really groovy people, two of them are from Denmark. You'll LOVE them. If they go back to Copenhagen and tell their friends they had dinner with an American rock star..."

It was not until then I noticed she was trailing an entourage of about a half-dozen. All dressed in hippie style, bright silks and gold chains, high suede boots and headbands dripping fake pearls.

She leaned close to his ear and I heard her whisper, "I'll get rid of them before dessert."

I left. I did have a date.

I got back late. Alan was sitting in a chair in the lobby, the kind nobody ever sits in, reading a book. He was alone. Somehow, he had gotten a film of grease all over his glasses. The knot on the silk scarf had slipped around behind his neck so he looked like a refugee from an elegant gallows. He was obviously waiting there for me or somebody else in the band to come along. I didn't want to ask how things went.

"Big waste of time, Fito," he said. "Big waste of time."

"You didn't do anything?"

"Yeah, I did something. I bought dinner for eight people, including two who did not speak any language I could understand. I still don't know who the fuck they were."

"She just stuck you for the bill? You didn't go anywhere with her?"

"I took her to a show and after that we ended up in her house where she ignored me and avoided me, just talking to her friends, so I left and wandered the streets. I spent over three hundred pounds and I didn't even get a goodnight kiss. Fuck it. Let's go up to Bob's room and get a joint."

In the elevator, I saw Alan quietly rubbing the tears from his face.

When I came here last year, you promised much to me
When I came here last year, you promised much to me
You led me on and teased me
You picked me up and let me down.

When I asked you here for dinner and
you brought all your friends
When I asked you here for dinner and
you brought all your friends
Here I am feeding half of London
And all I should be feeding here is you.

When I took you to the music show and
we wound up in your house
When I took you to the music show and
we wound up in your house
But you ran around and hid from me
You left me on the streets of London all alone.

Increasingly depressed and lonely, Alan talked often of death. He wanted to play for the people to make them hear his message, to

159

Skip (with camera) hopes Bear will fit into space suit at photo shoot for "Future Blues" album cover.

CANNED HEAT "FUTURE BLUES"

PRODUCED BY SKIP TAYLOR

CONTAINS THE HIT SINGLE—"LET'S WORK TOGETHER"

With the upside down flag signaling distress for planet Earth, the band strikes an Iwo Jima-like pose for the cover of "Future Blues"

keep alive the blues and save the earth, but he didn't like being famous. He never understood why people recognized him or would ask for his autograph, because he would never have done anything like that to anyone else.

He didn't want to have to learn to handle fans. He wanted them to listen to his songs and ignore him, and he was miserable that it only seemed to work the other way around.

His hit songs are all about getting away.

"On The Road Again:"
Well, I'm so tired of cryin'
but I'm out on the road again,
I'm on the road again.
I ain't got no woman just to call my special friend.

"Goin' Up The Country:"
And, I'm going to leave the city got to get away
I'm going to leave the city got to get away
All this fussing and fighting
Man, you know I sure can't stay.

Another song from "Future Blues" that reflected Alan's depressed and confused state of mind was "My Time Ain't Long."

Don't the moon look pretty shining down thru the trees
Don't the moon look pretty shining down thru the, shining
down thru the woods
Well I know, know my time ain't long.

I can hear the waves lapping up on the shore
I can hear the waves, lapping up on the,
lapping up on the shore
Well I know, know my time ain't long.

If a girl deserts me wonder what will I do
If a girl deserts me wonder what will I, wonder what will I do
Well I know, know my time ain't long.

We knew he was talking about getting away entirely, about death.

It started with the van the band bought him so he could sleep out in the woods without laying on the ground all night. Alan cracked it up, sending us all piling out of the rehearsal to see if he was okay. He confessed then that he did it deliberately: "I was driving along the freeway and all of a sudden I just thought 'Fuck it' and drove off the road." Fortunately, he wasn't badly hurt and he didn't hurt anyone else.

A short time later he tried—and failed—again. "Christ," he said. "I'm so fucked up I can't even kill myself right. I had all these reds to take and do myself in and I lost them behind the Topanga Corral when I was high or drunk or something and now I can't find them."

Alan was put under psychiatric care. This shrink, the genius, put the Bear in charge of Alan. She said Alan ought to go live with him, because he could take better care of Alan and see that he doesn't get all fucked up. My God, talk about the blind leading the blind. The Bear was a magnificent human being in his way, but he was nobody to put in charge of anyone's mental health at any time. It was like putting some berserk Viking in charge of little orphan Bambi.

Alan sang about the shrink in "Human Condition."

Well, it's a low down kinda condition
Been runnin' 'round my brain
says it may drive me insane
and every organism that I can hear or see
Seems to have the blues to me.
So I ran to the doctor
sat down on the bed
I looked up right at her
this is what she said
You're in a human condition
that's what's got you down
human condition, your face is full of frown
You've got to stand your ground.

The shrink put him on anti-depressant pills, which made him even more depressed because he wouldn't take them correctly. At first, those kind of pills make you sleepy and relaxed, just knock you out. You have to keep taking them. Then after some time, they start making you sort of normal, and then eventually, when you've been on them a few weeks, you're actually a little wired, a little juiced and ready to rumble. You have to take them for several weeks and go through this whole cycle for the right affect to kick in.

Of course, Alan lost the pills almost immediately. We were on tour in the South, driving from New Orleans to Mobile, and all of a sudden Alan remembers he left his anti-suicide pills in a motel room a couple of hours behind us.

Henry was driving. He slammed on the brakes, whipped a U-turn and drove like crazy back to the motel, but the maid had already cleaned up the room. She threw out the pills, the Dumpster was already dumped and we had to get the hell back on the road or blow the next gig.

That night, after the show, I tried to put my psychology training to work. We were all concerned about Alan, and I thought what we needed was to cry together. Crying can be very healthy, a relief for depression. That night in the dressing room, I got all the guys together and I started talking to them about Alan and how he needed us, and I created this very sad mood and I got them all holding hands. Except Alan.

He picked up on what I was doing. He just stood there and said "See, I can't even do this."

He was supposed to get more pills. We all made him promise he would. But if he could get his act together enough to buy more pills, he wouldn't have needed the damn pills to begin with.

A couple of weeks later, he quit Canned Heat, figuring maybe it was the band that was killing him. Canned Heat and living on the road and the crowds. His loss was a bummer for all of us, especially The Bear, who got very irritable, snapping at people.

But Alan could not stay away. Two weeks later he showed up at the Veterans Auditorium, where we were rehearsing again, trying to put together songs without him. He just stepped out of the darkness in the hall, wearing the same goofy brown corduroy trousers and sort of Persian-rug pattern brown and yellow shirt he wore on stage at Woodstock.

We just looked at him, unsure what he wanted.

"I missed you guys," he said. "You guys aren't the problem. You're the only friends I have. I missed you."

The Bear hugged him so hard he almost crushed him.

"I love you guys," Alan said. "You're my bros."

We all hugged him. We pulled him into the rehearsal and the next day we had him back on the road.

On September 3, 1970, we were supposed to leave for a festival in Berlin. That morning, the Bear called me. "Have you seen Alan?"

I said "No," thinking: Of course, I haven't seen Alan, he lives with you. How come you don't see him?

"I can't find him, man. He was here last night and now I can't find him. He'll miss the plane and fuck up the trip to Europe."

"Did you look up on the hill, up in the bushes where he usually crashes?"

Alan, being Alan, didn't actually sleep inside the Bear's house. He would take a sleeping bag out in the canyon behind the house, the house that's empty and condemned now, and he would climb high up on this steep slope and then go way back along a little ridge. There was a small clearing there that was sort of his bedroom, just a little opening in the chaparral and a flat spot on the ridge, where he could sleep on the ground.

The Bear said yes, he looked there. At least that's the way I remember it, that he said yes. I don't like to think about this part much. I wish I didn't even have to write it because I don't want it in my head any more.

We finally agreed that Alan had probably gone off to get some stuff for the trip and would meet us at the airport.

That afternoon, we were all in the limousine—Henry, Bear, Tony and myself—outside the TWA terminal at LAX. There was no sign of Alan.

Skip Taylor drove up and stuck his head in the limo window. "We can't find him. Nobody knows where the hell he is. If you guys don't get on that plane right now, you'll miss the festival, and we already cashed the deposit so we'd be in deep legal shit if that happens. Get on the plane."

He stopped for a minute. "You know what I think?"

"Yeah," Bear said. "We know what you think."

"I think Alan is dead."

He drove away. We all put on our stone mask faces and got on the plane. None of us wanted to say what we were thinking, like maybe if we said anything, saying it would make our fears come true.

Skip told me later he knew right away where he was going to look

165

for Alan. He just drove straight to the Bear's house, went out back and climbed up that long steep slope and pushed his way back through the bushes to the little clearing.

It was hot, mid-afternoon, and the sun was shining bright on Alan's body, stretched out on top of his sleeping bag, in his jeans and shirt. There was an empty gin bottle next to him, and a large, empty bottle of Seconal. His arms were crossed on his chest. Dying, he had composed himself the way he saw dead bodies portrayed in pictures and movies.

There were those who said later that it was all an accident. No it wasn't. It was a big bottle of Seconal, the preferred drug for killing yourself, the drug Alan bought specifically for that purpose before. Alan knew drugs, knew the difference between a buzz dose and a death dose. He was far too intelligent to overdose by accident.

He had a big smile on his face, like he had finally done something right, like he had finally showed us that he could do something skillfully, something harder than just learning to drive or pick up a girl.

I don't think that way. I am no admirer of death, no fan of surrendering forever. I have been way too close to too many other death-lovers in the years since I knew Alan. But it was Alan's life. The horrible part was that he never really understood that he was enough of a genius at the things he was good at that it didn't make any difference that he was a nerd the rest of the time. He was still ahead of the game.

And if he had only lived a little while longer, and tolerated our messy world, he would have seen that the supersonic passenger plane did not become a huge problem—America never built one—and that an entire environmental movement would spring up, that millions of people would join him in his fears for the Earth. "Poor Moon" was revived in 1995 by the Scottish band "Blues N' Trouble."

He could have sung to them and inspired them, the way Sting and Police did a few years later for the Green Peace movement in Europe.

But hell, that would have made Alan a really big star. And he would have hated that.

From the time he ran from the bullies when he was a little kid, he was looking for someplace where it would be safe to be himself, to have his brilliance all concentrated in one area and ignore the rest of life, twirling his hair around his fingers while he memorized the names of all the leaves. He never found that place and he could not bear to look for it anymore.

When we checked into our hotel in Berlin, the clerk handed the Bear a note to call Skip at once. We all went up to Bob's room. Before Bear could make the call, Skip called again.

The Bear listened. "Yeah. Yeah man. Well, it's not like it's a surprise, right? Yeah, we can do the gig."

He put down the phone. We all looked at each other.

"Yeah. he really did it. He really did it this time."

The phone rang again. It was the limo driver to take us to the festival. He was in the lobby.

Time to play the blues for the people.

We all trooped out to the limo. On the way to the festival we passed a joint around and I saw the Bear swallow something. Why did The Bear say he had checked the hillside and Alan wasn't up there? Because The Bear was just too fat and lazy to climb the hill, even with a life at stake? Because he didn't want to admit that to the rest of us? Did The Bear know he was up there, probably dead already? I don't know the answers but the questions will stay with me forever.

Backstage I sat with the drummer of Procol Harum, who was very supportive, the way the English guys always are at times like that. He had some coke and I took the biggest hit of that drug I had ever had in my life. I didn't want to think about Alan out there in the woods, then or now.

When they announced us, right after Procol Harum, some of the audience cheered but some others just sort of sat there, clapping quietly. We figured, well, some of them know and some of them don't.

The Bear picked up a mike, turned to face us instead of the audience, and started into an old, slow blues tune by Little Walter, a black legend out of Chicago who was one of the greatest harmonica players ever, a guy whose scratchy old records Alan loved to play for the other guys on long, warm nights in the house in the Canyon.

The Bear's voice was even lower and raspier than usual:

Last night I lost the best friend I ever had.
And now you are gone and left me
You know I feel so sad...

A sort of sigh and a rustle of whispers went through the audience. I looked at the other guys. There were tears in our eyes, but we played the gig to the end.

Coming right after us was Janis Joplin, who knew Alan and Bear well; she once tried to hire them as her backup band. As we came off stage, she stopped us. "I heard about Alan. I think it's a hell of a thing that you guys can play tonight."

We watched her sashay out on stage, not knowing that in just two weeks she'd be as dead as Alan, with a needle in her arm in a Hollywood bungalow.

Playing after her was Jimi Hendrix. By the end of the month, he made the proverbial three.

We hired Joel Scott Hill, one of the founders of the San Francisco group Moby Grape, and flew him in that very night to fill the vacant spot in the band for the rest of the European tour.

By the time we returned to the U.S., Alan had been cremated, which was what he wanted. Some time later, the Bear asked us all to come over to his house to smoke some weed and listen to some music. It had been a while since we'd done that. Sounded like a good idea. Regroup, get in touch with our roots.

We were laying around on the floor, getting ripped on pot and some truly horrible home-made wine when The Bear said, "I've got something I have to show you guys. Look at this."

He brought out a cardboard box, like a shoe box, but slightly bigger. He pulled off the lid. Inside there were things like chunks of coal and burnt sticks.

"It's Alan."

He had picked up Alan's ashes from the crematory.

"Let's party with Alan."

"Hey Alan," he says to the box. "Join the party, man. No wine for you, I guess, but what would you like to hear? A little Elmore James?"

He put on "Blues Before Sunrise" and placed the box on a little chair that was there for his kids.

The party went on. We all got totally wasted. Every now and then somebody would say something to Alan's box, tell him a joke or something.   At the end of the night, Bear took me aside in the bathroom. "Here, man. He was your buddy. You should have some of him too."

He handed me a dark glass jar with a wide mouth and a big cork stopper. In it were some of Alan's ashes. A lot of them actually, about a pound. I felt a little sick.

"I don't know, Bear...."

"Hey man, this is the best thing. Alan will always be part of Canned Heat. Nobody else has to know. Just us. Hell, we can take him to parties, maybe take him on stage if we want to. And it won't be any harder to get him laid than it was before."

Well, it sounded like a good idea at the time. A tradition. A very private one. It fit The Bear's passion for collecting things. He and Alan had collected all these old records. Now Bear collected Alan too.

I kept the jar.   Bear kept the box. Later on, his brother Richard got a box too. We didn't know then that Canned Heat was starting a long downhill run, that the trip down the slippery slope had started and was picking up speed.

So Alan stayed with us. His box had a place of honor at our parties, a silent witness from our golden years after we hit the skids.

Poor bastard couldn't escape after all.

BOOKER N' BEAT

photo: Philip Melnick

As the plane touched down on the runway at the Portland airport, we were enjoying the fame that our "Boogie with Canned Heat" LP brought us. Down in baggage claim, while I was checking to see if the limo was outside, I heard Bob's unmistakable roar:

"Hey, you guys. That's John Lee Hooker!"

We all turned toward the next conveyor belt and there he was, picking up a case containing his famous Epiphone guitar.

For a couple of seconds, we were in awe, then simultaneously we all ran towards him to shake his hand and introduce ourselves.

"How would you like to do a record with us?", Bob blurted out.

"Hey, I know who you guys are. And I sure like the way you boys boogie," said the man we'd admired for years. We quickly exchanged telephone numbers before heading off to our respective gigs that night.

It took over two years for us to get permission from Hooker's label, ABC Bluesway, to record with him. It was a very long, very arduous ordeal involving a tangle of legal issues that had to be resolved. Skip was talking with John Lee and told him it might be a "double album." To which Hooker replied: "If it's gonna be a double album, you're gonna have to pay me double money."

By the time "Hooker 'n Heat" was actually recorded at the Liberty Studios in Los Angeles, it was May 1970 and Canned Heat had the hit album "Living the Blues" on the charts, along with two hit singles, "Goin' Up The Country" and "Let's Work Together."

Skip did a masterful job capturing the spirit of this memorable session in the album's liner notes:

"He arrived for the session wearing a plaid cap, leather jacket, black satin shirt and some old dress slacks and carrying the old Epiphone guitar that had been around the world more than once. Once at the studio, we tried out about eight really ancient amps before finding the one that had that real "Hooker" sound, a sound we hadn't heard on John's records for a long, long time. We built a plywood platform for John to sit on while he played. An old Silvertone amp rested a few feet away. One mike on the amp, one for his voice, and one to pick up John's stompin', he never quits stompin! Never far away was a bottle of Chivas Regal and a cup of water to smooth it down.

There is another blues great who really shines on this album, Alan

"Blind Owl" Wilson. This is the last album that the Owl was to record, for he died suddenly, shortly after the album was finished. Hooker calls Alan "the greatest harmonica player ever." Alan's piano and guitar work were also brilliant as this album clearly demonstrates.

During the past decade, John Lee Hooker's appeal has been primarily to blues enthusiasts, but his human insight and compassion are universal in today's troubled times. Hopefully, with the availability of this album, a larger audience than ever before will be exposed to the talent of John Lee Hooker, Alan Wilson and Canned Heat.

This is the real 'boogie' old and new together. John Lee Hooker invented the 'boogie' thirty years ago and Canned Heat made it popular on today's music scene. The natural and logical fusion of John Lee Hooker and Canned Heat has made each of them famous three decades apart!"

The sessions were fun and challenging. Our familiarity with his music made us completely in sync and able to record most of the songs on the first or second take. With Hooker, it's just a matter of knowing his music, knowing his character and falling in with his emotion. There's no rehearsing or learning parts, because he's going to do it different every time. His music is so real and spontaneous it only happens once. That's the real blues.

It was such a good marriage, such a good combination of talents. Hooker was constantly laughing and clearly delighted with the results as we listened to the playback of the recordings. Sadly, the photo on the cover of "Hooker 'n Heat" shows us sitting around in a funky little room with a picture of Alan hanging on the wall. By then, he had already left this cruel world. Poor Alan, he was so far gone he didn't even get to see the project finished; he was dead before the mixing and mastering were done.

The record was a success. It got great reviews and brought Hooker back into the public eye at just the right time; a strong blues revival was happening and many of its originators were getting some long overdue recognition. We were particularly happy with the fact that the single "Whiskey and Wimmen" became a hit on the black charts. I remember how proud I felt driving around the LA freeways hearing it played on KGFJ, the famous rhythm and blues station.

John Lee Hooker tells Skip Taylor-"If it's goin' be a double album, you're gonna have to pay me double money!"

Blacks recognized what Canned Heat was doing and some even acknowledge that "They may be white boys, but they do sound good." In the late '60s and '70s, a lot of blacks started turning their backs on the blues. They didn't want to know about music that reminded them of the south and cotton picking times. It struck them as having too much of an Uncle Tom attitude. They were into riots, integration, and the new Muslim awareness. Martin Luther King and Malcolm X were national figures.

This abandonment of their own roots is painful for me to see and it should be even more painful for blacks to recognize that the blues tradition was being carried on by whites. If it wasn't for white artist like Stevie Ray Vaughan, The Fabulous Thunderbirds and Canned Heat, the blues would probably fade into obscurity because of a lack of interest among the blacks. Just look what they've done to their music in the '90s! It's mostly funk-oriented with no blues influence at all.

Even Muddy Waters, the legendary black performer, said before he died: "You guys are carrying the banner now." He was talking to white musicians. Fortunately, there are a few exceptions like Robert Cray, a young gifted blues player, who is keeping the blues mainstream by making it popular with both blacks and whites.

John Lee Hooker with Tony de la Barreda and Alan Wilson during the first "Hooker N' Heat" session, April 1970

Soon after the record was released, we went on the road, all over the U.S. and Canada. We had great times together and got to know each other well, developing close friendships. We did a number of memorable gigs including one at Carnegie Hall attended by Jackie Onasis and other New York VIPs. After a year, we each went our separate ways with John assembling his own band, although we still did occasional gigs together.

Like previous projects, we didn't look on our recording with Hooker as a commercial enterprise. It was an artistic endeavor we wanted to be long-lasting and legendary. Today, those records are in the Library of Congress. Collectors' magazines regularly list offers that range from $200 to $250 for "Future Blues," "Hooker 'n Heat," and other Canned Heat records in mint condition. The vinyl releases are very desirable. As further proof of how historical those sessions were, EMI recently released a CD of "Hooker And Heat" in a beautiful set similar to the Robert Johnson package, which also made history in the CD market. Once again, I haven't received any royalties or a penny from any of this, but that's a story for a later chapter.

Some years later, in 1978, we did another record together, called "Hooker 'n Heat Live at the Fox Venice," produced by Howard Wolf and recorded live in front of a boogie-crazed crowd at the now-closed Fox Venice Theatre in Los Angeles. John was our guest of honor, but we also had the Chambers Brothers and New Orleans piano player, Ronnie Barron, as part of the show. The Fox Venice was ideal for a live recording. The evening turned into a real party, and the audience didn't leave 'til 3:30 A.M. Bear's parting salutation summed it up then and now: "Don't Forget To Boogie."

The record, which was released by Rhino Records, was not as successful as the first one, but it had good acceptance, and by then, John's career had been stable for a few years.

In early 1987, the Canned Heat lineup included me, James Thornbury, Larry and Henry (who was back). I received a call from musician/producer Roy Rogers to do a session with "The Hook." This project was to be another attempt to get John Lee Hooker back in the limelight. Roy asked us to cooperate with him in helping Hooker by doing the sessions for a minimum amount of money ($150) and without claims to any royalties or residuals. We agreed immediately without a moment's hesitation, because we would do anything to help John, who by then was around 70.

Working with our idol again was a blast. The one-day session was held in San Francisco and we recorded four songs that resulted in a production that was better than any of us expected or imagined. "The Healer" brought John the highest degree of fame he had ever achieved and it became a worldwide hit with double platinum sales. Roy's idea to put different performers, influenced by Hooker, all on the same record backing John was an outstanding success and established him as a major producer. Santana, Bonnie Raitt, Los Lobos, Charlie Musselwhite and Canned Heat were all happy to be part of this historical tribute.

I was impressed that John didn't seem affected by his fame and fortune. He'd often call me just to say hello and rap. I felt privileged to receive phone calls out of friendship from a man I admired so much and who was so well-known now. These attempts by John to stay in touch made me respect and love him even more, since he was again proving the caliber of human being he was and that's very important to me.

In a "Rolling Stone" interview after the huge success of "The Healer," John was asked which band played his music best. He replied without hesitation: "The Canned Heat. I've always loved those boys and I still do." It felt so good to read that and immediately my thoughts turned to Bob and Alan who would have been really pleased.

Because we were part of "The Healer" project, I started receiving newspaper clips from John's publicity machine. I sadly realized that in most of these articles Canned Heat and Charlie Musselwhite were not even mentioned as part of the recording session. I was really hurt because we were the most blues-oriented performers and the musicians who were the most true to Hooker's music. Also, we were the ones that could have used the publicity the most, since Bonnie Raitt, Santana and Los Lobos (who were always mentioned), were rich, famous and not struggling like us. The press can be so superficial and reckless with the truth.

In 1992, when I was producing our "Internal Combustion" CD, I thought about Bear and how he would come up with different lyrics every time we played the boogie. One format he used quite often was to sing about John Lee Hooker, since he was the wellspring, the originator.

John Lee Hooker sure is a friend of mine.
He can pitch the boogie boogie and he'll do it all the time....

177

This gave me an idea. By taking some of the spontaneous lyrics Bob sang in those live performances years ago, I could reorganize them, add some lyrics of my own, and create a new song called "John Lee Hooker Boogie" as a tribute.

In one of my phone calls with John, I asked him if he would be kind enough to record the song with us; he could just say a few words or play a few notes on his guitar. Whatever he wanted. I told him it would be a great help to us, since we were struggling for recognition and credibility in the '90s.

Always the gentleman, he said: "I'd be happy to do it, Fito. Just get the session together and let me know."

I hung up very excited and grateful to my old friend.

A couple of weeks after that phone call, we played a gig in San Jose at a place called The Cabaret. When the manager told me that John Lee Hooker, with his entire entourage complete with bodyguards, was here to see us, I was thrilled. Not only did he come to dig our performance, but he got on stage and boogied with us until the end of the night. What a treat to have a man who's making twenty grand a night come to a joint and perform for nothing just to be with his friends. Again, I felt great love and respect for the man.

Since we were face to face, I repeated my request for him to perform on "John Lee Hooker Boogie." I kidded him:

"John, are you sure there won't be a problem appearing with us now that you're so famous? It would really be a big help to us."

"Oh, don't worry, Fito. Just contact my manager, Mike Kappas, at the Rosebud Agency and make sure you tell him that I said I want to do it."

By now, I'd hired our good friend Eugene Skuratowicz and his company Music Matters to manage the band, which considering our history and bad luck, was a brave undertaking on his part. Eugene made countless attempts to get John to perform with us. To make it easy for him, we offered to do the session in a studio only a few blocks from his house and to pick him up and deliver him within a couple of hours, since the basic tracks were already made. All he had to do was overdub a few words or a couple of licks on his guitar.

Every time we talked to him directly, he said "yes," but every time we talked to his manager, there were all kinds of complications and negative vibes. To add further insult, he started asking for large amounts of money and percentage points on the recording. Amounts he knew very well we didn't have, because it was a self-produced record on a limited budget. How ironic that just a short time ago, we helped John on his greatest project, graciously accepting $150 and no royalties. Eugene tried and tried, politely, in every way, to convince Kappas to allow Hooker to keep his word. But it got to the point where the manager wouldn't even take our calls. He just blew us off. Once we realized that getting Hooker involved was a lost cause, we recorded "The John Lee Hooker Boogie" without him.   Meanwhile, Hooker was appearing with acts that had contributed nothing to his success. I was appalled when I heard Hooker on Van Morrison's version of "Gloria." It reeked of commercialism...my idol had sold out and obviously had lost control over his music, his word and his life.

Shortly after the "Internal Combustion" CD was finished, I got a call out of the blue from Skip Taylor, who I hadn't seen in 15 years. With the help of some investors in Minnesota, he had just started a new record company called "River Road Records." He liked my project very much and decided to release it. I explained my problems about Hooker and his failure to keep his word. Although Skip was able to get through to Kappas, he too was pushed aside and our request was again denied. So the ever-inventive Skip came up with the idea of inserting John's voice from the original "Hooker N' Heat" into the new song.

In the typical cut-throat tradition of the music business, it only took a few days to hear from Kappas. But this time, it was his attorney contacting Eugene and threatening to sue because Skip used John's voice without their permission. Skip felt he didn't need to get permission to use material on masters he produced and had already paid Hooker for.

Kappas was just pissed off because we were able to get around his bullshit, so he decided to fuck with us. To this day, John's manager does not like us and we still don't understand why. We don't even know him. Tragically, he started threats of a lawsuit against Canned Heat in the name of John Lee Hooker. Of course, all of this took place without John knowing or having a say about it.

A final, killing blow came one night when I sat down to watch "Biography," on the Arts and Entertainment network. Pushing out of my mind the problems we had with Kappas and the attorneys, I settled down for what I knew would be a good solid hour of excellent entertainment. I watched and waited during the segments where Hooker and Kappas were being interviewed. At the half way mark, I was surprised that Canned Heat hadn't been mentioned yet. More time ticked away, and still no mention of us. Kappas meanwhile is talking about Van Morrison, Eric Burdon and others who were influenced by John, without any reference at all to Canned Heat.

By now, the show was almost over and not a word about Canned Heat. By the end of the hour, I had a knot in my stomach and tears were streaming down my face. One question after another flashed through my tormented mind. How could this be happening? Do they get the A&E Channel in heaven? If they do, Bob and Alan must have been crying along with me. If not, they were certainly rolling over in their graves.

Even if he didn't give us credit like Albert Collins always did for helping him with his career, he could have at least mentioned Alan or Bob. My emotions ran from blind fury one minute to total disgust and disappointment the next. I felt betrayed. In some ways, knowing that he's not responsible for the injustice makes it even worse. It's not uncommon that once someone becomes a "star," they put on blinders and build a wall around themselves to keep reality out— without caring who gets hurt.

I still talk to John occasionally, but I never mention these painful incidents. Since nothing can be changed, there's no use bothering him; he's too old and has little control over those events. I guess it's just another example of the cruelty of the music business.

OUTLAWS TURN CRIMINAL

"Draculaaaaaaa? I never even heard the name...."

This is how I looked when I was arrested by the FBI for refusing to go to Vietnam.

After Alan's death, we had a band meeting at our hotel in Berlin. To cover the pain, we were drugging ourselves even more than usual. Passing the chillum full of hash, Bob said: "Shit, man, I sure miss Alan. But the show must go on and we have to finish this tour one way or another."

"We have to keep the character of the band," Henry said. "We've gotta have two guitars or a keyboard.

"How 'bout Ronnie Barron, that piano player from Louisiana? He's great. Maybe Skip can track him down," I suggested.

But Skip had no luck. Ronnie had just disappeared. Tony suggested Joel Scott Hill. We all knew Joel because he and Tony had played together. He was good-looking and had a following. His singing was outstanding and his guitar playing was adequate. Best of all, he was available.

A few days later, Joel hopped off the plane and joined us on stage without so much as one rehearsal. One more example of the Bear's lack of business savvy, a pattern that was to repeat itself over and over again. How ridiculous to hire somebody as a full-time replacement for our most important member without giving it hardly any thought. What we should have done was finish the tour with him on a trial basis and then decide if he should join us. Bear simply wanted to have a good time and surround himself with like-minded people. He never wanted to pay attention to the painful details of the crisis we were in.

It wasn't that Joel didn't have the talent. The problem was his lack of commitment and a sense of order in his life, which later was to affect the whole band, not just himself.

He hadn't been with the band more than a week when he started:

"Hey, guys, I've been approached to make a solo album."

He was clearly more interested in his own career than in maintaining the good and lucky position we were in. We had the tools to do well. We were a big band and very famous. We were still making a lot of money, and we had the support of Liberty, our record company, which later became United Artists. Obviously, Joel thought he could do better on his own, like many other Canned Heat members. But none has ever done better on his own.

Basically, Tony and Joel were in Canned Heat for the wrong reasons. They didn't join like I did. They didn't think "I was born to play with Canned Heat." They didn't see the bigness of the band.

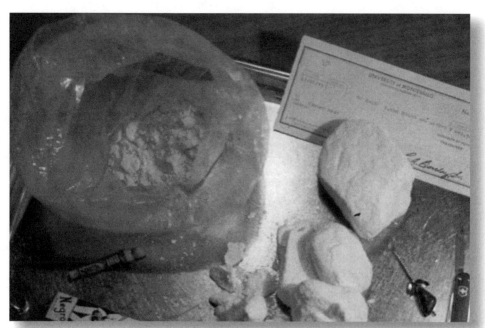

Colombia rocks

Skip Taylor sampling some of the best cocaine in the world in Bogota, Colombia.

183

Being searched—again—by police at European border.

Joel Scott Hill came in with the attitude that he was already a rock star. And Tony came in wanting to be a rock star, which is fine. But, what about the music? What about the blues? What about our art?

Both had enough talent to keep things going if they had the proper attitude. But they were more interested in partying with us and building careers as individuals. That's when it became clear that our pragmatic anarchy wasn't working any more and we lacked leadership.

The core had already been shattered by Larry and Henry's fight at the Fillmore, Alan's death and Larry's departure. Henry was back but his heavy drug habits were stronger than ever. And now we had Tony, who instead of getting into the music and learning from Henry and Bob, was picking up all their bad habits, especially Henry's, which included shooting speed and popping pills. To make matters worse, Joel came into the band with a heavy hard-liquor habit, which Henry and Bob embraced, adding to their already outrageous dope intake.

During the European tour after Alan's death, Canned Heat was

"The New Age" Band. L to R Henry Vestine, Richard Hite, Ed Beyer, James Shane, Fito de la Parra, Bob Hite (notice kilo of grass in Bob's hand.)

the headline act at England's Bath Pop Festival for the biggest paycheck in the band's history. But Led Zeppelin—unhappy that an American group was headlining an English festival—offered Skip a couple of thousand dollars to switch places. Without a second thought, we accepted the offer, feeling: "Who cares if we don't headline one festival?"

After a short rest, we set off for Canned Heat's first tour of Australia. We arrived at the Sydney airport on the same plane as Stephen Stills and his group Manassas. We breezed through Customs and were being interviewed in an upstairs lounge, when a Customs official came in and told us they were now going to search all of our equipment before we would be free to leave.

We exchanged anxious glances, as the official left. Each of us had our private stash and we had about a minute to dispose of EVERYTHING. I quickly put my grass into the coffee mug in front of me, while Tony was struggling to take a small package of speed and some joints out of his socks so he could insert them into the sugar dispenser.

At the same time, a panic-stricken Bob put his hand to his mouth. God knows what was in his fist, but with one gulp he swallowed it all, washing it down with a Coke, a look of urgency on his flushed face.

In the middle of the panic, Henry could be heard yelling to the shocked record company's Aussie PR guy: "Hey, dude, this is very important. Hang onto it and give it to me later." He handed off a plastic bag containing a few grams of speed and some syringes.

Within minutes, the official came back and announced, "Well, boys, we found it." Customs inspectors surrounded us, took us back to their offices and thoroughly strip-searched us, including that humiliating bend over and spread-the-cheeks scenario. Since we'd already gotten rid of everything, we were finally released.

Afraid to be caught with Henry's mysterious medical supplies, the panicked PR guy heaved the dope into a fountain outside the airport. That was really bad news. Vestine goes on speed binges, staying awake for days. But when they end, he sinks into what he calls "the big sleep," dropping into a coma-like hibernation that can last for days, sometimes for as long as two weeks. We tried to get him to time his ups and downs to the band's playing schedule. But without his stash, Henry collapsed into "the big sleep" prematurely, and the band was forced to tote him around Australia damn-near unconscious.

After the excruciatingly long flight and our shocking experience at customs, which left us in a bad mood, we still had to face a long, drive of several hours to the strange little town of Mulwalla near Melbourne in the state of Victoria, which became the site of the first Australian Pop Festival. We were put up in a little hotel in the middle of nowhere, and for entertainment we managed to get a couple of channels on TV—in black and white. This was 1971 and Australia was still very isolated.

Trying to keep Henry awake and aware for the performance, we scored about 10 Benzedrines, "whites," from some outback hippie, enough to keep 10 truck drivers awake for hours. In the fine Henry tradition, he popped them all, but a few minutes later he was again snoring on a bench in the dressing room. Later however, he managed to wake up and play a pretty good set, going back to sleep right after. This was the big sleep.

In a Woodstock-like atmosphere, and in spite of all the bullshit we'd been through, we managed to throw a good party with Stills' group and some Aussie musicians, highlighted by the Down Under rock pioneer Billy Thorpe and his group The Aztecs.

Even though it was a lot of trouble to get there and we didn't make that much money in comparison to what we were making in the U.S., it was a wise decision for Canned Heat to get exposure in that faraway country. It made our reputation in Australia and created a fan base that's loyal to this day.

Back in the U. S. prior to a southern tour, I stopped in to see my tax accountant Arnold Bernstein, who was getting ready to leave on vacation with his family. "I'm just about to head out the door. We're going to Northern California and we'll be visiting some of Alan's favorite spots."

I immediately flashed on the small jar on my fireplace mantel that had been Alan's home for more than a year. I said to Arnold: "You know I have a portion of Alan's remains in my house. Would you mind taking them to the redwoods that he loved so much? I'm sure it's the right thing to do." Arnold was very touched by my request. He not only did as I asked, but he added a Jewish prayer as he sprinkled the ashes among the trees. A few months later, Bob also took his portion of Alan to the redwoods.

Our friend was finally able to rest in peace in his favorite place.

During Mardi Gras, we played in a funky New Orleans place called the Warehouse. Our opening act was ZZ Top, a new Texas band that was just starting out and was happy to work with Canned Heat. They were nice, fresh and as I listened to them, I thought "these guys have something. They're going to make it."

But the most memorable part of the gig, was the stunningly beautiful brunette backstage, who came to me and introduced herself with a heavy Mississippi accent as "Pam the Barbiturate Queen." In spite of her beauty, she was stumbling and obviously very high, so I just said "hello" and ignored her, turning back to my roadies who were packing up my drums.

Shortly after, she walked into our dressing room and struck up a conversation with Joel, who was much more receptive to her Southern charm. They ended up spending the night together, while I had a good time with her friend, Joy Smith, who was a bit older, more relaxed and who went on to become a good friend of mine.

The following day, we decided to enjoy Mardi Gras, so we hit the streets. Watching Pam and the guys act like idiots, loaded on downers, alcohol and other things, I began asking myself why I was doing this, when I didn't really enjoy being high like that. After that, I quietly began cutting back on drug use, except for marijuana smoking which I still enjoy.

A few weeks after the southern tour, I was alone in the Laurel Canyon house I was still renting from Sonja, when the phone rang:

"Hi, Fito, this is Pam. I'm glad I tracked you down. I need your help desperately."

It was nice to hear that sweet voice with the warm Mississippi accent, but I wondered why she was calling me, when she was supposed to be Joel's lover.

I responded coldly: "What's up, Pam? Can't you find Joel?"

"I'm in big trouble, Fito. I got here from Texas yesterday and spent last night in a crash pad a friend told me about. God, this place is full of junkies and mean weirdoes. One of them punched me out. I took a bunch of reds and I got so depressed I slit both my wrists. I didn't really mean to but I just did it without thinking. Please, get me out of here," she pleaded.

I hesitated for a moment, not wanting to get into a confrontation with some riffraff over a girl I barely knew. But she persisted. She knew my weak spot. "Come on, Fito. Please pick me up. You won't regret helping me. I'll take care of you. I know how to make you feel good. I'll do anything you want."

My mind flashed back to a few days before when Joel had mentioned what a wonderful, luscious body she had and what a killer she was in bed.

I knew that Joel was in the middle of a divorce and wasn't even in town. Characteristically, I charged into another "rescue fantasy," got in my Aston Martin and headed down Laurel Canyon into a Hollywood side street. Pulling up in front of a shabby house, I beeped the horn and out walked Pam in a very nice dress. It was very tight and very red, an exact match for the bloodstains on the bandages around her wrists.

We walked into my house and as I was hanging up the car keys, she put her lips to my ear and her hand to my fly. "Oh, Fito, thank you so much for helping me," she whispered in that exciting southern drawl. "You're wonderful to do this. Let me show you how grateful I am. I always wanted you. Let me love you...."

She dropped to her knees right there and started sucking. My hands were wrapped in her hair and I kept trying not to look at the bandaged wrists. My knees were trembling so hard I could barely stand by the time she finished. It was one of the best blowjobs I ever had.

I didn't realize it at the time, but the bag she was carrying held everything she owned. To me, this was a combination favor/one night affair. But to her, she was moving in.

The next morning I had to split for a rehearsal, but I didn't ask her to leave, because I enjoyed the previous night and I knew she didn't have any place to go. So I let her stay, thinking it would be a temporary situation. At this point in my life, which was shortly after the divorce, I wasn't interested in settling down with anybody. But before I knew what I was getting into, she became my live-in girlfriend.

So now—even if I didn't want it—I had a new "old lady" and it was time to hit the road again. We had a booking in Miami on our way to Europe and we stayed at the then-famous Marco Polo Hotel on the main drag. The gig was at the Jai Alai Sports Center, where we were all doing some heavy duty drinking, right from the start. The show went well, but in the dressing room afterwards a drunken Joel was getting very antsy. He wanted to see Fats Domino, who was appearing at our hotel.

"Hey, Fito, c'mon. Move it. If we haul ass, we could make Fats' show in 30 minutes. I really want to see that guy."

We had rented two Cadillacs, so we told the other guys in the band where we were going so they could catch up later.

I can't believe I actually let Joel drive that night, but I must have been pretty drunk myself. Not too drunk to notice that Joel was weaving all over the road, but what the hell, I wanted to see the Fat Man's great band too.

We dumped the car in the front of the hotel, flipped the car keys to the valet park guy and headed into the lobby, crowded with short-haired rednecks in white shirts.

"Joel, check with the desk about the show; I'm going to the head."

While I was in the men's room, things went off the tracks. According to later reports, the scene went like this:

The lady at the desk was busy and didn't answer Joel's question about the show immediately, so he started yelling.

"Hey, bitch, I'm talking to you. We're gonna be late for the fuckin' show."

A bystander touched Joel on the shoulder and said: "Don't talk to her that way."

Swiveling to face the guy, Joel said: "Fuck you too. Mind your own business."

With that, the punches started flying and a full-blown brawl broke out. As I walked out of the restroom, I saw one of the rednecks holding Joel while another one broke a chair over his head and then used one of the legs to smash him in the face.

It all happened very quickly. I briefly considered joining in to defend my bro, but by then his face was covered with blood and the fight was clearly over. When the rednecks spotted me they turned, waving the chair legs.

"What about you, motherfucker? You want some too?"

Raising my hands in a gesture of appeasement I said: "No problem here, man."

I dragged my broken buddy to the elevator. The door opened and out stepped Bear, Henry and Tony, who had come in the back way. I'll never forget the stunned looks on their faces as they took in the lobby—strewn with blood, broken furniture and shattered glass—and me supporting the battered, bleeding Joel. Revenge was briefly considered and dismissed. After all, Joel asked for it—and got it.

The next day, a still-sore Joel managed to drag himself onto the plane as we set off for England. Arriving in London, Skip gave us the good news: "Hey, guys, I've leased a wonderful flat. This place belongs to King Hussein. No shit, it really does. The king of Jordan. We've got the royal pad on Grosvenor Square, right in the heart of Embassy Row."

It was a lavish four-bedroom, two-story apartment furnished with a beautiful grand piano in the living room. Antiques adorned the sidetables. The deal included a live-in chambermaid, a very pretty, but very proper, sort of Mary Poppins English rose. It was hardly a place for the likes of us.

Bear immediately took possession of the living room and made it his official bedroom and party center. Within hours, we got hold of a record player and a stash and made ourselves at home, rolling joints and cutting hashish on the elegant, richly varnished coffee tables.

Tony brought along his new wife, Cathy Rutherford, a leggy pretty blonde in the tradition of his first wife, the Queen of the Watusi, but classier. They took one of the corner bedrooms and I had a very nice, red velvet-walled suite next to them, while Henry and Joel took two rooms in the opposite wing.

Our roadies Ed Nett and Ron Stender together with our friend/hash connection RJ took the servants quarters next to the kitchen, which were certainly nice and comfortable. Somewhere in this period we lost our fancy British chambermaid. Because I was unpacking in my room, I don't know all the details, but I remember the horrified look on her face as she sprinted out of the apartment without a word, never to be seen again.

Terrific. We'd only been in the flat a few hours and already the placed reeked of marijuana and hashish and King Hussein's real estate agents would soon be getting an earful about depraved Yanks from their disgusted former chambermaid.

Our gig that night was at the famous jazz/blues club owned and named after the well-known English drummer Ronnie Scott. After the show, we met two lovely girls from Scandinavia. It didn't take much talking to get them to come back to the King's pad.

Within minutes, I had this beautiful, Twiggy-thin blonde sitting on my bed kissing me. Suddenly, there was a knock on my door.

"Fito, we have to talk to you a minute," said RJ chuckling.

I reluctantly disentangled myself. Closing the door behind me, a grinning RJ told me:

"You're not gonna believe it, Fito. This place is completely wired. There are intercoms in every room. Make sure you turn it on when you start fucking this chick. We're all listening in the kitchen. The switch is right there on the wall just beside the bed."

As I came back into the bedroom, I was greeted by a completely naked woman turning down the covers and dimming the lights. Clasping her to me, I discreetly reached behind her with my right hand, feeling for the intercom control. I dialed it up to the max as she wiggled and pressed against me.

Well, here goes, I thought. Here's one for the guys in the kitchen. I gave her a long slow tongue bath. She panted softly. I could picture the rest of the band, sitting around the speaker, unimpressed. She had to make more noise than that. I gently sucked her nipples while I flicked her clitoris. She let out a rolling moan "ahhhh, ahhh ahh." That was better. I rolled her over on her stomach, climbed aboard and gave it to her long and slow, then built up to the hardest, fastest strokes I could. She began yelling words in Swedish or whatever. I couldn't understand the words but the meaning was clear. She came with a wonderfully loud scream.

I went out to the kitchen to get some wine and a joint. The guys applauded softly. The Bear raised a glass to me. I took the stuff and headed back to the room thinking, "How the hell am I going to get her to sing an encore to THAT?"

The intercom caper continued through the whole stay. Whenever one of the band members brought a girl up to the place, we'd all retire to the kitchen, as if to leave them alone. We became scholars of female sex vocalization.

We'd make bets, based on their appearance, which category the latest one would fit into, a moaner, a single-worder, a complete-sentence chick or what.

There was only one who did everything, a tiny little Scottish girl with wine-glass tits and waist-length reddish-blonde hair who moaned, groaned, panted, gasped, yelled "yes, yes" and came in full sentences, like "Oh my god, I'm flying apart." She was one of the few women I've ever heard who had the full repertoire, and unknown to her, she had a dedicated fan club at each of her intercom concerts.

The rest of us used to beg Henry to bring her around more often, but he said she was married to a bobby and could only come over when she knew her husband would be tied up all day testifying in court. Somewhere on the Greater London police force, there is today

192

an aging cop, who will never know that once upon a time Henry followed his career with intense interest, cheering for every arrest.

With the apartment as our base during the day, we traveled to the surrounding areas to play gigs, returning to London each night. As the days went by, and without the chambermaid, the place started to suffer accelerated decay. The dining room became a permanent casino where poker was played non-stop in a cloud of smoke, amid empty food cartons, and liquor bottles of all kinds. Ashtrays overflowed, leaving more than one burn mark on the fancy furniture.

The Carpenters turned up in another apartment in the same building and Karen Carpenter, her death by anorexia many years in the future, dropped by a few times to get loaded with us.

One night in the middle of a poker game Henry and Joel got into an argument over cheating. They were both drunk and the scuffle that followed included flying chairs and smashing bottles. RJ, who lifts weights, broke up the fight, but that wasn't the end.

Shortly after, Tony and his new wife also got into a heavy, noisy and violent fight. So noisy it got me out of bed. Alarmed, I opened their door to find both of them bleeding slightly from face cuts and Cathy holding Tony's bass like a baseball bat, ready to wallop him again with it. It was such a brawl that a few minutes later two bobbies and one plainclothes man from Scotland Yard showed up. Evidently our diplomat neighbors couldn't take it any more.

We got an eviction notice the following day. Leaving the flat, I turned to look at the living room that had been the Bear's room. What a mess!!

On the Scandinavian leg of our tour, during a live radio show in Sweden, Bear was so hoarse from non-stop partying that in the middle of a song he stopped the music and yelled:

"Hey, guys, let's start again in a lower key. That good German hash sure screwed up my voice."

We were mortified. We were live on Sweden's most popular radio show. We wondered if they'd cut us off the air, maybe throw us out of the country. To our surprise, the show's audience, sitting at tables drinking tea or coffee, seemed delighted. Apparently we lived up to our reputation, bringing typical Canned Heat chaos to their very traditional, government-controlled radio waves.

After the show, a very elegant, friendly man, tall and dark haired in a quietly expensive suit with a silk turtleneck shirt, invited us to his home the next day for lunch.

Several Mercedes limos arrived at the hotel and took us to a castle with a long, circular driveway set off by landscaping that must have occupied a small army of gardeners.

"Wow, man, this guy must be royalty," Henry said. Not quite, only a count.

Still, I was impressed. Until then, the only counts I knew by name were Dracula and Basie and neither invited me to lunch.

The first person we ran into in the castle was his mother, who took one look at us, sniffed "Hello" and vanished. The dowager countess obviously disapproved of her son's taste in guests.

After lunch, the Count showed us around the castle and invited us to tour the grounds ourselves. In back was an acre of flourishing hemp plants—marijuana. They were about six feet tall and Tony instantly whipped a few buds off the nearest one and rolled a big fat, ultra-green joint. We passed it around. Nothing happened. Might as well have been smoking dandelions.

The count thought it was funny as hell when we told him his pot was a little on the weak side. "These plants are not for smoking," he laughed. "Only the female hemp plants can be smoked. These are male plants for making rope. You have to go downtown and see my friend Gunther from Hamburg, if you want the other kind, although you might try to make rope out of it."

As the limos headed down the driveway, he was still laughing so hard I thought his velvet bell bottoms would fall off.

Back in the States, we started the album "Historical Figures and Ancient Heads" and we were still big enough stars to get Little Richard to join us on "Rockin' with the King," which Skip had written about Richard.

The recording session began around 8 at night at Jordy Hormel's Village Recording Studio in West L.A. I brought along Lisa Morlas, a stunning 19-year old brunette with hazel eyes and ash brown hair. She was really getting off watching us lay down the tracks and I was getting off looking at her voluptuous figure in hip hugging bell-bottoms and a tight leotard.

Midway through the session, Skip walked in. Reaching into a big paper shopping bag, he fished out a baseball-sized rock of cocaine

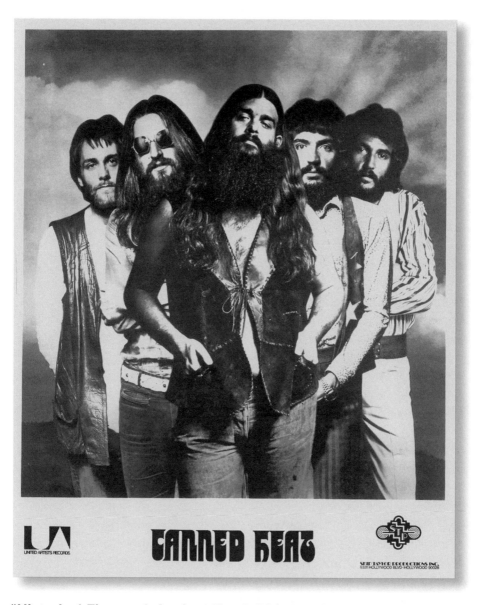

"Historical Figures & Ancient Heads" Lineup- l to r Henry Vestine,
Joel Scott Hill, Bob Hite, Fito de la Parra, Antonio de la Barreda.
Bear temporarily slimmer on "drinking man's diet."

and a chunk of deep brown hash.

"Where the hell did you get something like that?" I asked him.

"Nowhere around here," he laughed.

"You need another drum set, Fito? Just lemme know. We'll buy you the biggest goddam drums in the world. The bigger the better."

The roadies all laughed.

It finally dawned on me why Skip and the roadies were so upbeat ever since we got back from Europe. Why they suddenly had new cars and clothes. They'd loaded the amplifiers and drums with god knows how many kilos of the best North African hashish and smuggled it into the States.

I didn't realize it then, but this was the start of a pattern. Skip would buy dope, transporting it in our equipment and instruments, sometimes over international borders. This led eventually to some big time cocaine deals.

Their most profitable haul took place on a South American tour to Colombia. Skip had made a deal to bring Canned Heat and the Chambers Brothers to Bogotá. Included in the tour arrangements was Skip's use of the Presidential Suite at the elegant Tequendama Hotel. Even though we'd gotten used to luxury accommodations, this was truly deluxe. Not only was it a four room suite, but it came with a doorman, a maid, a cook and 24-hour limo service. But what made the suite unbelievably bizarre was the steady parade of vendors who appeared at the door selling everything from emeralds to alpaca sweaters to marijuana and cocaine.

The competition among drug dealers was fierce. One afternoon we were shooting the breeze with a guy selling grass and coke. To impress us, he covered the top of the dining room table with a large quantity of grass and over an ounce of coke. In the middle of sampling his wares, there was a loud knock on the door. One of the roadies quickly ushered the guy out through the kitchen, and the dealer—to our amazement—casually told us to keep the samples and give him a call if we were interested.

A few minutes later, Skip introduced us to Manuel, an elegant, aristocratic cocaine dealer. He took one look at the coke sample on the table and said: "Get this shit out of here." With the sweep of his arm, two thousand dollars worth of cocaine floated down onto the white pile carpet. Then, he emptied a bag containing lemon-sized hunks of pure coke onto the highly-polished mahogany table top and smiled.

After I left, Skip and the roadies purchased twenty kilos of pure cocaine from the debonair dealer, packing the stash in the speaker cabinets for the return trip to the States. It was an incredible deal. They paid about $40,000 for a haul that was worth over half a million dollars uncut on the street in LA. Skip told me later that he was sweating bullets when we got to Customs, but a friendly agent recognized the band's name and waved us through with barely a glance at our equipment. The band members and their friends enjoyed a very merry and very white Christmas that year.

As time went by, Skip's interest in dealing or doing drugs would replace his efforts as a manager, a loss which would haunt Canned Heat for years. But we were still riding high that night in late 1971. Around midnight a sleek, black limousine pulled up and out stepped Little Richard in skin-tight, shiny black silk pants and a glittery black cape topped off with a flaming-pink chiffon turban.

"Hello, y'all, I am ready to rock! Take me to that piano and shut up!"

During rehearsal, Little Richard started coming on to Tony, even blowing him kisses. "Oh, what a tall, gorgeous bass player. What's your name, honey? I'm sure gonna play good with you. Shut up!!"

Meanwhile, back in the recording booth, Little Richard's lover was flirting with Lisa, who was puzzled that a handsome, conservatively dressed guy, who was obviously gay, would be laying a line on her about how "hot and sexy" she was.

But what the hell, another weird night in L.A. Lisa and Tony just laughed off the mock advances. We wouldn't have cared if Little Richard showed up in a skirt and high heels; we admired his music and history so much that we felt privileged to be playing with "The King."

Although the sessions were fun and had a good feeling, they lacked Alan's creative input and the album showed it. United Artists pulled out all the promotion stops, including full-page ads in the music trades and a billboard on the Sunset Strip. But in spite of some good boogies, like "Cherokee Dance" and "Long Way From LA," the album didn't produce a top ten hit. We didn't realize it yet, but those days had already slipped away. Canned Heat was never to

197

have a top ten song again.

Over the next several months, we did a number of live shows with Little Richard where he really let loose. With us, he got down and dirty, digging deep into his blues/boogie roots. The combination of Canned Heat and Little Richard was definitely not your typical '50s revival gig.

But there was no downturn in the band's excesses. Flying to Detroit to promote the album, Henry and Tony were loaded on pills and booze even before boarding the plane. After a few more drinks, they got so rowdy the stewardesses refused to serve them. Tony was yelling: "Nurse, nurse, bring me another one," and when the chief stewardess came back to bawl them out, Henry spit at her.

Shortly afterward, the pilot stunned the passengers by announcing he was making an unscheduled stop in Chicago, where three FBI agents boarded the plane and arrested all the band members—except me.

I was sitting in the front of the plane in the non-smoking section. So as the feds led my colleagues away in handcuffs, I just looked away. "Band? What band? Rockers? Don't know any."

The gray-haired, very proper-looking old lady in the seat beside me watched intently as I discreetly took the joints I was carrying and slipped them into my socks at the first sight of the law.

"Please don't blow the whistle on me."

"Not me, young man," she said. "In my earlier line of work, you never finked on anyone, especially not for a little reefer."

I've always regretted not asking her who the hell she was and what she used to do.

In Detroit, I went to the club where we were to play the next night, not knowing what else to do. I figured at least ONE member of Canned Heat should show up to apologize to the audience.

I was standing outside, trying to work up my nerve to tell the promoter I was the only musician he hired who wasn't behind bars, when a limousine, one of the crummy, beat-up kind that hangs around small town airports, stopped in the parking lot. The doors opened and bodies fell out. Literally, just fell right out. Henry was still drunk.

The band had made bail, hired a limo, rode half the day across Indiana and Michigan, got a speeding ticket, almost went to jail again when Tony called one of the state troopers a Nazi asshole and they still made the gig almost on time.

A few days later, we boarded a plane to Chicago just a few minutes ahead of Kenny Rogers and the First Edition.

"How nice to see you, Mr. Rogers," greeted the stewardess. "Your friends from Canned Heat are already here."

Obviously aware of what happened on our previous flight, and fearing his band would be blamed for any new outrage Canned Heat might perpetrate, Rogers turned to the guys behind him.

"Hold it. Everybody back. We're taking another flight. Off the plane, guys. C'mon. Everybody off."

Mr. Rogers' army trooped back down the steps with the Bear shouting after them: "Fuck you, you lightweight mother-fuckers. We're 'living the life' and you don't know how."

On the road there were groupies, and then there were super-groupies, girls who took sex to such an artistically obsessed level they became part of the rock n' roll culture, like the Plaster Casters, the Butter Queen and Connie from Little Rock, who was immortalized as "sweet, sweet Connie" in the song "We're an American Band" by Grand Funk Railroad.

After a show in Dallas, this folksy blonde Amazon strolled into the dressing room. "Hi, y'all, I've got some pretty good weed here. And if one of you guys wants one of mah special massages, just tell me your room number and I'll be raht there with mah implements."

Swapping puzzled glances, we wondered what the hell "implements" meant.

The Bear took the bait and they spent the night together. "This broad is fucking incredible," he told us the next day. "You guys should have done it. She's the famous Butter Queen.

Bear gave the blow by blow. "She comes up to my room carrying a big canvas bag. First, she strips naked. Biggest tits I've ever seen. Then she pushes me down in the bathtub and strips ME. Then she reaches in the bag and pulls out a stick of butter and says: 'Roll over.'

"I didn't know what she was going to do with that butter, so I hesitated. 'Don't be a baby,' she says, grabbing my arm and flipping me over. She's STRONG, man. Then, she rubs the butter all over my back, all over my butt.

"She runs out of butter, reaches into the bag and gets another stick. She rubs it all over the back of my legs. 'Roll over.' This time I roll over. She mashes a stick of butter in my beard. She covers my chest with butter, my gut, she gets down to my dick and she covers it with more butter while she strokes it. Then my balls. Then my legs.

"I'm dripping butter like a box of popcorn. Then she starts rubbing me with her hands and licking it off. It took her hours, man. I came twice. By then, I was real glad she had more butter in that bag."

Connie from Little Rock was different. Unlike most groupies she didn't look at all slutty. She was a very slim brunette, with the manner and speech of someone born to a good family and very well educated. If you saw her on the street, you'd presume she was an uptight business executive in some field like telecommunications or maybe with a government agency.

In fact, 20 years after her infamous period, I ran into her again. She was a respectable schoolteacher who had run for public office. But the night I met her at the Holiday Inn in Little Rock in 1972, it wasn't votes she was looking for.

As we pulled into the parking lot in a couple of taxis after the gig, she came driving in behind us in a small car. Walking up to us, wearing a sophisticated black silk skirt with a little bolero jacket and a gold chain around her hips, she just said: "Hi, I'm Connie. Welcome to Little Rock. Would you like me to join you?"

We knew what that meant. We had heard about Connie from other bands. She was famous. First of all, she was famous for not being just a star-fucker. Which was good, because Canned Heat had no real pretty-boy stars. Some groupies would just go with the most famous guy in the band. They had hierarchies of their own. The top girl got the lead singer, the second best got the bass, on down the line. Some would take on two or three guys. But there were unwritten limits on who and how many. Connie, the other bands said, had no limits at all—the whole band, the roadies, the managers, everybody, as many times as they wanted, as long as the guys were reasonably clean and not crazy. She was reputedly one of the most artistic, mind-blowing fucks in the world.

I had heard traveling musicians rave about her in airport bars in London, New York and Los Angeles. She later appeared as a world-class groupie on TV shows, including "Phil Donohue" and "Oprah" and wrote an article for "Cosmopolitan."

And there in the parking lot I passed her up.

"Yeah, sure, we'd like you to join us," Bear told her. "You know there's eight of us?"

She smiled. "Is that all? "

I interrupted. "Make it seven man, I'm going to bed. Long trip. Really tired."

"Oh, c'mon, Fito. Stay with us," she begged.

"No, really. I'm bushed. I'm sure you'll have a good time with these guys."

I knew she would. I had already met Connie, and slept with her, a few years before.

Tony already had his arm around her waist and she flowed easily up against him like she'd been living with him for years, even as she reached for Henry's hand and begged me to come with them.

But I figured I'd let the rest of the wolf pack devour this chick. She had a great rep, but there were just too many of us for my tastes. If there had been another girl, then I would have stayed, but since she was the only one, I decided to get some rest.

As I lay in bed, I could hear peals of laughter in the hallway accompanied by doors constantly opening and closing. It sounded like a teen-age pajama party. And it went on all night. I fell asleep listening to her laughing, moaning, coming, laughing some more. Guys grunting and crying "Oh yeah" followed by girlish giggles.

Hours later, with dawn breaking, I heard a hesitant, soft little knock on the door. I knew it was her.

She stood in the doorway, wearing a white hotel towel knotted at one hip, with her clothes rolled up in a bundle under her arm. For some reason, she was on tiptoe. She had pulled her hair back into a ponytail with a rubber band. Her breasts were small but perfectly shaped. She looked very delicate and very young and very, very innocent. Her skin glistened with droplets of water from a shower, which had washed off all her makeup.

"Okay, Fito, no more put-offs. It's Connie time. I know you, you're not that tired."

I knew she had been screwed and banged and banged again all night long, and while that may have repulsed some, I found it was turning me on. Her sheer abandonment was exciting me, the erotic contrast between her innocent appearance and the glow of unbridled sexuality that seemed to light up her body. I could hear guys snoring in the other rooms, worn out. I was in awe of her determination to keep pushing herself to some new level of experience.

I was weakening, but I was still reluctant to do the same thing everybody else had done to her all night long.

Picking up on my hesitation as we stood in the doorway, she snuggled up to me, flattening herself against my bare chest and the boxer shorts I'd been sleeping in.

"Part of me is still a virgin. You could be the first."

"A virgin?" I couldn't help smiling.

"Yes. Really." She pouted and looked like I had insulted her.

"I've never done it in the ass. I'm ready now. I want you to be the first. I'll never forget you."

I'd never done it that way either.

"You got any butter with you?"

"What?"

"Never mind. Come on in."

We had no butter but I had some lubricated rubbers. I'd be an idiot to swear that was her first time, but from the way she writhed and moaned, it sure seemed to be.

"It hurts, but it's sort of a good hurt," she said later.

We went on for about an hour when there was another, more aggressive knock. It was our road manager David Weaver. "Hey, Fito, let's get the hell out of here. We're going to miss our flight."

As we said good-bye in the hotel lobby, Connie was beaming, her glow filling the room. With a smile on her face, she reached in her bag and pulled out a button, which she pinned on my jacket like a military medal for bravery.

Printed on it, in orange letters on a black background, was "Connie in Little Rock" and her phone number.

Pulling away from the hotel, I looked around the limo, packed with band members and roadies. Everybody in the car was wearing a Connie button.

On this same tour, another misguided promoter (thinking we were a "Top Pop Band") booked us into the Disney World Amphitheater for the Prom Night, a celebration for high school graduates from all over south Florida.

My Florida friend Noreen got us some LSD, which we dropped before heading for the park. We figured we'd have a ball on the rides, along with tripping during and after the show.

By the time we arrived for the performance, the acid had kicked in, which only heightened our surprise and disappointment when management told us that we were NOT permitted to go on any rides or socialize with concert-goers. Disney keeps its performers in a sort of gulag, as far away from paying customers as possible. We were banished to the underground labyrinth of tunnels and sterile dressing rooms used by the people who work at Disney. Here we were, wasted on acid in a room with no windows, shockingly bright lights, blazing white walls and no way out. Talk about a bum trip.

We were about to flip out from claustrophobia, when our time to play finally came. Like Carnegie Hall, the stage uses an elevator system to bring it up to audience level for the outdoor show.

The heat was so brutal, I took off my T-shirt. Within seconds, I could see the stage manager desperately trying to get my attention from the wings. His hands were clasped in a pleading gesture and he had a terrified look on his face. He was absolutely apoplectic at such a vulgar display. Between reading his lips and guessing from his body language, it didn't take too much to figure out he was begging me to put my T-shirt back on. He kept mouthing: "I'm going to lose my job."

The Puritan attitude puzzled me. Most drummers routinely take their shirts off when it gets hot. Surprisingly, we got invited back years later, but that time we didn't drop any acid.

This time while I was on the road, Pam took a job as a masseuse at Circus Maximus on the Sunset Strip, which really bothered me, unlike her bi-sexuality, which turned me on. In spite of knowing she wasn't right for me, I was falling in love with her. I was drawn by her beauty and her sensuality, which was heightened by her heavy drug consumption. She was really into downers like Seconals (reds) and Nembutals (yellows), which were such strong barbiturates that when I tried one, it knocked me on my ass for a couple of days. She would take more than ten in one day just to keep the buzz going.

While the combination of her job and heavy drug use created on-going friction between us, I still kept dreaming I would be the guy whose true love would rescue her. Maybe even result in a family. It was one of the most self-destructive periods of my life.

As I was reading the newspaper in bed one morning, the phone rang. A very pleasant voice said: "Hello, this is Agent Cox from the FBI." My heart dropped. "I'm calling to tell you that you have been indicted for refusing to serve in Vietnam. In about an hour, I'm coming to your home to arrest you. Please be ready to come downtown."

I had no notion that being busted by the FBI was such a civilized process. I sort of expected guys with tommyguns to break in my front door and throw me face-down on the carpet.

I jumped out of bed, cleaned up every roach and every sign of drug paraphernalia in the house, and took a quick shower. Within minutes, the doorbell rang. Standing there was a mature man of medium height, who very politely asked me if I was ready to accompany him.

I was taken to the Federal Building downtown to be fingerprinted and photographed, just like one of the Ten Most Wanted. Once inside, Agent Cox disappeared and I was left in the hands of some uniformed policeman. Noticing my long hair and beard, the cop with the camera turned to his partner. His voice dripping with venom, he said: "Look at this one. He really has that criminal look." It turns out they had just fingerprinted some of Charlie Manson's family members and in their minds anyone with long hair was a drug-crazed killer.

One of the prosecuting attorneys in the background overheard the comment and told them to cool it. He knew who I was and politely came to me and instructed me to sign a piece of paper. Within minutes, I had signed my release papers and was headed out the door.

On June 3, 1971 the U.S. Court of Appeals rejected my double jeopardy argument—I won one court challenge as a conscientious objector, but was immediately re-indicted and convicted this time—and a petition for a rehearing was denied. By October, my appeal to the Supreme Court of the United States had failed, but in an impressive bit of legal footwork, my attorney, good old J.B. Tietz, had persuaded the judge to sentence me to community service. To make amends for refusing to join the war because I wanted to play in a rock band, the judge sentenced me to....PLAY IN A ROCK BAND.

I was put on probation for five years and ordered to play free concerts at hospitals, prisons and other federal institutions. I was not about to question a sentence like that, though I sometimes wondered if the prisoners cheering us would have been such fans if they knew I was up there banging the drums as an alternative to being in a cell like them.

The band regarded the judge's sentence as a lark and primarily my problem. Henry ran across old friends from his outlaw biker days at some of the prisons. He had a regular family reunion at the federal prison hospital in Missouri. Half the audience were old pals, and when we went into "They Used to Call Me a Junkie," the place erupted with cheers, roars and catcalls.

The worst gig was at the Terminal Island prison just south of LA. Henry and Tony decided to turn the penance into a party by getting loaded before the gig. They showed up so drugged on downers Tony stumbled and fell off the stage during the performance. The prisoners figured out why and cheered like crazy. The guards figured out why and glared at us.

The whole scene made me extremely nervous. I was also getting increasingly pissed off at the other band members. At any moment, I expected the guards to simply announce that as long as Canned Heat was already in prison—and obviously belonged there—we might as well stay.

Disgusted by the general state of the band and that performance in particular, I decided to quit Canned Heat. I felt I brought Tony into the band and he betrayed me—and himself. Of course, being the stupid co-dependent that I was, I decided to leave, instead of firing him.

In the beginning, Tony was talented and promising, which was clear from his great performances on the "Historical Figures" and "Hooker n' Heat" LPs. Then he started abusing drugs with the same intensity as Henry and Bear. And to make matters worse, he flunked Canned Heat's attitude test: Tony wanted to be a rock and roll star instead of a blues musician.

The Bear was also disgusted at what was happening to the band. In a rare display of leadership, he called me a week later and convinced me to stay, saying that Tony was the problem and he was going to fire him whether I rejoined or not.

Meanwhile, Joel went nuts in a whole new direction. Wracked by guilt after booze and sex sprees, he became a fervent Christian and subjected us to Elmer Gantry-style religious tirades, urging us to repent for our sins. We also resented Joel for his attempt to use Canned Heat as a stepping stone to further his own career. Before the year's end, both Joel and Tony were out: Tony for being excessively bad; Joel for being obnoxiously good.

Bear's brother Richard Hite replaced Tony, while James Shane and keyboardist Ed Beyer were new additions. Although this 1973 incarnation was to be called The New Age band, not much had changed. Drugs, alcohol and "living the life" continued.

James Shane was a talented songwriter who wrote a number of tunes, including "The Harley-Davidson Blues," which made us even more popular among outlaw motorcyclists, who were becoming some of our hardcore fans. James worked hard to restore the creativity the band lost when Alan died. Some of his songs came close to being hits, but close only counts with hand grenades. The new music never reached the band's earlier level of success.

Unfortunately, Richard had acquired all of his brother's bad habits and addictions without having the Bear's charm and musical knowledge. Now, we not only had problems with Bob, but his increasingly-fat little brother was becoming a nuisance. To make matters worse, he was younger than us, so his musical taste was very different. He even liked The Beatles and other pop groups. But the real kicker was the fact that he was a Conservative Republican who voted for Nixon.

As we began work on "The New Age" album, the world of popular music was changing. The era of peace, love and mind expanding drugs was over. Grass and psychedelics were out; Polyester, plastic, cocaine and hideous disco music had come in. It was very easy for club owners and promoters to pack places without paying for live bands, crushing the careers of thousands of musicians. Around the world, people turned their backs on just about everything we stood for: appreciation of beauty, musical proficiency, live bands, creativity, and improvisation. They lost themselves in a sea of lights, dancing to lame, repetitive quarter note beats and picking each other up for one-night stands.

With the times and public taste turning against us, we soldiered on trying to maintain our tradition as the band that mixed country blues with rock and roll. During the sessions produced by Skip

Taylor, we came up with songs like "Keep It Clean," "Rock N' Roll Music," and "Election Blues," in which Bear, disgusted by Nixon's re-election, growled:

The election's over. My man didn't even finish the race.
Nixon's on the throne again, baby,
We may go so far right that we may fall.

It was a good try but our time was over. Our album was also a last spasm for United Artists, which was faced with trends the company's executives didn't understand and a new age in music that was passing them by.

Before our European tour to promote the album, Henry and I were sitting in a coffee shop on the Sunset Strip with a clearly depressed Bob.

"Fito, man, I feel like shit. I can't do this stuff forever. I gotta straighten up. I talked to a doctor today. He said I'm fuckin' killing myself and I have to get healthy or die. I feel like an old man sometimes."

"It won't happen unless you understand that you really have to change," I replied. "Like go a diet. You could get in shape. Lots of guys do that, why not you?"

Henry thought this was hysterically funny.

"Yeah, Bear. You can eat fucking salads and run around the streets in your shorts every morning. Get little ripply muscles in your gut," he said laughing out loud.

Bear was inspired. "I'm going to do it. I really am."

This made me very happy. I could see Pamela slipping away. Henry was hopeless, but maybe I could help keep the Bear up and roaring.

"Just watch," he said to Henry as we left.

The next night we were back in the same coffee shop and Bear ordered a massive steak with three fried eggs. Between bites, he would slip a bottle of scotch out of his pocket and pour a splash into his water glass.

"Hey, great diet," Henry teased. "Condemned man's last meal?"

"Fuck no," Bear answered. "I'm on a diet. This is it, starting now, I'm really going to get in shape."

"For Christ's sake, Bear," I said. "That's practically one whole cow you've got on your plate."

207

"It's a new diet, man. The drinking man's diet. You can drink all you want and eat all you want so long as it's just protein. You just have to avoid carbohydrates. I read a book about it. You can lose a lot of weight this way."

He slipped another slug of scotch into the water glass.

"Bear, that's gotta be bullshit."

"Hey Fito, don't be such a pain in the ass. You're just naturally a skinny little guy. I need some help. This is supposed to be a great diet. And this one I can stick to. Scotch and steaks. Hey, man, I can do that."

It was like the Bear to find the one health regimen in the world that was probably worse for him than his usual body-destroying way of life. When he didn't lose weight, he supplemented the steak diet with speed and cigarettes, which did make him lose weight. But the more pounds he lost, the crazier he got and the raspier his voice became.

The European tour was a bummer. Even European audiences, who had always embraced jazz and blues as something artistically valuable from America, something with no European equal, were turning away. Clubs we'd played at repeatedly simply stopped hiring live bands.

In France, after a performance at the Olympia in Paris, this funny-looking, tall, friendly Frenchman called Phillipe Rault came to our dressing room and invited us to record with Memphis Slim and Clarence "Gatemouth" Brown, the famous old black bluesmen. It was close to midnight and we were wasted from a two-hour gig, but this was not an invitation musicians like us could turn down.

We took all the uppers in Henry's stash and drove to a beautiful castle on the outskirts of Paris where the recording studio was. The session was a pure blues encounter. We were really jazzed about being able to play with some of the first generation masters.

The session started with Memphis Slim. Although he was already in his 60s, he had this beautiful young French woman sitting next him at the piano, constantly caressing him and serving him drinks, food and whatever his heart desired. Like many other blues and jazz performers, he had become totally integrated into French society. He even carried fancy business cards saying "Monsieur Peter Chatman."

208

Most of the songs were first takes—no rehearsals, no overdubs. The real thing. He was a great piano player, with gigantic hands that took him anywhere he wanted on the keyboard. He would explain an idea to us, play a few bars and we'd cut it. It wasn't perfect, but it had that certain magic that comes with spontaneity.

A few weeks after the tracks were finished, Phillipe, the producer, came up with the idea of adding the Memphis Horns to make the music tighter, more colorful and more appealing to a broader audience. The album, called "Memphis Heat," was reissued as a CD in the early '90s.

Unlike our session with Memphis Slim, the one with Gatemouth Brown was a disaster. The uppers had worn off, and we were exhausted, when Henry and James decided to mess with the tuning on Gatemouth's guitar while he was in the men's room. This triggered an argument that ended up in a shouting match that killed the session's "vibes."

(Henry and Gatemouth weren't fated to be buddies in the best of times. Gatemouth was a deputy sheriff back home in New Mexico and black to boot. Henry was an outlaw with a confederate flag tattoo.)

Although Phillipe got them to shake hands and the session went on, the night was ruined. We managed to record only a couple of decent tracks. The album was called "Gate's On The Heat," but in reality, there are only two tracks that feature Canned Heat. I know we didn't play on the others. They must have brought in some other musicians to play on the rest of the album without giving them any credit.

We came back to the United States to a new set of problems. Disco took away a lot of the fans, but we were still a great band and hundreds of thousands of people still loved us and our music. We started out playing in honky-tonks and roadhouses and we'd never really stopped. We could go back to that. We could take less money. We could drive the van to gigs instead of flying. We could hang in until the people recovered their good sense and ditch the disco crap.

One afternoon Skip sat us down at a long table in his office and rolled out a big highway map of the United States.

"The good news. You've got gigs in Sacramento; Denver; Tucson; Gary, Indiana; a place outside of Houston and Pensacola,

Florida.

"Great," said Bear.

"No, not so great," replied Skip. "The bad news: You can't get to these places."

"What do you mean, we can't? We can drive. That's a lot of driving, but we can do it. The roadies can drive and we'll sleep in the van."

Skip tossed a yellow legal pad on the table showing the mileage between cities.

"You'd have to drive almost six thousand miles, Bob. And it would take two vans for all the instruments and the roadies."

"So what?"

"Haven't you read the papers? Those vans get about nine miles to the gallon. Didn't you notice those long lines at the gas stations on your way over here? There's a gas crisis. See this column here?" He pointed to the legal pad. "That's what all these club owners would pay, all of them together." It was a very small number, much smaller than anything we would have received in the '60s for playing just one venue.

"In all honesty, you can't afford to go much farther than Bakersfield," said Skip. We were stunned.

"I could only get one local booking for you in the next five weeks," he added. "The club owners think all live bands are poison and you guys are the worst poison of all. They've got this idea that you attract the hordes from hell instead of upscale guys in leisure suits."

"What are you trying to tell us?" asked Henry.

"You're broke, guys. The money's gone and there's no more coming in. To be blunt, don't sit by the phone waiting," said Skip, shaking his head sadly.

The elevator wasn't working so we had to leave by the back stairs. The exit door was stuck, so Bear gave it his best shot, twice. It wouldn't budge. We had to call a janitor to open it.

As Bear walked down the street holding his shoulder, I could hear him muttering, "Shit, shit, shit."

With the disco scene so strong in the U.S., we headed south of the border for a couple of months to earn some money, even though we had some concerns about the kind of reception we'd get from the government. The last time we performed in Mexico City, during the golden age days, we played at the wedding of Alfredito, the son of President Diaz Ordaz. After our performance at *Los Pinos,* the Mexican White House, we were invited to sit at a table between some high-ranking diplomats and a powerful *generalísimos* and his military entourage.

As I approached our table, I heard an anguished cry from Bob: "Alan, no! Don't do it!" It was too late. A spaced-out Alan, whose eyesight had always been bad, had just plopped his guitar smack in the middle of the bottom of the exquisite, multi-layered wedding cake. He mistook the first tier for a table.

After that disaster, we were surprised to get our new work permit without a hassle and we were welcomed with open arms. Our fans still thought of me as the only local star to join a top band in *"El Norte"* and they loved *"El Oso,"* The Bear.

We became stars again at gigantic, jam-packed rock n' roll parties then popular in Mexico called *"Reventones,"* from the Spanish word for "explosion." Within the walls of a reventon venue, anything goes. Forget fire laws. Crowd control was executed by shooting automatic weapons into the air when the wave of people would get out of hand.

At one performance, the crowd pushed forward so forcefully that front row spectators were crushed against the stage causing some to throw up and others to pass out. They were quickly tossed hand to hand over the heads of the crowd to get them out—just like today's mosh pits but much more hard-core.

Once the band was inside, we weren't able to get out until the reventon ended hours later due to sheer exhaustion. There were no cops brave enough to enter these arenas, which were organized in what are known as "lost cities" within the huge metropolis—the largest city in the world. Even though these were dangerous times, we were getting off on it.

My life at this point was in total turmoil. I'd lost my wife, my current girlfriend was a mess, Canned Heat was barely alive and my life had no direction, when I got this unexpected call from my father in Mexico.

"Son, this woman came to see me and claimed to have had your child. At first, I didn't believe her. I thought she might be looking for a free ride now that you are famous. But when I saw that precious little face, looking so much like you, any doubts washed away. You have to come and recognize him and give him your name." Evidently, he was the result of a one-night affair in Mexico with a woman who used to call herself Vivian.

I fell instantly in love with my son, who would become my friend and ally for the rest of my life. With a sense of great pride, I immediately gave him my name. Little Adolfo had already spent the first years of his life in a stable home environment with his grandparents. He was so well mannered and intelligent.

Sometime later I brought him to the U.S. and we both became citizens.

Unfortunately, by the time I was able to bring him to the States, I was not a rich rock star anymore, so I had to figure out a way to earn some money to take care of my family, which at this point consisted of me, my five year-old son, my half-sister Magdalena, who was taking care of him, and Pam—when she was around.

But I wasn't as bad off as the other band members, who had nothing to fall back on and who spent their money as though they'd go on making it for the rest of their lives. Thank God my father had insisted on my sending him money from each check I received during the "Golden Age," so he could invest it in Mexico.

It was a tough time, but I had to face it. No more rock star. No more good living. I thought, "Get used to it, Fito." I sold my beautiful 3.0cs BMW car that I'd bought just a year earlier, but I couldn't bear to part with my BMW R75 motorcycle. I was back to getting around on a motorcycle—just like my early days in Mexico

We lived on bread, cold cuts and that classic American contribution to survival cuisine—peanut butter and jelly sandwiches. And thanks to the credit extended by my Altadena milkman, we had a steady supply of milk. He was a good man who allowed me to fall three months in arrears and still kept leaving bottles. I never saw his face; he came and went in the dark of night, but I will never forget the gratitude I felt toward him.

I scrounged for money. I bought broken-down old cars, fixed them in my garage and sold them for a few bucks more, ruefully remembering how I had laughed at Henry and his Harley mechanic fantasy. I sold used amps the band could do without. I went back to the Topanga Corral, where the whole Canned Heat phenomenon began, and picked up some work as the house drummer, backing big names like Lowell Fulson, George Harmonica Smith, T. Bone

Walker and Big Joe Turner for $25 a gig.

Bad as it was, there was a lesson there, a lesson I learned and the other guys fought. The old days were gone for good. We would have to live in the present and that meant I would never again depend solely on Canned Heat for my living. Yes, I was still born to play with Canned Heat and I was going to stay until the bitter end, whenever that came. But in the mean time, I had to get some things going outside the band.

The other guys didn't see it that way. They figured that we were in a temporary slump, that any day now things would return to normal. We'd be rich and famous again. The lifelong party would crank up and the money would roll in again. It was a dream, a beautiful dream, and they could not bring themselves to wake up.

I looked around and found one source of income right under my nose: marijuana. By now, I had been smoking it regularly for years, regularly enough that one of my neighbors had shared a few joints with me, just sitting around listening to old records on summer afternoons.

One night he appeared at my door, while I was going through pockets looking for change, trying to figure out how to get twenty bucks to buy some food for the family.

"Hey, man, could I score some weed off you? I have some friends over and we're totally out."

I got a baggie from the back of the closet.

"Hey, cool. That's great. I'll give you forty for that."

"No. I don't think I paid that much."

I knew perfectly well I had paid less than twenty.

"No man, that's cool. That's the going price around here. I'm not going to cheat you or anything. Here, take the forty."

I took his money. "Can you use any more of this? I know where to score some more."

"Well, hey, yeah. I could use some more later, like next week."

I wished him goodnight and sat there thinking. I had enough contacts in the music world that I could get weed a lot cheaper than what people around here were willing to pay. Until then, I hadn't realized we were getting a good deal. Best of all, I knew Mexico, where the weed came from, and I knew it very well. And I knew that pot sold in the United States for about 20 times what it cost in small Mexican villages.

Hell, I had been aiding and abetting dope smuggling for years, without making any profit, just playing in Canned Heat and letting the roadies and managers hide hash in the speakers coming home from foreign tours.

Hard times had come, time to start dealing myself.

I rounded up some grass from friends and began retailing it to the guy next door and his friends, who brought in other friends. It was all cash, no taxes and sometimes we had more than peanut butter sandwiches to eat for a change.

As soon as I had about a grand together, I flew to Mexico City. My father wanted to have some work done on his mint condition white 1964 Ford Galaxy in the U.S. and I was to drive it back and forth, a great opportunity to bring a load of weed to the border.

When I arrived in Mexico City, I quickly called my half brother Flavio, who by then was getting high and had a lot of connections due to his charming and outgoing personality.

"So where is it that you can find this incredibly cheap weed?" I asked him.

"A village near the volcano Popocateptl. They have some of the best *sativa* in Mexico with purple hairs. Come on. You're going with me."

On the way to a remote Indian village in my dad's car, we developed a plan. He would go with the Indians to look over the crop, while I would guard the cash payment in the car, communicating by walkie-talkie to close the deal and turn over the money.

"I realize going to this little village way out in the mountains isn't like buying a new shirt in a store, *hermanito*, but when the people take one look at the car, they'll know who we are and why were here. They'll know we must have a lot of money in the car, because that's the only way you can buy weed. Isn't this awfully risky?"

"It's a chance we have to take," answered Flavio. "Sure, they can take us out in the country somewhere and stick a pistol in our face and take all our money and still keep the weed. But what are we going to do, report them to the cops? Hell, two of them ARE the cops," he said laughing.

But we managed to buy at least half a dozen loads. Luckily, we never got caught.

That was phase one. So far, so good, sort of. Now for phase two. One of our roadies said if I could buy wholesale quantities of weed in Mexico, he could get it into the United States. He wouldn't say

**One of the loads brought from Mexico,
waiting on my bed to be packaged.**

how. He just said that if I could get the weed to Mexicali, I should call him and he would meet me there.

The roadie's secret turned out to be a drainage culvert that ran right under a fence at the border in a remote area of Arizona near Ajo. During the day, we would transport duffel bags loaded with marijuana to the culvert and carry them through it in an elaborate operation which involved depositing them on the Mexican side. Then, my roadie would travel to the middle of the desert near Organ Pipe Cactus National Park with a couple of girls posing as "innocent campers" where they'd spend a couple of days in the wild establishing their outdoorsy bonafides to passing Border Patrol officers. At night, he would crawl through to the culvert under the border, grab the duffel bags, drag them back to the van and split for L.A.

Meanwhile, my brother showed up with one of his connections, a mean looking Indian from the State of Guerrero known as *El Talentos* (The Talented One) in a funky old border hotel in Mexicali. This time they not only had the marijuana bags, but they also had about a pound of heroin, saying that as long as we're smuggling the one, we could smuggle the other. For added attraction, *Talentos* offered to front us the heroin at no cost until we sold it in the U.S. He also hinted that organized crime figures knew what we were up to and we better smuggle the heroin and keep our mouths shut. Although he was armed, we flat out refused. Taking only the weed, we never saw *El Talentos* again. I heard a few weeks later that he was killed in a shoot-out with the *Federales* in the Sierra Madre Mountains in Guerrero.

One evening, as my roadie was leaving the culvert for his night time run to LA, he was busted by the Border Patrol. With shotguns leveled, the officers surrounded the van in the middle of the Arizona desert. While this was bad, it was not as bad as it would have been, had we accepted the heroin package from our Indian buddy. The roadie was tossed in jail for a few days, but eventually went free, after paying a heavy fine and being placed on probation.

With that, my criminal days were over.

My brother, on the other hand, stuck with it and soon after got caught by Mexican police in a hotel room in Mexico City with two .45s, a couple of underage girls, and 20 kilos of marijuana. He was sentenced to serve 5 years 3 months at the infamous Lecumberri prison, called *El Palacio Negro,* the standard Mexican sentence for weed possession for sale.

On appeals from my mother, I sent Flavio the few extra dollars I could scrounge up, so he could buy "the right to a cell," then a bed and blanket, and other essentials for survival—like decent food. The Mexican prison system works on the premise that you have to buy the right to live.

During this time, Bear and I became big fans of a '30s actor named Dwight Fry, a druggie who appeared in many old movies, most notably as Igor in the original "Frankenstein", and Renfield, the bizarre servant, in Bela Lugosi's "Dracula." When asked if he knew the bloodsucking count, Renfield would respond with a shriek: "Draculaaaa? I've never even hearrrrd the naaame." This line became a part of our outlaw shtick.

Stoned on weed, the Bear and I would have laughing, mock-rehearsals practicing how we would react to police questioning: "Fito? Bear? I've never even hearrrrd the naaame."

This period in the band's life hit a dangerous point. Bob's house had become a beacon for all kinds of misfits, outlaws and outright criminals. The music playing sessions, where nice hippie girls and

"Junkie Robbers" posing after the Ventura heist.

musicians hung out and learned together, had been replaced by a cesspool of ugly characters common to the Topanga area throughout its history.

This, along with being broke and disillusioned, brought out Bob's dark side. He started to proudly brag about knowing Manson family members, relatives of the Dillinger gang and other low-life practicing criminals. These people had now become his audience and his mentors. I'd even get calls in the middle of the night inviting me to dine on steaks ripped off from the local supermarkets. Adding to this degenerate environment was the proverbial non-stop, hard drug use, highlighted by shooting heroin and cocaine, topped off by getting drunk and taking all kinds of pills.

Eventually, some of these people actually took over his house—with his approval, of course, since they were providing him with money, food and drugs—and more importantly—adulation. One time, a couple of these characters went to nearby Ventura, a small city about 60 miles from LA, and committed armed robbery by assaulting an old lady who owned a jewelry store specializing in fine turquoise. The hundred thousand dollars plus worth of loot was her life's savings and the theft triggered a heart attack on the poor woman shortly after.

That night, an enthusiastic Bob, laughing with the rush criminals get from pulling off a heist, called me.

"Fito, you've got to come over. These guys have all this jewelry and they want to sell it cheap or trade it for some weed. This is a great chance to pick up something nice for Pam."

I traded some weed and a few dollars for a couple of beautiful bracelets, a ring and a belt buckle that must have been worth thousands, but it didn't feel right. I was afraid, but I did it anyway.

Meanwhile, the Ventura County police were enraged that an old lady had been ripped off, so they went on an all-out manhunt, which really wasn't necessary. A day or two after the robbery, the stupid girlfriends of the criminal-junkies, along with Bob's new girlfriend Susan, went to a fair in Ventura wearing some of the stolen items. Someone recognized the jewelry and tipped off police.

The next day, there was a knock on Bob's front door. When he opened it, he was confronted by a burly, plainclothes cop, who looked and acted just like "Popeye Doyle" out of the "French Connection." He started right in giving Bob the third degree:

"All right, I know you know all about the robbery your friends pulled off in Ventura, so tell me where the fuck they are or you're going to be in deep shit as an accessory to a felony."

Bob knew he didn't have to let the cop in without a search warrant, which was a very good thing, because the loot and the two criminals were right there hiding in one of the small bedrooms.

A pale Bob, holding his breathe, managed to say: "Jewelry? Robbery? I've never even hearrrrrd the naaame."

This time The Bear got lucky. As the cop turned to leave, he looked back angrily at Bob, knowing he'd been lied to, and said: "I'll be back with a warrant, asshole!"

Within 24 hours, one of the criminal-junkies was apprehended and confessed to everything. That same afternoon, I also received a phone call from my friend Alicia, who had been called earlier by the police because they had my house under surveillance. She warned me to expect a call from the cops, so I set up my recording device to tape the conversation. When the call came, I hit the "record" button.

The officer identified himself then said: "I know you're not directly involved with the robbery, but you've purchased some stolen property and we know you're involved with drugs. We're not interested in putting you away, but we expect you to cooperate with us and immediately return all the jewelry in your possession."

I replied: "Yes, sir, I'm sorry. I'll cooperate, but I must have your words that I won't be arrested and harassed any more."

"You have my word. Our only interest now is to recover the stolen property. We already have the people responsible in custody."

"Fine. I must tell you that I have just recorded this conversation. Just tell me what to do and where to meet you and I'll be there."

He gave me instructions to meet at a parking lot on the border of LA and Ventura counties. I jumped into my father's—fancy but very Mexican—white Ford Galaxy that I drove up from Mexico.

Showing up at the rendezvous, I was immediately surrounded by at least 10 police cars complete with flashing lights and officers with guns drawn. I thought: My god, what an over reaction and waste of taxpayers money.

I quietly got out of the car and handed over the small package of jewelry. Not a word was exchanged, until I asked if I could leave.

"Yes," the cop said.

I quietly drove away, my Mexican plates and the giant taillights of the Galaxy fading into the night, thanking God that the police kept their word.

Given the reputation the band already had, word of our escapades spread around the rock world grapevine. Between truth and hype, we were now truly certifiable as the baddest guys in rock n' roll, dangerous to be around and genuine criminals to boot. As the years go by, our reputation goes with us; whether its cool or a millstone depends on the times and who we're dealing with.

This picture was on the front page of the Los Angeles Times &
New York Times. It was the inspiration for the name of the boat
cannon in Francis Ford Coppola's "Apocalypse Now." Twenty
five years later, the trooper in the picture came to visit me.
"Fito, I'm the one in the picture, laying on top of the howitzer,"
he said, as he hugged me and cried. Here is his unit pin and
hand written note.

9

TOO OLD TO BE POPULAR
TOO YOUNG TO
BE LEGENDS

D. TROOP 1st OF
THE 1st CALVARY
AIR MOBIL AIR ARMOR,
AIRRIFLE, CANNED HEAT
PA SHAYKIN
H.N.I.C.

On my way back from Ventura, I couldn't wait to tell Pam that everything had gone well and according to plan, but when I walked in my feeling of exhilaration was immediately deflated by an unpleasant sight that had become a regular pattern. The house was filthy with dirty dishes piled high in the smelly kitchen, the bed unmade and Pam loaded on barbiturates, nodding off on the sofa in front of the TV.

Pissed off at the scene, I lashed out: "What the fuck have you been doing all day? The house is a mess and so are you!"

With an air of disdain that made it clear she didn't want to deal with it, she said: "Ohhh, Fito, you know I'm the kind of woman that likes to be taken care of. I'm not a worker." She opened her robe slightly so I could see her breasts. "Come on. Why don't you relax? Pop a downer and let's have some fun." Pam was typical of so many young, pretty women who rely on their beauty and sexuality to get them through life. In Mexico, this kind of woman is called a "porcelain doll."

I was flooded with a feeling of loss for my wife Sonja, who was not as pretty, but was a real partner. My father was right, when he said "Sonja is the best woman you'll ever have." It was obvious that my relationship with Pam was disintegrating. There was a lot of love and a lot of sex, but we were just too different.

Within a few days the band was on the road again, this time for a Midwest tour. It started in Detroit, a city well-known for its party-hearty attitude and fringe groups like John Sinclair's radical White Panthers, the Translove Energies hippie colony and the rock band MC5. In previous years, we'd played in clubs like the famous Grand Ballroom, where it was so crazy people would actually make love on the floor, and the East Town Theater, where the shows would start at midnight and go on 'til everyone was exhausted in the early morning hours. During various gigs in the Motor City, speed and other drugs were rampant and I was introduced to THC, MDA and PCP (angel dust).

Our first stop was a union-controlled Masonic Temple, where we got totally whacked and played to a half empty hall. A few in the audience were as wasted as we were and having a ball. But as the show went on and on, people who were not as high started to leave. We were so stoned, we didn't realize we'd been on the stage for over an hour and half, a half hour longer than our time slot.

Our roadie finally shouted in my ear: "Fito, the promoter is flipping

222

Band on board pirate radio ship for Radio Veronica in the North Sea. "An outlaw band and an outlaw radio station."

out. Not only are they losing money 'cuz the place is half empty, but he doesn't want to pay the stagehands overtime. If you don't stop in the next couple of minutes, we're not going to get paid."

As the song ended, I yelled to Bob: "We gotta stop and we gotta stop now or we won't get paid. The promoter isn't gonna pay any overtime."

Bob refused to get off the stage. He turned to me with a maniacal look set off by blood-shot eyes and pinpoint pupils and screamed: "Don't bother me." Then, with a devilish grin, he shouted: "We'll pay to play."

So we did, playing on for hours and jamming like the good old days, playing for ourselves, for the joy of it and as a way to work out the increasing pain, until somehow we realized that virtually the entire audience had left the theater. Only a few very loaded diehard fans remained in the front row.

Holiday Inn® OF ATLANTA

175 PIEDMONT AVE. N. E.
ATLANTA, GEORGIA 30303

IRENE NUCKOLI
DIRECTOR
SALES & PUBLIC RELATIONS

January 3, 1972

Mrs. Nita Reynolds
CARLTON TRAVEL
6301 Laurel Canyon Blvd.
North Hollywood, California

RE: CANNED HEAT
    HOLIDAY 'INN AIRPORT
    DECEMBER 15, 1971

Dear Mrs. Reynolds:

I am sure that you will be as surprised to hear of the
following as I was.

The Canned Heat Group which stayed at our HOLIDAY INN
AIRPORT on December 15th went swimming in the Pool
<u>Nude</u> in the early hours of the morning, not only disturb-
ing the guests but also showing no respect for the
HOLIDAY INN AIRPORT nor your Company's name.

We were pleased to have had business from you. Holiday
Inns are known for being Family Type Motels and we can
not expose these people to groups like Canned Heat.

I would appreciate hearing from you about this matter
as soon as possible.

Sincerely,

Irene Nuckolts

IN/bb

photo: Steve LaVere

This is what the horrified guests of the Holiday Inn saw that morning.

In Illinois, we played at another huge arena with several other bands. In these kinds of facilities, the backstage entrances are designed to accommodate large trucks so there are huge, automatic security gates that roll up like giant metal carpets.

Bob showed up in a good mood, already drunk. Grandstanding for the other musicians and people backstage, he grabbed the bottom edge of a gate as it was slowly being rolled up. Our roadie Ed Nett and I exchanged horrified looks, as Ed screamed: "Don't do it! Don't do it!" But it was too late.

Bear rode it for two stories into the air, until he had to let go to avoid getting his fingers crushed in the roller mechanism. The 300 pound, flying fat guy landed straight up on his feet, but the fall injured his legs so badly he never fully recovered and had to perform from a wheel chair for over three months. He was never able to carry his weight gracefully again or even enjoy taking a walk. After that incident, Bob would complain loudly every time there was a long walk or steep stairs to get to a stage, enter a plane, or go anywhere longer than a block.

When we returned to LA, we received a visit from the Swedish Count we met in Europe. He showed up with his driver/bodyguard in a stretch Cadillac limousine at James Shane's ranch in Topanga Canyon, which we used for rehearsals and partying. Because the ground was soggy from a recent rain, the limo only managed to make it half way up the long driveway before it got stuck in mud.

We got a call from the distressed driver's car phone and James promptly jumped into an old funky jeep to rescue our royal friend. But instead of bringing him to the ranch, we moved the party to Bear's nearby house because that's where Bob's record collection was. I'm sure our royal friend wasn't ready for what came next.

As the evening progressed, a lot of pot was smoked and other drugs and alcohol consumed. In the kitchen, picking at some food, was a famous Mexican writer and a good friend of mine, Parmenides Garcia Saldania. (He was the one who singled out Canned Heat as the band that "married country blues with rock and roll.") He was pretty drunk—as always—and he began a tirade against the concept of a monarchy. Stumbling out of the kitchen with a pot full of broccoli in his hand, he got within a few inches of the Count's face. With slurred speech, he started in: "So, you're a

Count, huh? You think you're better than us? Did you know that Mexico was the first country in the Americas to kick royalty in the ass and out of this continent?"

The mood of our distinguished guest quickly changed from amusement to discomfort. Concerned that Parmenides was offending our titled visitor, the Bear took three long steps and decked the Mexican. As he hit the ground, boiling broccoli flew all over, stinking up the room for the rest of the evening.

The Count took it all in stride, even ignoring our fallen friend, who ended up spread-eagled in the center of the living room until the following day.

Toward the end of September 1974, I was surprised to open my mail and find an envelope from the White House. Inside was a fancy, official document—complete with a presidential seal. President Ford had granted amnesty to conscientious objectors. A feeling of reconciliation had swept the country and we could live our lives without the ghost of Vietnam.

As the gigs dried up, the band spiraled from anarchy to insanity and my private life with it. I sought refuge from the madness with my motorcycle and Pam, but my co-dependency was becoming increasingly deadly. I developed a duodenal ulcer that made my life a constant misery. After my doctor saw the results of my x-rays, he stood in the doorway of his office and pointed his finger at me:

"Adolfo, you have a great big, bleeding ulcer. No more speed. No more cocaine. You can smoke all the grass you want and I would even recommend fucking a lot. Relax. Take your medicine and be careful with the food you eat." All of this was okay for the symptoms, but not for the cause. That's where my MD failed.

Because of the turmoil with Pam, I decided to go back to my Beverly Hills therapist Melvin Kinder, who made it clear that my stomach problem was not just from excessive partying or drugs, but the real cause was my tormented relationship.

I'll never forget him asking: "How long are you going to indulge in your rescue fantasies, Fito? Until it kills you?"

Driving home from his office, I knew "this was it." As much as I loved her, Pam had to go. A couple of days later, after a long talk, we agreed to break up. I bought her a little 2-door Opel Kadet, gave her some money and we parted friends.

Back on the road, at a concert at Aaron Russo's famous Electric Theatre in Chicago, I met a lovely young Polish girl named Debbie. She had big green eyes, a stunning figure and an enchanting smile. There was instant chemistry, and we hit it off so well, I invited her to ride along to our next gig in Findley, Ohio so we could spend more time together.

When she showed up the next morning, our tour manager David Weaver asked to see an ID because she looked so young. The driver's license she showed us said she was 19 years old, so she jumped in the car and we cuddled all the way to the gig. Her innocence and beauty made me feel great. I was very upset over the break up with Pam and this was a new beginning.

After the performance, we arrived at our hotel to find a message from a small private airstrip near Findley. Debbie's very worried parents had chartered a private plane in Chicago and were on their way to "rescue" their little daughter—who was really 17—from the sinister clutches of Canned Heat's drummer.

Although I liked her a lot, I respected her and we never got it on, which was a good thing. I was shocked to discover that because Debbie was underage, I could have been charged with violating the Mann Act for taking a minor across state lines.

While David grabbed Debbie and took her to the airport to deliver her to her parents, Richard Hite and I jumped in our rented car and headed out of town. Debbie made it clear to her parents that nothing bad had happened and that she lied to us about her age. Years later, she spent time with me in LA but our relationship never really flourished. On the plus side, our narrow escape from the long arm of the law became the basis for our song "Highway 409."

In what appeared to be the start of a new era, Skip was able to interest Atlantic Records in the band because two of the label's executives, Jerry Wexler and Ahmet Ertegun, loved blues music and had become enormously successful signing Eric Clapton, Aretha Franklin, Ray Charles, Led Zeppelin, the Allman Brothers, and the Rolling Stones.

To get us out of our contract with United Artist, Skip advised us to sign away all of our future UA royalties, because we were about $30,000 in the hole and hadn't sold enough records to cover our advances, not to mention the costs we'd incurred up to that point. With Atlantic interested in us and ready to give us a push, it seemed like a good decision—at the time. We didn't know that in a few short years all of our recordings would be re-issued in a completely new format called compact disk and whoever owned those rights would make a lot of money again. Sadly, the introduction of CDs would bring renewed income to many of the biggest names in '50s and '60s pop music, while Canned Heat would be frozen out once again.

After the contracts were signed, Atlantic sent us to their top recording studios at Muscle Shoals, Alabama to work on a new album. While waiting for the record company executives to pick us up at the small empty airport, The Bear tried to buy a candy bar from a vending machine, but the machine gobbled up his money without dispensing the candy. Bob immediately began pounding and kicking the machine, until the front cracked open, spilling out a variety of candies, potato chips and crackers.

When Henry, the Dixie patriot, saw what had happened, he felt Bear had insulted the honor of the South by kicking a southern vending machine. What followed was a giant, drunken brawl that ended up with both of them rolling around on the terminal floor, hurling insults. At the same moment, several cars pulled up with the Atlantic people. This was their first introduction to Canned Heat. The fighting drunks looked up, realized who was standing there, and in shame and silence got into the waiting cars. What an embarrassment for the rest of us.

Working on the album "One More River to Cross," under the guidance of producers/musicians Barry Becket and Roger Hawkins, was an enlightening experience. They had a long history of developing great sounds in their funky studio down in the deep South, so they suggested adding horns to most of the tracks and even jammed with us on several songs. It was a good effort, but it wasn't really Canned Heat. The music industry was still in the mid-'70's period of adjustment.

Once again, due to lack of leadership, we were not as prepared as we should have been for those sessions. Since Alan and Larry were no longer involved, this had become an on-going problem that I was aware of, but was not able to remedy because I didn't have any control. It was basically Bob's band and was being run Bob's style.

A bizarre footnote to the album was Henry's decision to call himself Henry *Loquisimo* (ultra-crazy), saying "I used to be mad, now I'm totally crazy." He insisted on being credited under that name on the record label and with ASCAP.

A month later I returned to LA and my son, who was now seven. He was a great source of joy and a wonderful kid, but I still felt a void because my love for Pam ran so deep. I let her move in to my Woodland Hills home, and just like before, it was a yo-yo relationship. We'd enjoy long bike rides and romantic nights with everything going well until she would give in to her dark side and start taking hard drugs again. Sometimes hiding them from me, sometimes not.

To promote "One More River to Cross" and to refresh the identity of the band, we decided to add horns after listening to the tenor sax/trombone combination created by the Jazz Crusaders, who were doing very well at the times. We hired two excellent musicians to go on the road with us. One was saxophone player Clifford Solomon, who we knew from the Ike and Tina Turner band as well as Sam and The Goodtimers. He had great credentials, having played with Lionel Hampton and the legendary blues singer Charles Brown. He was one of the best musicians I've ever played with. The second addition was trombone player Jock Ellis, who was also well-known in our circle and who played in several famous jazz and Latin bands. This unit was quickly nicknamed "The Horn Band."

We started our tour in England where we rented a funny, mid-size bus named "The President." It had a totally tacky interior, including ridiculous little tables decorated with velvet covered lamps. It was operated by a weird-looking, very straight couple (he the driver, she the stewardess), who were definitely NOT ready for the experience they were about to embark on.

Skip also managed a band featuring Harvey Mandel, our former lead guitar player, so he thought it would be great to sell us as a double bill. That also meant double party and double trouble. The tour was a total circus. There were eight members of Canned Heat and our road manager, combined with four musicians from Harvey's contingent plus his cousin from Chicago. Ed invited his beautiful blonde girlfriend and Skip was with a gorgeous English blonde named Carolyn, who was our tour manager and his girlfriend—at least in the beginning. Carolyn went on to promote a number of English bands and eventually married Roger Waters, leader of Pink Floyd.

We plunged through Europe for several weeks until we hit Amsterdam, where two Arab-looking dudes backstage at the concert hall turned us on to some of the best hash we'd ever smoked. After buzzing with us, they offered some it for sale. Naturally, just about everybody in the bus pitched in to buy some of the killer hash.

After the show, we had to drive overnight to the next gig in Paris and the bus was total madness. Within minutes of hitting the road, someone got out the just-purchased hash.

"What's that awful smell coming from the back of the bus?" yelled Skip. A putrid, dung-smelling odor was floating through the bus.

"Fuck. We'd been ripped off!" bellowed Bear. "This ain't no killer hash. This is camel crap wrapped in twigs and stems from somebody's goddam lawn!"

In our frustration, we kept lighting up more and more pipefulls, refusing to believe we'd been taken and hoping somehow to catch a buzz like we did earlier with the fucking Arabs. Naturally, all this did was to worsen the smell.

Skip ordered the bus driver to stop. "Are you guys crazy? We're going to be crossing the border into France in a few miles. Get that shit out of here."

Everybody passed their share of the camel crap forward and Bob tossed it by the side of the road.

"OK, guys," said Skip. "Does anybody have any other drugs?"

A ripple of soft, innocent "no's" could be heard throughout the bus, as heads popped up from the seats like ducks in a shooting gallery, each person denying possession in order to protect his small, personal stash.

When we reached the border, the bus still stunk and we all looked terrible after a gig with no sleep. We couldn't have been more of a red flag for the French officials.

Entering the bus, one of the *gendarmes* looked at the spectacle and immediately gave the order: *"Allez, allez.* Everybody out!"

In a scene much like the one in "French Connection" when Popeye comes into the bar, the ping of pills hitting the floor echoed throughout the reeking bus. As we walked out, I grabbed a couple of downers out of my pocket and gave them to Henry, who stood in the middle of the bus popping any and all drugs people were handing to him.

The *gendarmes* instructed us to stand outside while they searched our suitcases. When they got to Bob's, they found a little zippered sidebag, which they opened revealing about a hundred red capsules—Seconals.

The officer turned to us. And we turned to Bob. With a look of surprise and complete innocence, he shrugged his shoulders, lifted his hands and said: "Geez, I forgot I had 'em."

So they marched him off to the customs office under arrest. Now, the mood of the officials turned vicious and the search intensified with the addition of three more officers.

I had half a gram of cocaine and a couple of joints, which I'd been saving to share with everybody at our performance at the Olympia in Paris. When these were found in my wallet, I too was marched inside, to be followed shortly by Skip, Harvey and Henry.

On the first floor of the building there was a medium size room with four desks. They told us to sit down, so they could process the paperwork. After about half an hour of sitting around, the pills Henry popped started to take effect, resulting in a real attitude.

Standing up on very unsteady legs, a very belligerent Henry yelled: "What the fuck's taking so long? What the hell are we doing here?" He then turned to an officer holding a transparent plastic bag confiscated from his suitcase. It contained about 50 syringes, three of which had a dark substance inside. Henry pointed to the loaded syringes and exclaimed in his version of French: *"Vitamin B douze! Vitamin B douze!"*

Knowing that syringes aren't illegal in Europe, Henry conned the official into thinking the needles in his possession were for vitamin B12 injections. Of course, in reality, the dark substance was heroin. The officer seemed puzzled not knowing what to do, so Henry in a bold move simply grabbed the bag and walked out.

There was "a failure to communicate" all around the room. We didn't speak French and the gendarmes didn't speak English. By now, they were probably wishing they hadn't searched us. They seemed confused about what to do with us, when suddenly an elegant, dashing, dark-skinned man in an officer's uniform appeared. It was clear he was the Chief Inspector.

Once again, my knowledge of history came into play. I just knew this guy had to be Algerian or Moroccan, so I immediately approached him and began speaking in Spanish, which seemed to strike a chord of empathy. He not only understood me, he seemed to like me. He signaled me to follow him upstairs to talk in private. As I passed by Skip, he handed me a copy of the contract for our Paris gig, along with a copy of "One More River To Cross."

I was able to convince the French-Algerian that we were not big time drug traffickers but just musicians, gypsies—not criminals. I acknowledged the possession of drugs, knowing it doesn't pay to play games once you're caught.

"We're in your country to entertain," I said, "and we'll be gone in two days. Please, let us go. There could be a riot at the Olympia if we don't show up."

He looked at the record and the contract, paused for a minute, and then picked up the phone to contact the Olympia. I could more or less understand the conversation. He was going to let us go and we would be a little late for the show.

While he was on the phone, I took a couple of steps back and turned to look out the window. I was stunned! There was Henry sitting in the bus shooting the heroin he had just taken back from the hands of the officials. I quickly turned back, hoping the Chief wouldn't see what I saw. He scribbled some figures and then informed me that we would have to pay a stiff fine of $500 U.S. dollars each—in cash, right then. Even though this was a hell of a lot of money for us at the time, we were relieved and happy to be on our way.

When the Chief handed me back the contract, I made a point of giving him the record as a gift. "I hope you enjoy it," adding, "Don't Forget To Boogie." For the first time, a smile crossed his face, as he said: *"Bon voyage."*

I returned to LA and my dysfunctional relationship.

One day Pam just vanished. I couldn't find her anywhere, but my instincts told me she was probably getting high. I looked for her at her job and at the homes of several friends without luck. During the search, I was overwhelmed with feelings of insecurity, jealousy, and

233

Pam looking good!!

frustration. I couldn't live with her and I couldn't live without her. Even though my shrink had advised me, I couldn't find the strength to break up for good.

Driving down Santa Monica Boulevard in Hollywood, I spotted an Opel just like hers going the opposite direction. Burning rubber, I did an immediate U-turn. I tried to catch up to the car, but wasn't able to. Then, reality came crashing in. "This is crazy! I better stop driving right now."

I pulled the car over to regain my composure. I spotted a small bar on the corner. Doing something completely out of character— since I don't like drinking or bars—I quickly ordered two shots of cognac to calm down, but they had exactly the opposite effect.

Pam in the pool.

Fito and Pam

Instead of feeling relief, I became more depressed; I went back to the car and broke down in tears.

I drove towards Lookout Mountain Drive off Laurel Canyon hoping Pam would be at Jannell's, one of her closest friends. Finding the door unlocked, I walked in and called their names. No answer. When I got to the master bedroom, I found them naked, wrapped in each other's arms, looking very beautiful and very loaded. So loaded they never heard me.

I grabbed Pam and shook her. "Why did you disappear? I've been looking for you all day. What the fuck is going on?"

It took Pam several minutes to regain consciousness. When she did, she acted like I was a stranger. That's when I slapped her hard enough to make her nose bleed. I was enraged and the cognac had gotten me drunk to the point that I did something I'd never done before or since. I hit a woman. I was so broken and ashamed, I turned and walked out.

As I was leaving, I overhead a crying Pam tell Jannell in her soft Mississippi accent, "I'm fixin' to drive ma'self off a cliff and end it all."

I sought refuge a few doors down with our roadie Dennis Parins, who was home with our mutual friend Joy Smith. Seeing how disturbed I was, they lit up a joint to comfort me, as I broke down and related the events of the day.

Our conversation was interrupted by the sounds of an ambulance, a police car and a towing truck.

"My god, she really did it!" I shouted, as the three of us rushed out to see what had happened.

Pam had indeed walked out, got in her little white Opel and drove over the cliff right next to Jannell's house. She didn't kill herself, but she damaged her knee and totaled the car I'd given her.

After being released from the hospital, she ended up back at my house in Woodland Hills. Both of us prisoners of love and incompatibility.

Even though Skip had decided to no longer manage or produce the band, Atlantic Records decided to give Canned Heat another shot, this time at the Criteria recording studios in Miami with the legendary producer Tom Dowd credited with a stellar list of R&B artists, including Ray Charles and Aretha Franklin. The label understood that the "One More River to Cross" project was not really us. Under the guidance of this top-flight producer, they planned to create something with mainstream appeal that would save our careers, just like they did with Eric Clapton and his records "461 Ocean Boulevard" and "Derek and the Dominos."

The label and the producer were very serious about the project. They did everything possible to make it a success. Tom came to see the band play in New York so he could familiarize himself with our style and personalities. We flew to Miami for a session to select material, analyze it and record a demo, which they gave us as "homework." We were to rehearse and polish the material back in LA in preparation for the real recording session a few weeks later.

Our rehearsals, which were few and far between, degenerated into chaos. We had never been given homework before. With few exceptions, we had either been produced by Skip or ourselves. Now, due to Bob's lack of leadership, Skip's abandonment and the on-going anarchy, we simply didn't have the organization or discipline to rehearse properly and take advantage of our last opportunity to have a major label interested in getting us out of the hole we were in.

Weeks later, when we showed up at Criteria, nothing had changed. We hadn't done our homework. And it was immediately apparent to Tom Dowd, who nevertheless went ahead and coached us and produced the album. Dowd's style was very compatible with the way we liked to play. For the most part, he avoided overdubbings and looked for a natural "band sound," which he achieved by positioning us in a semi-circle so we could see each other and get the same feeling as a live performance. It was the right way to record Canned Heat. The album came out pretty good in spite of us and our shortcomings.

Unfortunately, the stupidity reached a climax during those sessions when "living the life" became more important than playing the music. We now had three confirmed heavy drinkers: Bob, Henry and Richard. Our all night parties at the hotel were notorious and our bar bills were record-breaking. The guys even took pride in them. We were supposed to be working, but they turned it into an orgy of consumption, be it drugs, alcohol or food. They wantonly showed no regard for Atlantic or the other band members, who knew this was wrong but didn't have the power to change things.

As the sessions went on, Bob's throat got worse and worse, but it wasn't due to singing. He was caught in a vicious circle: first hoarseness, then drinking to forget about it, which lead to more hoarseness and shame, which in turn, resulted in more drinking. It got so bad towards the end, he wouldn't even show up for the sessions. I clearly remember Tom Dowd saying: "He's only harming himself." But he was wrong. Bob was harming all of us.

We managed to finish the project. But after their experience with us and the realization that Canned Heat was out of step with the current trend, Atlantic decided not to release the album. They turned ownership of the tapes over to us and let us go. It was the most serious blow to the band's career since Alan's death.

In my first attempt to exert some influence over the band, I mentioned the Dowd/Miami project to some Mexican record company executives who were friends of mine. They expressed interest in the album and liked my idea of translating a couple of the songs into Spanish.

Even though Skip had distanced himself from the band and put his brother Jim, a school teacher, in charge of Canned Heat, the tapes somehow ended up at Skip's house. I was determined to rescue the project, so I kept calling, but they just ignored me. It got to the point where Skip wouldn't even take my phone calls. Each time I called, he was "in the shower."

Months went by and Skip rented his house to Keith Richards, who was writing material for another Rolling Stone album. After a night of heavy-duty partying when everyone was asleep, a log rolled out of the fireplace and set the house on fire. Our Criteria master tapes vanished in a puff of smoke. Richards didn't notice the fire until he woke up too late to do anything except get out.

Fortunately, copies had been made of the masters and outtakes. Once I got hold of the material, I kept it for two decades, waiting for the right moment to release it. In 1997, Barry Ehrmann, a record executive with a new label called Paradigm, expressed interest in reviving the project and I was able to assemble a good selection of the sessions, even though the copies were in pretty bad shape. Some even fell apart while we worked with them. Fortunately, we were able to save them by transferring almost everything to digital audio tape (DAT) and then we brought them back to life on a Pro Tools system at Oasis Mastering Labs. It was very gratifying to finish the project and release the material on a CD called "The Ties That Bind" twenty years after it was recorded.

Because of my deteriorating financial conditions, my father reluctantly sent me some of the money he'd invested for me in Mexico during the glory years, but not until he extracted a promise from me not spend it foolishly. Taking his advice, I began investing in American real estate, buying, renting and selling houses. I also invested in European automobiles. I gradually built a financial base outside the band, which saved me from the tough financial fate that most musicians—famous or not—typically suffer.

Although staying with Canned Heat looked like more trouble than it was worth, I somehow couldn't leave; we were a band of brothers once, and perhaps we could be again. I just couldn't kiss off that great day I introduced myself to Bob; the band had become a home I couldn't leave.

With Bear's doping and boozing making him increasingly dysfunctional, I began to rise in importance within the band. Over occasional protests, mostly from his brother Richard, I took charge on the road; I became the behind-the-scenes administrator. My English was fluent and my business sense was growing quickly now that I understood how things work in the U.S.

Meanwhile, Bear had married Susan, a friendly, good-looking woman who wrote him love letters he used to share with me. I remember one in particular in which she tells Bob how warm and wise he is and how happy she feels being next to a man that knows so much and has so much music in him. Unfortunately, the relationship was to be short and very, very tragic. The Bear and Susan started shooting cocaine, speed, and heroin. They got drunk, they screamed at each other, they made love and got mad again.

After our disastrous meltdown with Atlantic, Canned Heat was rudderless, drifting hopelessly at sea. Skip had simply faded away. His cocaine habit plus the Playboy bunnies was a hell of a combination for a business manager. Looking back, Canned Heat should have been as popular as the Grateful Dead, because Canned Heat was a better band and had three worldwide hit records. But The Dead had it together in spite of not having hit records. They had good management and a vision. They saw themselves as more than a '60s band; they created a legendary band, which made them one of the top money-makers in the music world into the '90s.

At this point, Howard Wolf, a well-regarded Hollywood manager I'd met during my days with Los Tequilas, became our manager and we got a gig at an upscale California ski resort in Mammoth Lakes. Unfortunately, the place had really bad vibes as far as Bear was concerned. He couldn't relate to the whole jet set ski scene, so he insulted the audience to a degree we had never seen before. Stumbling around the stage, he shouted: "So, you think you're hot shit, you yuppie candyass motherfuckers? Well, we are the shit! And if you don't like it go fuck yourselves, you uptight upper-class motherfuckers. You don't know nothin' 'bout the blues!" Unlike the tough, cynical blues and biker addicts who were the core of our fans, the sensitive yuppies walked out. Who could blame them?

Disgusted, James Shane, Ed Beyer, and even Henry quit the band that very night.

After his parents died, Henry inherited a substantial amount of money. He married for the second time (to Lisa, a nice Jewish girl and daughter of a Beverly Hills doctor), and decided to move to South Carolina to pursue the life of a southern gentleman.

An accident also influenced his decision. Tanked and loaded, he got into a car crash on Topanga Canyon, injuring a friend who sued him, which quickly did away with a lot of his inheritance. The police were amazed to discover that no one in the history of the LAPD had ever been arrested with such a high level of alcohol in his system.

To fill in the blanks, we hired two talented, blues-oriented musicians: Chris Morgan on guitar and Gene Taylor on piano and lead guitar. Chris was a friend of Richard's and Gene was one of the best boogie-woogie piano players around. He also played good lead guitar and had a look and attitude that was perfect for Canned Heat. He was a big, friendly fellow with a long beard.

After a show one night in Indiana, Richard got very drunk and very obnoxious, which lead to an argument with me in the hallway at the Holiday Inn. Bob overheard us and opened his door.

"I'm going to give it to him," I said, wrapping my Swiss army knife in my hand to make my fist more powerful; Richard was twice my weight and several inches taller. Bob nodded his approval, so I threw a couple of punches, flowering Richard's drunken face with blood.

After the first couple of blows, Richard threw all his weight against me, wrapped me in a bear hug and started to choke me. We crashed right through the dry wall. I was really pissed. I could out box him, but the moment he used his weight to wrestle with me, I was dead meat.

Gene Taylor, hearing the commotion, came out of his room and immediately grabbed us by the throats. With his strong, piano player hands, he choked both of us: "You assholes better stop this right now!"

A few seconds later, the furious hotel manager showed up just as we were heading toward our rooms. David Weaver assured him that Canned Heat would pay for the damages and that we'd behave ourselves from then on.

My relationship with Richard went rapidly downhill after that, resulting in a similar fight a few months later. How awful to have to play and live with people who are so fucked up that violence is the only recourse for solving problems.

In spite of the trends and the odds being against us, an English agent named Barrie Marshall contacted us and introduced us over the phone to a gargantuan German wrestling promoter called Karlo. Even though music was not his bag, he was fascinated with The Bear and Canned Heat, so he decided to hire us for a European tour.

He had just inherited some money and knew he wasn't going to live long, which was sad because he was such a nice person. He was grossly overweight and suffered from a number of illnesses, including narcolepsy, which made dealing with him very difficult, because this form of sleeping sickness would cause him to suddenly fall asleep, sometimes in mid-sentence during trans-Atlantic phone calls and negotiations with club owners and agents.

Although Karlo booked us into nice, large venues, they were only 25 percent full because Europe was totally caught up in disco music. This had a very negative effect on the morale of the band and Gene Taylor, who was young and immature, couldn't deal with it. One night, as we were eating in a charming cafe in Biarritz in France, Gene blew his top because he couldn't get a pizza. He quit the band—and the tour—right then and there.

Ian Flooks, who was doing his first tour with us as road manager, suggested we ask Stan Webb to fill in on lead guitar because his band, Chicken Shack, was our opening act. He accepted immediately, briefly making him the only Englishman to ever be a member of Canned Heat. Clever Ian later became a famous agent/manager for Police and Sting.

When we returned to the States, we hired Mark Skyer from Chicago, an excellent singer and decent lead guitar player, we'd met on our European tour with the "Horn" band when he was playing with Harvey Mandel.

It had been more than two years since Atlantic dropped us, but we were still hoping for a record deal. We didn't entertain any illusions; we knew no major label would touch a blues act like us during this period, so we tried a smaller company. Takoma Records, which was owned by John Fahey, the guitar player/musicologist who originally brought Alan Wilson from the east coast, was based in LA and run by Jon Monday, who was friendly, very professional and loved blues music. This was a real artists label and we would be their biggest act.

Half way through the negotiations in Jon's office, Bob (whose health was in steady decline) released a fart so bad that there was no way we could ignore its existence. We tried to continue talking business as though nothing had happened, but it didn't work.

The putrid smell had permeated the room to such a degree that the Takoma executive looked up at us, dropped his pen on the desktop and said: "Well. (pause) The meeting is over." He got up, extended his hand, said good-bye and fled the room. He simply couldn't stand being there.

As we walked out of the office afraid our deal had fallen through, I turned to Bob: "You asshole. Why didn't you get up and go to the bathroom before bombing the room? You screwed up the whole thing!!"

"Geez, guys, I just couldn't help it. It just came out," he replied.

A few days later, I was notified that our contracts were ready to be signed. What a relief. Luckily for Canned Heat, Bob only killed the meeting, not the deal.

The farting had become a real problem. When we were touring in our 15-passenger van, Bear would always plop himself on the long seat (for three people) right behind the driver. After a few joints, he would fall out. While sleeping, he would occasionally shoot an awful, loud, smelly fart. We had to carry giant-size cans of Lysol, so we could be prepared. When one of his earth-shattering rumbles would happen, we would urgently get up and start spraying Lysol throughout the front of the van. The combination of odors, of course, was even more revolting.

After a particularly offensive fart and our Lysol countermeasure, Bob woke up very angry. He sat up, turned his puffy face towards us in the back of the van, and said: "You are a bunch of lightweight motherfuckers." And promptly fell back to sleep.

In an attempt to finally release us from our tormented relationship, Pam decided to move back to Mississippi. This time, I was the one who wanted her to stay because I always felt so lonely and devastated, but she prevailed and left LA.

A few months later, I received a phone call from her; she was desperate and in tears. She had married an old boyfriend and was extremely upset and suicidal.

"Oh, Fito, I miss you so much. I'm so unhappy."

"I miss you too, baby, but now that you're there, you have a new life. Try to make it work. You know I wish you the best," I quickly hung up.

A few months later I received a phone call. She was back in LA and had a decent job working with computers. She also had a new boyfriend she'd just broken up with because he recently broke her arm and beat the hell out of her.

This Pam was much more jaded and damaged than the one who had left me barely a year ago. She no longer took care of herself, letting her weight and appearance go. Her barbiturate habit had now turned into a heroin/cocaine habit. Even her love toward me didn't feel the same. But she still managed to manipulate me, triggering one last rescue fantasy.

In an effort to hide the miserable situation she'd been in with her abusive ex-boyfriend, she asked if she could stay at my house in Burbank, when her mom and some other family members came to visit her in Los Angeles. When her family asked about the bandages, she told them she hurt herself in a fall.

I invited her family over for a barbecue one evening and decided her mother needed to know the truth. I told her Pam was in serious trouble and needed psychiatric counseling and hospitalization as soon as possible. Her mother suspected things weren't quite right, but she couldn't believe her daughter was in such desperate straits. She listened to me, but didn't do a thing. She obviously didn't agree with my assessment. Pam's ability to deceive had worked better than my truth-telling.

A few days after the visit, I received a call from a very disturbed young woman: "You don't know me, but I desperately need your help. Your friend Pam has stolen my husband Larry and turned him into a heroin addict. We're only in our 20s and we just got married. We were very much in love until that horrible woman seduced my husband at work. She's destroying our lives! Please, you've got to help me."

I was stunned. I knew Pam had a dark side, but I never thought she would do something this rotten.

"I'm so sorry, but there's not much I can do. Pam is very sensuous and that gives her power. I'll have a serious talk with her, but I can't promise anything."

Prior this call, I suspected Pam was messing around because my phone would ring and when I answered, the person would hang up. And, occasionally she would ask to spend the night in a hotel so she could get away from everything and get high. Clear signs of infidelity.

The same day the young woman called about her husband, I had my final confrontation with Pam. "I don't ever want to see you or hear from you again, Pam. I am absolutely exhausted. And now, you've not only insulted me, but you've done something very rotten to that poor young couple. You used your sexual powers to turn that stupid kid into an addict. You've destroyed that family. I'm finished with you forever and you are to leave my house within 24 hours."

This time was for real and she knew it. I had never talked to her this way before. And more importantly, I had never looked at her that way before—with true anger.

Within a few hours, the idiot kid pulled up in a beat up pickup truck to get Pam and all her belongings. Two weeks later, I got another call. This time it was Linda, Pam's friend and lover.

"Hi, Fito, I know you don't want to hear about Pam, but I just had to call you to tell you she's not doing well. She's back at the massage parlor and keeps missing work. She's worse than ever and I'm very worried. I'm sorry to bother you."

"Yes, you are bothering me. I don't want to hear about her or her problems. I'm finished with her," I said, hanging up. This time I was not going to be co-dependent. I had finally learned to control myself and ignore my "rescue fantasies."

A couple of months later, in the fall of 1977, I received another call. This time it was her sister Glynda.

"Sit down, Fito. I have something terrible to tell you."

"Pam is dead, right? I knew it was going to happen."

"She died of a heroin overdose in a motel room in Burbank where she was living with a guy named Larry," said her sister.

It was a cold, desolate feeling, but I was no longer able to react. I was totally worn out. There was nothing left.

Glynda, sensed this and simply said good-bye without giving me any details about the funeral, knowing I wasn't going to show up.

I tried so hard. But Pam was like so many others I knew then. She started down a road that went right to an early grave, but she wouldn't get off it. My love wasn't enough to pull her back and I wasn't about to go with her. Much as I loved her, much as I shouldn't have, I was just not going that way. There's a lot to be said for being alive and sane. Dead men play no blues.

A few months after her death, I received a card from her mother. "Fito, we love you, no matter what. I should have listened to you, but now she's at peace. God bless you." It was deeply gratifying for me to receive that card. I didn't hear from any of her family again until December of 1996 when Glynda contacted me during a tour through Florida, re-establishing our friendship.

On stage, I didn't feel the pain somehow. The rush of the music always took over. I'd drum like hell and forget all about Pamela. But when the night was over, she was always there in my head. I saw that beautiful face on a lot of hotel room ceilings. It was a long time before she went away.

My business ventures expanded to include a partnership in a recording studio in the funky east Hollywood area of Melrose Avenue and Western. My partner was Bob Safir, an engineer who had a lot of talent but little equipment, so we entered a one year agreement where I would invest around $10,000 to modernize his studio with new mikes, cables, a new 16-channel board and an 80-8 tape recorder from TEAC. It turned out to be a small, professionally run studio that made money and the relationship allowed me to learn more about the production end of the business, including how to engineer a session.

Together with Larry Taylor, we produced a traditional New Orleans-style blues album featuring the virtuoso piano player/singer Ronnie Barron. Running those sessions was a pleasure and an education. I engineered the whole project and mixed it with Larry. Most of it was done live, with overdubbings only on the horn sections with Jerry Jumonville, another excellent musician from Louisiana.

We called the album "Blue Delicacies" and Howard Wolf helped us find a deal where we made a little money. Unfortunately, the people we licensed the record to never released it. They printed about 1,000 copies and then canned the project, using it only as a tax deduction, which is all that they wanted it for.

Once again, the artists get fucked, especially Ronnie, whose talent never gained the recognition it should have. It was truly heart-breaking for me, because this project was one I was particularly proud of, even taking into account all my award-winning records.

When my agreement with Bob Safir ended, I decided to build my own recording/rehearsal studio at my house in Mar Vista to see if we could revitalize the band. I had the space, a double-size garage, which was ideal. With the help of a musician/builder called John Sholdung, I got the necessary permits and we built it from scratch. It turned out to be a much bigger undertaking than I anticipated, but again, it was a wonderful learning experience in terms of sound-proofing, acoustics, and construction in general.

My friend Jeff Addison, who goes back to my Sot Weed Factor days, knew a lot about engineering and gave me a book called "How to Build a Recording Studio," which became our bible for the year it took to complete the project. The studio was built almost entirely by out-of-work musicians. It was really something to see this eclectic mix of artists covered with dust, banging nails (and sometimes their fingers), installing roof shingles and building insulating walls. When the studio was finished, I named it Panzer Productions, again reflecting my passion for military history. Owning a studio was hard work, but a wonderful experience. Unfortunately, it was too late to change Canned Heat's destiny.

At the same time I was running my studio, we started recording our "Human Condition" album at Takoma's studio on Pico Boulevard in West LA. We invited the Chambers Brothers to join us on some of the songs, and on the others, we used the vocals of Mark Skyer, along with Bob. The title was taken from one of the last songs Alan wrote, but wasn't released until this album. The rest of the material was a combination of country blues with a touch of rock and roll. It was a nice effort, but the time was just not right for another hit.

During our negotiations with Takoma, our manager Howard Wolf discovered that the band's name had never been registered, even though Canned Heat had been performing for more than 10 years. On the morning of January 16, 1979, I was surprised to get a call from Bear asking me to join him at the Santa Monica Outlook so we could register the name Canned Heat by filing a DBA (Doing Business As) that would appear in the newspaper. I was particularly pleased that he asked me instead of his brother Richard.

By having me sign the DBA papers, I formally became co-owner of the band's name, which signified his acceptance of me as a co-equal and heir-apparent. He knew if anyone was going to keep the band alive, it was me. He was tired of the pressure of leadership, and with me by his side, he knew there would be someone to share the burden.

Meanwhile, the friction between Bob and Richard was getting worse day by day. The excessive drinking, the sense of futility regarding our careers, and the lack of money was taking its toll even on their bond as brothers. One day after a big argument, Richard quit. Within days, Mark Skyer and Chris Morgan walked out, reducing Canned Heat to only the Bear and me.

During this period, the Dan Akroyd and John Belushi movie "The Blues Brothers" was released, making the blues scene suddenly fashionable again. In spite of the popularity of disco, a new generation of musicians interested in the blues was appearing on the scene. One of them was Mike Mann, a.k.a. Hollywood Fats, the son of a Beverly Hills doctor and a rich kid who turned his back on affluence at an early age and dedicated himself totally to his guitar; he became an outstanding and very unique musician of legendary proportions. He formed "The Hollywood Fats Band" that included our ex-bass player Larry Taylor and they worked small nightclubs in the LA area. They established a good reputation, but were never able to get beyond that plateau of limited exposure and even less money.

Knowing that Bob and I had disbanded the "Human Condition"

band, Larry approached us and suggested we contact Ronnie Barron and join forces with him and Fats. It was a great match up, particularly because Bear and Hollywood Fats were both tremendous eaters. While they were downing hamburgers in a greasy spoon in New York, they decided to call themselves "The Burger Brothers," which gave this unit its quirky identity. Even though this combination was plagued with all kinds of problems and lasted only a short time, it was one of the best Canned Heat lineups in years.

We were happy to get any gigs we could, which meant ending up in a bar in Victorville, a long way from the Fillmore and the Hollywood record studios and an even longer way from the arenas of Europe. Victorville was a truck stop in the lonesome sandy nowhere between LA and Vegas. The crowd was hard core blues people: outlaw bikers, ex-cons and asphalt cowgirls, the scufflers and the scuffled, the raptor-eyed people you see hitchhiking in the Western American desert, far from town and traveling light.

As we started to play, Bear, who'd been washing down reds with beer for two hours, took the mike and asked the crowd: "Hey, you'all live here?"

"Yeahhhh," came the answering roar, playing their role in the show-biz ritual, setting up some shallow hometown compliment.

"Well, you're fucked!"

The crowd fell silent.

"I mean, FUCKED! Anybody who has to live here is hopelessly fucked."

Shit, I figured, there goes another audience, just like the crowd Bear drove out of the bar in the ski lodge at Mammoth Mountain a few months earlier, calling them yuppie candyass motherfuckers. This audience was made of cooler stuff. They thought about it for a couple of seconds. Then they laughed. Then they cheered. I guess they liked Bear's spirit. Or maybe they just figured they really WERE fucked and gave Bear points for accuracy.

Bear went on a real tear that night. Maybe he figured he had to give the people a hell of a good time after telling them they were all fucked. More likely it was just the reds and the beer, but he pulled out all the stops and sang 'til he had to sit down on the floor and sang from the floor until he had to lay down. Then, he tried to sing another number on his back, but just collapsed and lay there snoring. Luckily, Ronnie was an excellent singer, so he took over and

"Burger Brothers" lineup- L to R- Hollywood Fats, Fito de la Parra, Bob Hite, Larry Taylor, Jay Spell

we finished the show with that mountain of flesh snoring right there at the front of the stage.

At the end of the evening, no one was about to get a hernia lifting the giant sleeping Bear, so we left him there until noon the next day.

As we shook him awake, he roared: "What the fuck happened?"

"Shit, Bear, you're in Victorville! Don't you remember?"

We left the Bear out cold on stages all over America. At the Topanga Corral it had become the norm. We'd often find Bob wandering aimlessly the next morning, walking in a total fog towards his house after a night of rage.

Another memorable incident on tour was our visit to French Canada. Without a word of explanation, Ronnie Barron walked off stage during a performance in Montreal to do some coke. When the time for a piano solo came, Larry, realizing that Ronnie had disappeared, went into a screaming fit on stage.

At the same he was playing, he turned and yelled: "That Ronnie is a flaming asshole. I'm going to quit." In a fury, he then proceeded to slam the neck of his bass against my cymbals as the band played on. Poor Larry. He always wanted things to go right. Here he was again with the Canned Heat, having to deal with all the madness.

The audience, which as usual was made up of the gritty, hard-bitten types who were still Canned Heat fans, took all this in stride.

In the dressing room after the show, Ronnie, noticing how pissed off we were, approached each band member, and pointing his index finger went around the room: "I'm better than you, better than you, and better than you." And then he stalked out.

It's a shame that the most talented musicians are often the hardest to get along with. Even if Ronnie's music was great, we simply couldn't handle his unpredictable temper and his uncivilized behavior on the road. He was fired shortly after this incident, although we had pain in our hearts because we were friends.

Larry found a replacement in Jay Spell, a fantastic blind piano player who grew up with Ronnie Milsap and attended the same school for the blind. Fortunately, he provided the same musical excellence as Ronnie Barron, so we were able to maintain the same level of quality.

Fats and Bear were a great combo and constantly fed off each other. At the Topanga Corral one night, we were playing with Big Joe Turner, whose talent was as considerable as his size. In fact, he was even bigger than Bob or Fats, which is really saying something.

After our performance, a young, foxy white chick starts coming on to this giant of a black man. As she curled her body around his and started to caress him in a very personal place, Big Joe smiled down at her and said:

"Oh, no, honey. I'm too fat to fuck; suck my dick."

Needless to say, Bob and Fats immediately adopted the rhyme and could frequently be heard chanting the mantra, especially if a great looking girl was present.

Another memorable evening was a rowdy gig at Culver City's Veteran's Auditorium, when Frank Cook showed up in our dressing room. It had been over 12 years since I last saw him at the Topanga Corral, the night I was introduced to Canned Heat and he didn't let me sit in. I was chatting in a corner with a journalist friend when Frank came in to talk to Larry and Bob. After they exchanged greetings, he turned towards me and without even saying hello, declared—with the same American arrogance I'd seen before: "I changed your life."

I looked at him without answering. His remark was so absurd and his manner so impolite he didn't deserve a response.

In September 1979, Canned Heat was invited to the 10th anniversary of Woodstock, which was held at an outdoor stadium in Brookhaven, Long Island, instead of the original location at Max Yasgur's farm. The Canned Heat lineup was a strong musical force, with Bob not only shining as the great blues singer he was, but also as a performer. He created a fun environment with his "Get Down And Boogie" attitude and his wisecracks with the other guys in the band.

Unknown to us, the show was recorded and the tapes were secretly kept until 1995, when Barry Ehrmann, who was then with King Biscuit Flower Hour, contacted me to see if I would mix and master those tapes. I gladly accepted and entered a release agreement. The "Canned Heat in Concert" CD was mixed in Frankfurt, Germany. While working on it, I was delighted the live performance had gone so well. It's the only recording in existence featuring Hollywood Fats and The Bear together.

While the concert was a great party, it was too early for nostalgia. We were too old to be popular, but too young to be legends. At this point, Woodstock was not a symbol of an era, it was just passé.

Al Bennett, the former president of United Artists/Liberty Records (remember the man who bought Canned Heat's publishing royalties for $10,000 to help get the guys out of jail in Denver years ago?) wanted to release a Canned Heat record with his new company, Cream Records.

During negotiations with Bob Todd, who was to produce the LP, the room suddenly filled with a revolting smell. Thinking of the famous fart that ended the meeting with Tacoma Records, I turned to Bear: "Are you trying to kill the meeting again?"

Bob blurted out with injured innocence: "It wasn't me. It was

Larry."

Our reputation was for drugs, death, brawls, and crime—now record company executives had to fear room-clearing flatulence.

Al Bennett liked Canned Heat and was willing to invest in the band, but he warned us not to do a blues-oriented album; he insisted on rhythm and blues to keep up with the changing times and to make us more commercial. Cream had acquired the Stax Volt catalog, which included some great songs, so we listened to dozens of tunes and finally picked out some we liked. We were not used to this kind of approach, but we really didn't have a choice. Having any record company interested in us was all we could ask for.

Hollywood Fats was a great blues guitar player, but this contrived music bothered him and made him lose interest. He also had trouble getting a sound the producer was happy with. As a result, Bob Todd brought in Mike Halby, an R&B singer and guitar player, to finish the project the way he envisioned it.

Mike did a good job and when the sessions were over he asked if he was going to be a member of Canned Heat. Bear and I discussed it, and even though he wasn't a blues player, we liked his singing and his desire to be in the band, so he was hired as a permanent member.

After the album was completed, Mr. Bennett suffered a family tragedy and his interest in the LP faded. Our enthusiasm wasn't very high either, because we were forced to play music that really wasn't our bag. As a result, the record wasn't released until years later after Bob's death, when our ex-bass player Tony de la Barreda took an interest in it while he was with RCA in Mexico.

At the same time Fats and Larry were working on the Canned Heat album, they kept their own blues band going. It was very good, but they only played small clubs where they could get familiar with the acoustics and get comfortable with the sound. Canned Heat worked just the opposite. We only played one-nighters; we were always in different places where we had to adapt to the acoustics of each venues. Besides, our rock-oriented attitude made us a louder band and this made it even more difficult for Larry and Fats to find the "comfort zone" they had with their blues band.

Naturally, this created a lot of tension. Larry and Fats began complaining about Canned Heat in general, and me in particular, because they couldn't "get off." The two kept up such a steady stream of criticism, I wanted to quit. I'd given my life to this band,

and the unrelenting pressure of these two with their superiority complex was something I didn't need.

At a meeting without the Bear, I told Fats and Larry: "Since you guys don't like the way I play, and you're constantly putting your blues band above Canned Heat, I've decided to pull out and let you guys do anything you want with the band as long as Bob agrees. Go ahead and combine the other members of the Hollywood Fats Band and turn that into Canned Heat. Maybe that way you'll be happy at last." I was so disgusted, I was quitting and giving them my share of the band.

To my surprise, they didn't accept the offer. They were worried that their frontman/harmonica player, Al Blake, wouldn't like being second banana to Bob. I didn't understand their reasoning because the Bear was an extraordinary frontman and I didn't think there was a conflict.

When I told Bob about the meeting and my desire to quit, he was angry because he had picked up on their attitude too. He said I should never have considered quitting.

"Fuck them, if they don't like our band," he bellowed. "You're my bro and you are Canned Heat's drummer. I don't want to be in the band without you. Fuck Larry, he doesn't know how to have a good time." I was touched by Bob's display of loyalty.

Eventually this magnificent lineup dissolved. Larry and Fats wandered off and continued with their band. Amazingly, Henry returned to Canned Heat and this time he wasn't drinking. He actually stayed dry for a year and a half and only smoked grass. What a pleasure to see a healthy Henry on the wagon and with his head screwed on right. His playing was extraordinary. Canned Heat now had three originals back on deck, plus Jay Spell and Mike Halby.

Tragically, Bob's relationship with Susan was deteriorating at an accelerated pace, which caused him to drink even more. One night a very drunken Bear crashed his VW van and the impact hurled him through the windshield. His nose and a cheekbone were broken, resulting in surgery on one of his eyes. He never regained his sweet expression. He may have been big and fat, but he was a good-looking man. Now he was no longer handsome.

It was the end of a false dawn: The star had burned out.

HELL IS JUST ON DOWN THE LINE

"The Bear" with his namesake.

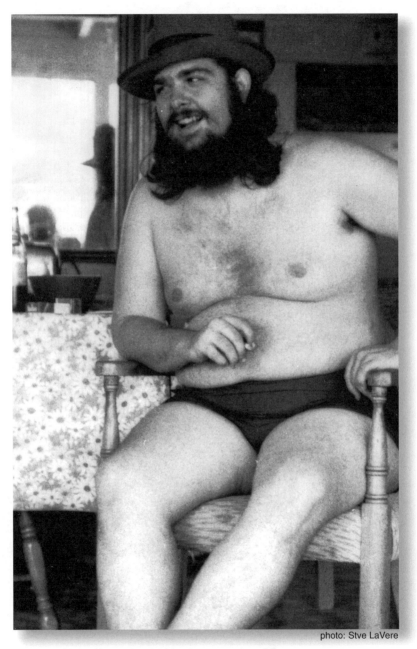

photo: Stve LaVere

The jovial friendly Bear

"La montaña humana del blues" (the human mountain of blues)

Once again we found ourselves without a bass player, so Jay Spell got in touch with a bass playing-buddy called John Lamb, a totally square Mormon from Salt Lake City and a comically out-of-place character, who quickly became horrified by our Canned Heat lifestyle.

Although Howard Wolf, with his tough, give-no-quarter Hollywood management style, was still our manager, he was running out of steam. I learned a lot from Howard. One day, while he was giving me detailed instructions for an upcoming tour, I asked: "Howard, why do you run the band the way you do?" Looking at me with steely eyes, he snapped: "This is Hollywood. The ocean is full of sharks...but I am the barracuda."

I didn't know it yet, but the first stop on the tour was to become a turning point not only for the band, but for me personally. Shortly before our appearance at the Keystone Club in Northern California, we were hanging out in the dressing room, smoking a couple of joints, downing a few beers and starting to feel that heightened sense of excitement performers get just before they go on stage. I hated to break the mood, but I reminded Bob, "Howard gave us very specific instructions: 'Get paid before you play'." A dark look crossed Bob's face. He hated all the squabbling over money. More importantly, he didn't want to be denied a chance to drink in the adulation of our diehard fans; he didn't want to miss a chance to boogie with the people.

As Bob started for the stage, I grabbed his arm: "We've got to find out what's going on with the money."

In the promoter's office, I put it on the line: "We're not going to play until we get paid."

The promoter glared at me like a heavy in a B-movie: "Do you know who you're talking to?"

"Hey, I like you. We like playing in your clubs. But we gotta get our money first."

Bear couldn't stand the face-off. "Come on, Fito, let's go play."

"Shut the fuck up, Bob. I'm calling our manager," I said, reaching for the phone.

"Howard, we haven't gotten paid, but Bob says we should play or the promoters will blackball us at his other clubs."

The Barracuda isn't about to budge. "I don't give a fuck who they are or how many clubs they own, Fito. They've been messing with me for weeks over the deposit and they still haven't paid it. Don't

258

Bob, shortly before his death. The abuse was showing

play until you get paid. "

As I hung up the phone, it was clear I wasn't about to budge either.

The promoter casually reached over to open a floor safe: "Hey, guys, relax. Look. Everything's cool." We could see stacks of bills neatly bundled.

Sure that everything was settled, Bob headed for the stage, at which point the promoter quickly closed the safe.

I insisted: "Sorry, but we need to get paid BEFORE we play."

Opening the safe for a second time, the owner grabbed a bunch of bills and threw them at me: "You guys will never work for me again."

Thinking about it now, it's pretty funny. Me, the Mexican mouse, roaring at Bob, the elephant. It was the first time anyone had overruled the Bear in front of outsiders. Today, it gives me a certain satisfaction knowing that Canned Heat has outlived all three of the promoters' clubs.

During this unruly back-office showdown, it was clear that the torch had been passed. I was in charge, not Bob. The Bear would sing on, lurching toward his destiny, still hungrily seeking love and sensation, still starved for the orgiastic togetherness that in the golden years could unite all of us playing old records in the living room, or a stadium packed with thousands of stomping fans swept up by a thunderstorm of blues. But right now the band was barely clinging to life, kept alive only by willpower. The bad boys need a grownup to take care of business or these real life blues brothers are dead for sure. And I, once the new kid at the door, get the job by default.

I was not only born to play with Canned Heat, I was born to keep it alive.

By now, Howard Wolf, who would go on to represent Hollywood heavy-hitters like Henry Mancini, had lost interest in the band so we decided to let him go. Mike Halby introduced us to an agent called Eddie Haddad and to show what he could do, Eddie set up a month-long tour of U.S. military bases that became a touring nightmare because the military wouldn't pay to transport our instruments or roadies.

At each gig we were forced to pick up instruments from local service bands, which meant playing with different instruments at each location. To make matters worse, sometimes we played two sets a night in different places—one for the officers and another for the enlisted men. But we weren't about to complain. We all needed the money. Fortunately, the organizers assigned John Bell, an extremely efficient, very nice Brit with a great sense of humor, as our tour manager.

The first gig on the U. S. Armed Forces tour was Edwards Air Force Base in California. When it was time to leave the hotel for the performance, Bell arrived with these impeccably dressed, ramrod straight officers. After being introduced all around, we headed for the van.

Sitting there waiting, we realized: Bob was missing. Why isn't he here? Suddenly, Big Willie, our road manager, came rushing up shouting: "I cannot deal with this! Fito, you have to help me! You have to come up and help me dress Bob."

"What do you mean? We're already late. Everybody's waiting."

At this point, Bob was drunk all the time, day and night. Earlier that day, he was obviously smashed, but I expected him to be at least a little sober by now. But this time, he just couldn't sober up even if he wanted to, he was so ill.

Racing to Bob's room, Willie and I threw open the door. The Bear was on his knees in the center of the bed wrapped in a sheet, sobbing. There was shit all over the room, all over the bed and all over the sheet.

I couldn't believe it. "Bob, how in the hell did this happen?"

He cried even harder: "I can't stand it. I want to die."

Physically, he was so damaged he couldn't even hold his bowels. At the same time, he was so drunk he couldn't get washed and ready for the gig. We worked as fast as we could, but it still took us over 20 excruciating minutes to drag him to the shower, clean him up and then get him dressed.

Meanwhile, all the brass was waiting downstairs.

Here we were. The first stop on the tour and we're already late.

Of course, once Bob was washed up, he started yelling "fuck this mother-fucker," and "the attitude" started all over again. During the performance, he was still so drunk, so damaged, that he collapsed on the stage and we finished the set with him laying there—just like we did in Victorville.

Two days later we were off to Europe. Since I'm a military history freak, I was really looking forward to playing at bases that were crucial in World War II. I got a lot more than I bargained for.

At Alconbury, an air base made famous during the Battle of Britain, I discovered that "swinging" was a favorite pastime. I guess all these young people were bored and taking drugs, so recreational sex was a natural next step. In fact, there may have been as much swinging inside the close-knit military complex as there was in the music business. We found that once you were in the network, you could have a great time with service wives whose hobby was group sex and whose husbands got a kick out of it.

After our performance at Alconbury, an Air force sergeant who was a big Canned Heat fan brought his very attractive wife up to our dressing room. "This is my wife. She's going to go back with you guys. Please take care of her and treat her nice." (This was the first time a guy actually offered us his wife for a couple of days.)

Back at our hotel in London, Henry and our new-found-friend started swilling Jack Daniels. Eventually, we ended up doing all kinds of things with her, including fucking her with a banana while licking her clit. When we woke up in the morning, we looked around for the delectable dildo only to discover that the omnivorous Bear noticed it earlier on the night table and automatically scarfed it.

Our next gig was Bitburg, the famous German Luftwaffe base where Ronald Reagan laid a wreath of flowers as a gesture of reconciliation with Germany; it caused all kinds of criticism from the Jewish community because a couple of SS soldiers were also buried there alongside the Wermacht pilots and soldiers. We, of course, were there in the late '70s before Reagan and at the height of The Cold War. The drug scene was very heavy and I was amazed to discover that some of the guys who were assigned to assemble and maintain small nuclear warheads were sitting right here in our dressing room after the concert getting ripped out of their heads on hashish and marijuana just a few hours before they'd be zipping around the Fulda Pass practicing with live ammunition.

"Shit man, tomorrow we have maneuvers with our tank platoon. It's already two in the morning and here we are getting fucked up with the Canned Heat."

Coughing out a cloud of smoke, Bob passed the chillum: "Don't worry, bro. Take another drag."

Out the dressing room window I could see the tanks lined up and ready for action. One thought crossed my mind: I sure hope the

Russians aren't planning to attack us tomorrow. It was funny and scary at the same time.

Our last night in Europe was spent partying with the secretaries and wives of NATO honchos. The next day we were leaving for the longest flight I'd ever taken, from Brussels to Manila in the Philippines.

At the beginning of the USAF tour, we were skeptical about the kind of reception we would receive because Canned Heat was basically very anti-establishment. We were war protesters. We were anti-Vietnam guys. But as the tour went on, I remembered what my teacher told me: "Don't worry. You are going to make people feel. They'll do anything you want."

After years of being stuck in military bases all over the world, these audiences were ready for anything that brought them a touch of America. We were playing the blues and barrel house piano, boogie-woogie music and they loved it. In officers' clubs everywhere we went, wives of admirals, generals, and other high ranking officers would come on to us—some of them a little drunk—grabbing our legs, hugging us and thanking us for being there. It was obvious these women weren't part of the establishment and didn't give a shit. They wanted to boogie. And we made it happen.

My teacher was right. Music was the answer.

Towards the end of this hellish 30-gig tour, we found ourselves in Okinawa, a 794 square mile island off the southern tip of Japan famous for one of the worst World War II battles in the Pacific Theater. On a beautiful, sunny afternoon while I was walking next to the swimming pool at the Hilton Hotel where we were staying, I was surprised to see an old Samurai-style Japanese cemetery right there on the hotel grounds. As I was reflecting on the 162,000 Japanese who died defending the island and the 11,000 Americans who died taking it, my thoughts were abruptly interrupted by the sound of five amphibious assault vehicles popping up out of the surf. Suddenly, the hatches were thrown open and I could see these killer Marines with their tattoos, huge muscles and strong necks. I'm thinking, these are the bad-asses we're going to be entertaining tonight; these guys are going to identify with Canned Heat, even though they know we don't support everything they believed in. We have a common bond: We are bad and they are bad.

Okinawa carried a heavy vibe and I felt it that night. By the third song, the Marines were starting to get out of control. To make matters worse, Bear was really feeding off it and getting loose. "You Marines, you bad-ass, mother-fuckers, you think you are bad? We're going to show you what bad really is. We're going to play such fucking boogie, you'll get down and never come back."

By now we were really getting it on. Unfortunately, Jay still hadn't gotten used to the full-blast, fry-the-amps, boogie-rock that is Canned Heat's specialty. And being blind, he developed particularly sensitive hearing so the volume was piercing his pain threshold. Desperately trying to shield his ears, he scrunched beneath the piano and played from the floor, reaching up and over the keyboard with his right hand while holding his left over his ear. All we could see was his disembodied hand plunking back and forth on the keys in a hopeless attempt to finish the gig.

I developed a lot of respect for Jay on this trip. He had to memorize the layout of every hotel room in order to find the shower, the electrical outlets and the light switches. He was just amazing, traveling under such difficult conditions with all the one-night stands. He was totally self-sufficient, absolutely immaculate and in many ways he did his job better than people who could see.

Meanwhile, the music was blasting away and John Bell came up behind me and started shouting, but I could only catch a few words: "Tell, Bob..." and then something about "chicks." Actually, he was yelling:

"Tell Bob to COOL IT because there's a general here with his wife and kids and some chicks." It seemed the general in charge brought his family to see the band, much like our infamous performance in Portland, Oregon, where parents brought their teenyboppers not knowing what Canned Heat was really about, not realizing they were going to encounter a sour/drunk Bob Hite and a very crazed band.

By now, beer cans were flying all over the place and Bob was not cooling it. In fact, he was getting worse and the Marines were right with him! The Bear had no way of knowing a general was in the audience. All he could see from the stage was a bunch of drunken Marines going nuts, so he roared into the mike: "Fuck this, fuck that." The audience (at least, the majority) was caught up in the excitement, screaming "Right On!" back at the stage.

Without warning, two dozen MPs swarmed the auditorium and the stage. An officer, pointing an index finger at us, barked: "Stop playing."

And we did. Instantly. Right in the middle of "Dust My Broom."

He grabbed the mike from Bob: "Everybody. Back to barracks."

The general must have been very pissed off and very disappointed. Our tour manager and our agent were mortified.

The tour ended in Osaka, Japan and we headed for Tokyo to catch our awful 15-hour flight home. The six hour bus ride to the airport was a total nightmare through horrendous traffic. By the time we finally arrived at our terminal, I was totally exhausted and starting to get dizzy. This quickly escalated into a sense of being overwhelmed by the crowds, the lines, and the congestion.

The flight was quite uneventful until I reached U.S. Customs in Hawaii. When I opened my briefcase to get out my passport, my wallet was missing. Vanished. Gone. So was all the money I'd earned, along with $1,500 that belonged to the band, plus my Mexican Military Card, my ID, and my Mexican Passport. I was furious. I wanted to kill myself.

After the month-from-hell, I wound up back in Los Angeles without a penny to show for the experience. Worse yet, I was in debt. I would lay on my bed crying. The tour was to be our big break: I was to come back home with three thousand dollars to pay my mortgage and a few bills, buy a little grass, lay back a little. But here I was, owing the band $1,500.

Not surprisingly, Lamb and Spell quit the minute they got their feet back on American soil. Frankly, I was surprised they even finished the tour. They were quiet, decent guys.

You need an outlaw mentality to survive with Canned Heat.

So the '80s began with all of us looking straight down a well-greased chute to hell.

The Bear was a mountain of ruin. His ankles were shattered, his face had been pulped by the two car crashes and his system was stewing in alcohol and drugs, as Susan lead him into deeper and deeper pits of debauchery.

He got into fights. He was hoarse all the time. He got even fatter and farted continuously, like some sort of berserk outboard engine.

Finally, even the Bear's spirit was starting to break. He wanted to be loved. Hell, it was only a little over 10 years ago that he was loved by millions. He ate it up. He wallowed in it. That was why he played the music, so the people would love him. That's why he invited footloose musicians to his house and played records for them all night long and why he got up on stages and sang till the club owners turned off the lights to make him stop. He hungered to make people happy and educate them about the blues.

It was beginning to come through to him that maybe he would never be loved by that many people again, that maybe our time was truly past. A lot of the '60s musicians that were there with us in the golden age were gone by now. Morrison, Wilson, Hendrix and Joplin. His remarks about dying increased.

"Maybe Alan had the right idea, Fito. Alan was up there on the stage at Woodstock. Alan heard all those fuckers cheering, man. He was there for all the fun, but he'll never have to play bars next to junk yards, man."

During an appearance in a small night club in Northern California, Bob shot one of his long, rowdy, loud farts on the stage, but this time he had the bright idea of putting the microphone next to his ass to amplify the noise. Laughing like hell at a table down front was a towering outlaw motorcyclist wearing a denim jacket with the arms cut off and patches and chains here and there. The biker, who stood about 6'4" and weighed over 400 pounds, had a face like a flamed-out boxer, a face I knew. He had been showing up at our gigs all over California and Nevada for months. I remembered seeing him talking to the Bear at the "Tribal Stomp" in Berkeley, the anniversary of the birth of the Avalon Ballroom organized by founder Chet Helms. The Bear said the biker was a fan, a really gung-ho fan, who had given him some righteous coke. He was putting a lot of miles on his Harley just following us around. Bear got the idea he owned a biker bar in a small town on the northern California coast and wanted us to play there someday.

After the performance, the biker looped his arm over the Bear's shoulder and shuffled him off into the dark, initiating Bob's last—characteristically hair-raising—management decision. It never occurred to me that the little chat the biker was having with the Bear that night, while waking him up with line after line of cocaine, was going to determine the future of the band for the next couple years.

Back in L.A., Bear gave me a call.

"Fito, I think I know how to get the band moving again."

I waited to hear whatever brainstorm Bear had come up with to make yet another try at a comeback. Now that we owned the band together, he was consulting me. I felt good about that but I didn't see anything coming our way to be optimistic about. I couldn't see any way out of the band's slide, but I was glad the Bear was accepting me as his partner. He had a respect for my business ability. I wasn't rich, but I had my nice house with a recording studio in Mar Vista, some rent coming in from other properties, a car, a motorcycle, girls I could afford to treat nicely. I was healthy, and although I had probably tried just about everything, I wasn't addicted to anything.

Bear knew by this time that if Canned Heat was going to survive, I was going to have to run it. It wasn't just that I had it together and he didn't. We loved each other and we still loved our idea of the music. We were the survivors, us and Henry and Larry. But Larry was back with the Hollywood Fats band and Henry had married again and moved to South Carolina where he was going through his "southern roots" phase. Henry had become a born-again Confederate, a Dixie chauvinist. He joined the Ku Klux Klan, which even by Henry's standards was truly bizarre behavior for a man who made his living playing music created by black geniuses. We had to fly him in from his chitlins and grits refuge for every gig or rehearsal.

"We need a new manager," The Bear said. "I sort of hired one."

"Who?"

"The biker."

"The biker? The giant guy with the real long hair and tattoos who's been following us around on a Harley? The guy who looks like a locomotive with feet? Bob, this is your idea of a manager? Somebody to deal with the record company accountants, the straight businessmen, the club owners, things like that?"

"Fito, you gotta talk to this guy. He has a lot of really great ideas. He believes in us. He knows what we should be doing. He understands our music and he really wants to be our manager, which is more than you can say for those other assholes in the suits. I told him I thought it was a good idea, but that you have to go along with it."

"Okay. What happens now?"

"What happens now is he's coming over to your house this afternoon to talk to you. Promise me, you'll listen to him. Just listen to him. Give him a fair chance."

That afternoon the biker showed up at my house, sat down and casually laid out two lines of cocaine big enough to wire all of Mar Vista for the rest of the year. I'm thinking: "Am I going to have to finish this talking to this guy?"

Later on, I found out that was the way he often got what he wanted in business dealings—just lay down blow until the other person wound up so loaded they'd agree to anything. Things always seem so clear when you're wired on coke, even the nuttiest ideas are so easy to understand and so reasonable.

But I have a rule against mixing business with pleasure. This guy had a big selling job to do if he wanted to convince ME he should be our manager, and I'm not getting a heart attack from his cocaine while he tries. Also, the whole thing with Pamela left me with an ulcer that didn't like cocaine. I take a couple of hits now and then but stay far away from that big coke rush that kills people.

I was thinking, fuck, I don't want to do this. I don't even want to talk to him. This long-haired, rowdy biker, this is no proper manager—not like Skip and Howard Wolf and all those Hollywood sharks. Then he started telling me his plans, how we're going to be stars again, how he's going to have me driving a Rolls Royce, telling me he's absolutely convinced Canned Heat is going right back up to the top, we just need him to make it happen.

"Hey, c'mon, man," I said. "Look at Bear, look what kind of shape he's in. Hell, look at all of us. Look at the times. Look at the record companies, look at what they're buying. We can play, we can get some gigs, we still have a lot of fans. But being rock stars and all that, that's fucking over, man. Look at the stars today—they dye their hair blonde and wear women's makeup and white three-piece suits. We can never be part of that. Can you see Bear dressing like Boy George? Can you imagine Henry trying to look like David Bowie?"

"It doesn't matter, Fito. NONE of that matters. I'm going to put everything into this and we're going to fucking DO it. There's no other band like Canned Heat. There are millions of people out there who need your music. You play music that's so old and yet so new, and it says things so many of the rest of us want to hear. You guys are great and I'm going to make the world see that."

I was sort of stunned. I was used to fans, we still had plenty, but this guy, this hulking menace, he's just on fire with how great we are. I listened to him and I thought: this guy believes in Canned Heat more than any of us.

"What about resources? Backing? This is a tough business and it takes money to get ahead. Can you back us with whatever you make off some biker bar up north?"

"Fuck the bar. That isn't where the backing comes from."

He was a Hells Angel and had backing from several other outlaw clubs. He also had other business dealings, which I didn't have to know about. Maybe somebody else would have been scared off. I was intrigued. After all, by this time, Canned Heat had a reputation as a bunch of hot-wired druggies who played to exorcise their personal demons instead of for money, with a wildly unpredictable lead singer who sometimes insulted his audiences.

Okay. Thinking about it in a detached, business-like way, what could be so wrong about throwing in with the outlaw bikers?

After all, they're another bunch of long-haired guys with personal demons, who despise disco music and its androgynous pussy fashions. We've always had a lot of bikers among our fans. "The Harley Davidson Blues" that James Shane wrote for the "New Age" album in 1973 is one of our most durable numbers; we get calls for it all the time.

With the bikers, we would be going where we were wanted instead of pounding on locked doors. And our rep as outlaws? The dope, the crimes? Hell, that just made us regular guys.

Besides, what did we have to lose? It couldn't get any crazier than it was already, could it? (The answer was yes, but that took a while to learn.)

I asked the biker whether he really wanted to get into this tough business, telling him the story about Howard Wolf being ruthless and his reply: "Because this is Hollywood and the ocean is full of sharks. But I'm okay because I'm a barracuda."

"Fuck that," the biker said. "I'm the killer whale."

So I asked the 400-pound, pony-tailed, tattooed outlaw his strategy for making the band successful again, and he answered: "Strategy? I don't know nothin' about strategy. I'm just gonna push."

He was known forevermore as "The Push."

In truth, we never knew his real name. He gave us a name, but it didn't take long to figure out that it was a phony. The Push seemed to have a lot of names, depending on where he was and who he was with. His bros in the Angels called him by a different name than his girlfriends used. He had a driver's license in a name I'm SURE wasn't his.

Well, we all had our little idiosyncrasies in Canned Heat. If our manager wanted a mobile identity, so be it. Nobody asked him why he needed one. The Push was not the kind of guy you asked real personal questions.

He was so delighted when I told him he was hired, he picked me up by the shoulders, lifted me a good three feet in the air and kissed me on the forehead. "The Push" was in.

His first move was to bring in a bass player, one of his biker friends, a huge Chicano called Ernie Rodriguez. He was not as good as Larry, but then I always had trouble finding anybody even close to Larry. But Ernie had a good personality; he was reliable, he looked good and he sang great.

Shortly after he joined the Canned Heat family, The Push and Mike Halby negotiated the production of "Kings of the Boogie" with Jerry Barnes, a top-notch engineer and manager of the United Western Recording Studios in Hollywood. Unfortunately, this was to be Bob's last performance on a record. Maybe he felt it. He was already on the path.

I suggested an idea for the album based on the obscure blues tune, "I Tried" by Larry Davis, one my favorites from Duke Records in Texas. After Bob put his words to it, and we added a couple of breaks, it turned into a prophetic, gritty message. It was the last song Bob wrote and recorded. It still gives me goose bumps to hear it.

My life keeps me worrying
Hells just on down the line.
But I keep on speeding,
Fast life is a dog-gone crime.
Drinking rotgut whiskey,
Sniffing good cocaine,
I'm always getting in trouble
I think I'm going insane.

Meanwhile, Bear's natural inclination to hurtle out of control down the slippery slope of life was getting a horrifying boost from Susan, who was even farther out of control than he was.

Susan was a nice woman when I first met her—not very well educated or classy, but pleasant—although always a little spacey.

Like, shortly after she gave birth to their daughter, Roseanne, she told me: "It was a groove, I was on acid the whole time. It was like the whole world was coming out of me, like I personally created everything, like I was God the Mother."

Well, maybe that was a lot of fun for Susan, a milestone taste of the divine and all, but how much fun was it for Roseanne, who must have been squeezed down the birth canal with a jolt of acid in her blood? Psychiatrists are still debating just how traumatic it is to be born and how the experience affects you psychologically for the remainder of your life. It certainly can't be good to go through it with your unformed little baby brain hopping and popping with acid visions.

Susan had two children, Shawn and Daphne, from a previous marriage with Richard "Get Yourself Together" Moore, a nickname he picked up when he started with us as a young recording engineer on our LP "Living the Blues." Later, Richard was to become a well-known teacher and outstanding recording engineer.

Susan not only got heavily into drugs, she was using even more than the Bear. God help the Hite family. He was actually the more responsible person, compared to Susan. They were living on food stamps and I loaned them money now and then, especially when Bear would tell me his electricity was being cut off and the kids' food would spoil in the fridge. Things continued to spiral out of control. Bear cracked up his Volkswagen van, smashing his face on the windshield and then Susan wrecked their other car.

One day I got a frantic call from the Bear, totally freaking out. "I don't know what to do, Fito. She's gone into a coma and I can't get her out."

"How did it happen?"

"Well, we were shooting some cocaine."

I was furious. "What do you mean? Don't you know how bad it is for you to shoot that shit?"

I was deep in my co-dependent phase, always lecturing Bob, always trying to convince him he was really screwed up and should try to pull out of it, to get a grip, always telling the roadies not to get the Bear any drugs, not to bring booze to Henry. It was like trying to stop a wave from the ocean with your two hands. But I loved them both. I felt I had to do something.

Susan lay in the house in a coma for about two days before Bear did anything about it. He kept saying a doctor friend of his had told

271

him she'd come to on her own. All this time, of course, the kids were there, playing in the other rooms, friends were coming by, getting loaded with Bob. The house was total chaos. Finally, there was no other choice but to take Susan to the hospital.

Bear called me from County-USC Hospital in east L.A.: "She needs brain surgery."

He didn't have any money; he was going to have to get the bill paid by Medi-Cal. A few years earlier he was a star, filling arenas from Woodstock to Berlin. Now, he was living on food stamps and they were going to drill open his wife's skull on welfare.

When I arrived at the hospital, the Bear was walking slowly around the lobby, looking totally dazed. "They sucked her brain out," he said, crying.

I don't know the medical details, but she'd had some sort of mild stroke from the cocaine overdose, rupturing a vein or an artery in her brain. He said they used a vacuum hose to suck out dead tissue. When she finally came to, she couldn't recognize Bear or anybody else, not even her children. Bob was devastated.

"They got the good stuff with the bad stuff," he wept, which wasn't very sophisticated as medicine, I suppose, but was really prophetic. Because if Susan was destructive even before she got her skull sucked, she was hell on a lightning bolt after the operation.

It was a big day for Bear when he came into her room and she looked up and said "Bob? You're Bob, aren't you? Big, old funny Bob." The big guy was so overcome he couldn't speak. He had really been afraid she would never again know who he was. And when it came to being loved, loved as a man, she was all he had left. By the time she could go home, she was walking again and could recognize most of the people she knew before the operation.

I went to Mexico City for a couple of weeks and the first thing I did when I got back to LA was to go over to the Bear's place. Susan met me at the door and grabbed me, yelling over her shoulder, "Hey, Fito's back." Then she gave me a big kiss. Not a welcome-home kiss, which I expected, but a real deep French kiss, shoving her tongue as far inside my mouth as she could. When I tried to break loose she grabbed my hips and started humping me, giggling and shouting, "C'mon, Fito, let's see it. C'mon, ya little Messican prick. Let's see yer little Messican prick."

She grabbed my crotch, hard, squeezing viciously.

I tried to push her away—she had an insane strength—when

Bear came in from the kitchen, wearing only a pair of brown, baggy shorts. He looked at me, and a strange expression flickered across his face—disgust? resignation? It vanished quickly and he just plopped heavily down on a couch, his big belly quivering and his eyes closed. He was drunk.

So was she.

Drunk, stoned and bad crazy.

Bob had asked me to visit this time because he wanted to play some records and do a little research like we used to do in the old days. Unfortunately, we'd be listening to a record and Susan would come charging into the room, screaming at him, things like: "You're an ugly fat bastard with a tiny dick who can't even fuck any more." At first he tried to ignore her, but she chased him from one side of the house to the other, shrieking at him while he tried to get away. It was total chaos.

That frightful, sad day I realized how much our old record listening parties had degenerated. The sense of communion, the education, the beauty of it all was finished. The communal meetings of sharing music and learning from Bear had turned into drunkenness and madness. The sense of grace was gone.

Somehow after the operation, Susan became a complete madwoman. A whole new Susan, a much worse Susan than the one with all the brain cells. She took to hanging out in bars, picking up guys. She must have seemed like an erotic dream come true to those guys. She was still in her early 30s, not bad looking, wildly aggressive sexually, the dream girl you never, ever meet, who walks up and grabs your dick without saying a word. I sometimes wondered what those guys felt like when her hair fell forward in bed and they could see the Frankenstein stitches up the back of her skull, feel this sort of empty depression under it. When they realized that this was a crazy woman with a head full of mush. Half full, only.

That fateful day, Bob cooked a pot of chili just like the old times and he wanted me to stay for dinner. But after that incredible display of family dysfunction, I got up and said good-bye. We didn't even hear a complete song. I walked out of his house leaving him in sadness and shame, half drunk with his crazy wife.

I didn't want to see the Bear anymore after that. The band had very few gigs and every time I saw him and Susan together, it turned into a nightmare, with them getting stoned and drunk and screaming at each other.

I figured she should be put in a hospital somewhere, but then, the Bear should have been in an institution himself. Two addictive personalities out of control. Who was going to take care of who? It was like a whirlpool, getting tighter and tighter, faster and faster. Finally, a social service worker came by during one of their stoned fights. She went right to a judge and got an order to take their kids away, putting them in some county care/foster home program.

That did it for Bob. It gave him the strength to do something. He knew things had to change. He was not a fool, he was still an intelligent man. And he loved his kids. Losing them hurt him immensely. His home was so important to him. In a way, he was this old-fashioned guy who got all sentimental over love songs, who wanted to live in a house with a white picket fence with his adoring wife and great kids who loved him. Papa Bear and his cubs.

At the same time, he wanted to live the life of a blues singer, to be on the road with the band, drinking, taking dope, grabbing groupies, belting out songs 'til dawn to cheering crowds, the life of the party night after night.

Instead, he's got Susan drinking straight bourbon to get down, shooting coke to get back up, fucking anyone else she can get her hands on and screeching at him that he's too fat to fuck and his dick's too skinny.

When they took his kids, he finally kicked Susan out and told her he was getting a divorce. It took two of the Push's big biker friends to carry her screaming out of the house. With all she had done to him, the breakup still left Bob hurting deeply. This, of course, just made him drink more and take more drugs. He cried all the time, "I wanna die, I wanna die."

One hot, summer day he asked me to come over and give him a ride to one of our rare gigs. The night before, while he was asleep, Susan broke into the house, took what little money he had and drove away with his car.

The guys in the band began talking about taking care of Susan. We all figured there was no band without The Bear, and there wasn't going to be any Bear if Susan kept bleeding him. There was even talk about kidnapping her and driving her to her family in El Paso. The plan was to turn her over to them and explain that she was very crazy and would surely kill herself if she ever got back to California. It was a desperate time, and there were those of us who loved the Bear that much.

Meanwhile, The Bear set up a meeting with former Canned Heat agent Irv Azoff, now a Hollywood big shot. The Bear was excited when Azoff agreed to meet with him. He was convinced that the clouds were parting, that Azoff would use his connections and power to help the band get a new start.

He arrived at Azoff's office at the appointed time with Mike Halby in tow. A recharged Bear told the secretary: "Hi, I'm The Bear."

Puzzled, the secretary said: "Who?"

"I'm The Bear from Canned Heat."

"Who, from Canned what?"

"I have an appointment with Irv Azoff today at 3."

To which she replied: "Irv? Irv is not even in town."

Devastated, Bear took the only money he had—cash he'd hid from Susan in order to get the electric power turned back on at his house—and spent it on a gram of cocaine, beginning his last binge.

Bob showed up at the Palomino that night already pretty drunk, but the band sounded brilliant in the first set. A tough band—Mike Halby, Ernie Rodriguez, Henry Vestine, The Bear and me.

The Bear jumped on stage and was spraying attitude all over. "Fuck this place. We are bad motherfuckers and you people here, you are going to see some bad shit tonight, the real fuckin' stuff, the real boogie."

The place was maybe 70 percent full, which was good for those days. We didn't realize that this was one sign that the long, awful disco times were coming to an end, that the people were coming back for us, getting down again, out for live bands and boogie. And here we were, this sort of wounded band, this name from the Stone Age that struggled to keep from sinking in the swamp through this whole decade, this whole fucked era.

And there was Bob right in front of them, the legendary Bear himself, the fantastic fat man of all those stories they'd heard, erupting on them like a volcano: "Now, you motherfuckers, you're going to see the real thing. We are the Canned Heat and we are b.a.a..a..d."

And he was right. We opened up the gates for them that night, gave them the genuine Canned Heat *pachanga,* right over the edge.

During the break between the first and second sets, we went outside where there were some tables and chairs, to smoke some joints with a few friends and fans. One of them had a little vial of heroin.

I don't do heroin, I don't like what it does to me. I'm afraid of it. I saw what it did to Pam and to the guys in the Rolling Stones and to lots of other friends and lovers. But I have to admit, I took a little hit that night. We were playing good, we were in the groove. We felt confident and tough and like really bad dudes. So if we screwed up our heads a little, maybe we'd play even better.

We're on our home turf. When it's all over, I can just go home and crash with my girlfriend Michelle. (Shortly after all this was over, she tried to kill me, but that's another story.)

As the Bear ripped the vial from my hand, I told him "Hey, this is strong stuff." I had taken a little tiny piece up my nose, about the size of half a matchhead, and felt it right away, a sort of sick dizziness. I was already sorry I took it.

But Bob didn't give a shit. He's drunk, he's rolling, he's doing the Bear thing. He grabbed the vial and just, whoooooooosh, sucked the whole vial of smack up his nose.

"Hey! Don't do that," I said.

It was too late. The vial was empty.

"This shit is not even going to get me high," he said. He's laughing. He's growling like the Bear.

"That's very dangerous," I warned.

I wasn't thinking about anything really permanent happening to him, I was thinking about him going into a coma and ruining the set again, the way he did many times before. Here we had some people to listen to us for a change, and they were really up for us. We could still hear them clapping and cheering inside.

The Palomino was a famous place, not some junkyard toilet on a two-lane road in the desert. We could get our careers back on track, if we built up fans in places like this, but it won't happen if we screw up another 10 years.

But I wasn't in charge of the band, The Push was. He was there and he was pissed off that Bear took the heroin. In the biker culture, heroin is looked down on, *verboten*. Guys like The Push figure real men take speed, smack is for losers. The Push knew Bear too well to waste time blaming him, but he wanted to find the guy who brought the heroin "and fuck him up right now."

Too late. Bear was too far gone to sing the next set. We walked him around, we walked him into the dressing room, trying to keep him on his feet.

And then came the true Canned Heat touch. Sort of funny in a way. A couple of bikers were hanging out in the dressing room. "Is he too fucked to sing?" one of them asked.

"Don't worry, man. We'll fix him right up. He's got to sing."

And under his nose they stuck a mirror with two giant lines of cocaine, each one almost as long as my foot. Either one of those lines would have given me a heart attack.

"This will straighten him right out, man," one of the bikers said. He and his buddy grabbed The Bear, who by now was just a zombie, and they stuck a straw in his nose and the platter of coke under it. Bob did what he always did, maybe only by reflex.

He inhaled it all.

I was worried about our next set in five minutes and there he was passing out again.

Well, we were used to this. And he was not actually out cold yet, he was sort of stumbling and mumbling.

In all this confusion, there was one voice of reason. Sonny Barton, a friend/partner of The Push and a former president of the Galloping Gooses, really understood the gravity of the situation, unlike the rest of us who didn't realize this was an issue of life and death. More than once, he said: "This man has to be taken to a hospital." We heard him, but no one was listening.

The Push turned to Jorge Reyes and Pepe Carcamo, a couple of Mexican kids, friends of mine who had a nice big van and knew where I lived: "You guys take Bob to Fito's house so Susan cannot find him and fuck with him. Give him a massage, feed him something, stay with him all the time."

Of course, I already had Henry with all his problems staying with me, so now I'll have both problems living in my house. I could have refused but we weren't like that. We were like a family, like your own blood.

In the dressing room, some girls were also waiting for us, so I put them to work giving Bear a massage, kneading this semi-conscious mountain of beard and flesh. I looked at him: "You're not going to be able to perform now, right? You are not going to be able to play the set, so I'm sending you home."

He could not speak very well, but he could see. He gripped my arm very hard for a long time, for maybe two minutes, and said something like, "I'm leaving."

It was very heavy.

I didn't understand at the time; but now I think I do. It's always painful for me to think about, but maybe Bob knew what was coming. I think maybe he felt death closing in, that maybe he knew this time The Bear had finally found his cave, his long sleep.

My manager said "he was leaving you the band." I don't know if he was doing that, or trying to say: "I'm dying, you're on your own, Fito." Or maybe he was just trying to tell me we'd have to get through the next set without him again.

When I die, if I ever find him again, I'll ask him.

If we'd known, we'd have called the paramedics, but he didn't look any worse than he did on hundreds of other nights. He was able to sit up in the van. He couldn't speak but he could understand what we said to him.

As the van pulled out with Bear wobbling in the back seat, we headed back to play the second set.

Good set, too. So good we got a standing ovation. I have to admit, I went home wondering if Canned Heat could exist without Bob.

Actually, I was feeling good, a little high from the great set and the dope, and I had Michelle with me; we were going to go home and get it on and have a good time. I figured I'd deal with my new roommates later, the problem bros, Henry and Bob.

Turning from Palms Avenue to Redwood in Mar Vista, I spotted a patrol car and an ambulance parked in front of my house. I looked at Michelle and Henry. "Fucking Bear! What kind of shit did he get me into now?"

The two Mexican kids came running out in shock. "Bob is dead, Fito."

It was like a building fell on me.

These guys were friends I trusted and still do. They said that the Bear was out cold, snoring, as they swung onto the San Diego Freeway to Mar Vista, but he suddenly began making a choking noise, like "Uggghhh uuuuggghh." They were desperate, but unsure what to do. Actually, they were very close to a hospital, the Veteran's Hospital in Brentwood. But being two guys from Mexico, they didn't know that.

Pepe, who was a masseur for a football team, started massaging Bob, hitting him in the heart, trying to do CPR. And he got him back. For a few minutes there, Bear was breathing again. But by the time they reached my house, that big heart had stopped for good.

According to the roadies, it took a half hour for the paramedics to arrive. Feature it: two dudes with heavy Mexican accents, calling from Mar Vista: "There is this guy, we think he's got a heart attack. We think he is dying."

I don't mean to say that the paramedics were racist, but you know how the system is. If you call from Beverly Hills or Bel-Air, you don't wait 30 minutes.

The paramedics tried to revive him but it was too late.

It was April 5, 1981. The Bear was gone. He was 38.

Inside the house, Bob's body was already covered. Years later the pictures of John Belushi's body being hauled out of the Chateau Marmont brought back this flood of memories of the night Bear died. I thought, there they are, the Blues Brothers, making big-bellied mounds under those death sheets.

Bob was the original blues brother. Belushi and Dan Akroyd in their movie were just caricatures of what Canned Heat was; but Belushi was into that role. He really "lived the life." All the way.

The cops, including some plainclothes vice guys, asked us all kinds of questions, to which of course we knew no answers. "Dracula? I've never even heard the name."

Did we know if he ingested any drugs?

Nope.

"Did you guys take any drugs yourselves?"

Nope.

"What did he die of?"

We weren't going to tell. With all the times we've been busted and harassed, after all that bullshit, cooperating would just get us in more trouble.

I didn't want to have to start answering questions, like who gave what drug to who, and how much, and where do we find these nice people so we can lock them up.

Who gave him the heroin? Who gave him the cocaine? Who is legally responsible for this, so we can charge them with murder? Who is morally responsible, so they can feel like killers all their lives?

Fuck that. The Bear did it. Nobody but him. Should I have grabbed his hand, pulled the dope away from him? If I had tried, he would have punched me out.

It was written. He wanted to go.

It was ironic: Too much fame had killed the Owl and lack of fame killed The Bear.

Alan took his bottle of pills up the hill because, among everything else that tortured him, he could not reconcile a rock star's life with his lonely fear for the trees and the moon. The Bear lived as recklessly as he could because once he had tasted the worship of thousands of fans, life had little meaning for him unless he could get another hit of that wonderful drug.

It was 5 in the morning and I was crying in the living room with Henry, crying for Bob and for Canned Heat as well. I remember that moment very well, because with Henry in a permanent mental haze, Canned Heat had dwindled down to me.

Me, the kid who got captured by all those American rock and blues records in Mexico City in the '50s, a time and place so far away by then that it might have been on another planet. Me, the quiet little drummer who couldn't speak English, who was naive enough to try to become a naturalized rocker in the land of an art form's birth. Me, who got off the train at Mexicali a nice middle-class Latino kid and became a man in this carnival of chaos, who had learned that death and the blues aren't married by accident.

It had come to me, all the glory and the misery, and I had to take it because I was the one who survived.

A part of me died with The Bear. I loved him and he loved me—probably even more than I loved him, because he did everything more. He drank more, ate more, doped more, sang more and died more.

But Canned Heat did not die with him.

Because far across the Pacific, the sun was rising in the west.

LET THE PUSH DO HIS DANCE

Fito with "The Push" and his "bag."

At this point, Canned Heat, by all logic, should have been dead. Even Top-40 rock bands from the '60s were having a hard go of it in this era, and the skull-and-crossbones life of ask-no-quarter pirates had finally killed both of Canned Heat's best known performers.

The Push and I had been negotiating a two month tour of Australia just before Bear's death, and even I believed the band was doomed now. But Peter Noble, the Australian promoter, assured us "The people will accept you as you are. Australia still loves Canned Heat."

So we hired Rick Kellogg to play harmonica, sing and help us finish "Kings of the Boogie." (Bob had done less than half the album.) Wolfman Jack wrote a touching dedication to The Bear on the liner notes. "...I really loved him...Bob's not gone...he's just backstage someplace...."

Henry called this incarnation of Canned Heat "The Mouth Band," because of its rowdy, beer-drinking, "let's party" mentality. We were a big hit with the Aussies, especially the bikers who typify the hard-living, blue-collar, white blues fans who are our natural audience. We began returning to Australia regularly, becoming one of the most popular blues/boogie bands in the country and using it as a springboard to return to Europe.

It took years before we could see this, but we had hit bottom and stopped sinking. It was my band now and I tried to bring a touch of order and responsibility to the group, to at least keep the chaos on the rails. Little by little, it paid off. From here began a long, grueling uphill road, keeping our old fans and building a generation of new ones, especially in Australia and Europe.

But all that was still far in the future.

One afternoon as I was mourning Bob's death, Michelle came to me in a rage about a petty argument she'd had with my friend and neighbor Jeff over some lost Quaaludes.

That was the final straw. I told her to leave. She was part of the chaos that was ravaging my life. She was madness.

When I first met her, she was an ex-call girl who went by the name of Pam. She was beautiful, bi-sexual, and a lot of fun, but she was not the kind of woman you want to spend the rest of your life with, in spite of all the sexual high jinx. After seeing the movie "Story of O," she developed a taste for spanking and S&M. Out of the blue, while high on drugs and sex, she decided she was French and wanted to be called Michelle. She even started speaking with an accent. It was clear that her life in the fast lane was beginning to take its toll.

The last straw came a few weeks after I kicked her out, when she tried to kill me loaded on speed and other drugs. She showed up at my house late at night brandishing a stolen .357 magnum. I grabbed both her hands and pushed her against the wall outside the entrance, fighting the strength of drug-madness. As I struggled to hold her hands flat against the wall so she couldn't aim the gun and shoot me, half-drunk Henry peeked out the door, stumbled towards her and gripped the pistol by the barrel, ripping it from her right hand.

After the police arrived, the officer who checked the gun, discovered that she had loaded the wrong ammo which is why I'm around to tell the story.

Meanwhile, the cop, who was trying to handcuff her, got caught up in a wrestling match with her screaming, kicking, biting, and resisting arrest. It was a sad thing to have happen to a nice woman who I cared for and thought of as a friend.

The incident reminded me of my father's observation about women: "The problem isn't getting them. The problem is getting rid of them."

Following the Bear's death and this attempt on my life, I was sick of Canned Heat, sick of the rock n' roll life, sick of crazy people around me killing themselves or trying to kill me, sick of L.A. with its lunatics and criminals, prostitutes and druggies. They had exhausted me. I had to get out. I also wanted my son to finish high school away from the mad whirlpool that had become our life in the city, so we moved to San Marcos, a small town in San Diego county, 120 miles south of L.A.

A few weeks after our return from Australia, The Push organized (if that's the word) his first Canned Heat tour, a circuit of biker bars in Northern California—his kingdom. In the years that followed, we may have hit just about every hardcore Harley hangout in the country. Push didn't think in terms of jet travel to giant concert halls, he thought in terms of driving to places he'd hang out in himself, someplace where he could wear his colors and nobody would stare because the other guys were wearing colors too.

As we're climbing into our van the first day of the tour, I asked The Push for our itinerary. For a split second he was puzzled.

"Itinerary?"

"You know, the list of places where we play, what time we go on, where we stay, how much we get. All that stuff."

"You just go where I tell you to go and play what I tell you to play. And don't worry about the money. If I have to, I'll pay you out of my own pocket. That's the itinerary."

The Push's management style was to approach bar owners and suggest that if they just play their cards right, and are real nice to him, the famous Canned Heat will perform, attracting outlaw cyclists and misfit fans from miles around. In effect, his standard tactic was to use the same approach that worked on the Bear—feed the club owner line after line of coke and speed until the prospect of packing his bar with bikers actually sounded like a WONDERFUL idea. When the Push got through with a lot of these club owners, they were so fucked up they'd agree to ANYTHING he said.

Even by the standards set by the band's previous managers, his organizational and administrative methods were unique. Draped over one shoulder he carried a massive leather pouch, a sort of rawhide mailman's bag stuffed with cocaine, speed and huge amounts of cash that appeared from god-knows-where, maybe $20,000 in small bills at a time. He rented a small car to use as an office, making the back seat his filing cabinet. As time went by, the car got funkier and funkier, the back seat filling with contracts, letters, receipts, sweat-encrusted T-shirts, paper cups, copies of "Easyriders" motorcycle magazine, empty beer bottles, half-eaten tacos, pictures of the band, pictures of his old lady and oily Harley parts.

From this point on, a lot of our income came out of the big bag. Money and drugs went into the bag. Money and drugs came out of the bag. Account books were sort of like his itineraries—it was all in The Push's head, or simply didn't exist.

But The Push was not a lout, not a barbarian. He may have been short on polish but he was very savvy, both intelligent and street-smart. He was a gentle giant who loved Canned Heat with a passion, loved it more than any of its members, and he loved being in the music business. With us, he figured he'd found a career, and he was just as seriously ambitious as Skip ever was.

The Push's style of life on the road left even us in awe. His favorite breakfast was to order a large pitcher of Pepsi Cola and a whole

My friend "Haakie" doing his thing

roast chicken. Out of the bag would come a quart of mayonnaise and a jar of white powder—speed. He'd put one or two heaping spoonfuls in the jug like sugar, and bury the chicken in mayonnaise. Then he'd scarf down the bird, chug-a-lug the meth-cola, pay the bill with a wad of currency from the big bag and we'd hit the highway.

The Push himself usually drove. When all that speed took effect, he'd crank the van, carrying eight people and pulling a trailer loaded with a ton of instruments and luggage, up to about 85 miles an hour and hold it there, eyes narrowed, jaw clenched. He saw it as his holy mission to get us to the next town as fast as possible. Nothing interfered.

One day, as we raced up Interstate 5 in a thunderstorm, our roadie Willie "The Block" points out the window: "We better stop at that station over there; we're almost out of gas."

The well-cranked Push, totally wired into his driving, growled back in exasperation: "I ain't got time to stop for gas!"

We all looked at each other, impressed by this display of Push-logic, but nobody dared to say a word. Of course, the van sputtered to a halt a few miles down the road. "Willie, go get some gas," snapped The Push. He was convinced that because Willie mentioned the low gas gauge, it was all Willie's fault.

Throughout our outlaw biker years, I carried a gun, a little .25 semi-auto pistol. The Push was always teasing me about its small caliber. "That's only a .25," he'd say. "If you shot me in the head with that, it would ricochet right off. All you'd do is get me mad."

One afternoon The Push was driving at top speed in the fast lane on the 101 Freeway when we came up on a guy tooling along in a beautiful, red convertible, a Jensen, one of those expensive British sports car that's not made any more. He got behind the car and gestured nicely with his hands for the guy to move over.

When the guy didn't pull into the right lane, The Push drove right up to the guy's bumper and hung there, clearly signaling that he wanted this guy to get out of the way. He was in one of his "don't have time to stop for gas" moods. If the Jensen driver knew what he had behind him, he probably would have pulled over and waited for us to get a mile ahead. Instead, the guy just hung in there. So The Push stuck his head out the window and politely yelled: "Get the fuck out of the way, you stupid asshole."

An obvious idiot, the driver of the car ignored us, reached down, grabbed something, and waved his left hand in the air. He was holding a brick and making throwing motions.

By now, both vehicles were going 80 miles an hour.

Great. A macho asshole. The kind of guy who sees an entire vanload of stoked rowdies barreling up behind him and decides to threaten them with a brick rather than let them pass.

The Push shouted: "Fito, give me your gun." You didn't argue with The Push in that mood. I handed him the gun.

He aimed at the brick waver and bellowed: "Come on, just try me."

Seeing the gun, the Jensen's driver swerved to the right, letting the van pass. Laughing uproariously, we took a look at the driver. His face had turned white.

Of course, the guy got off the freeway and immediately called the police. A short time later, a patrol car was following the van as we got to our exit. By now, I had disassembled the gun and put it among the drum parts where it would be hard to find.

Seeing the patrol car about to pull alongside, The Push jumped out and hid in the bushes, shouting: "Willie, you are me. You take over and you tell them you are me."

When we came to a stop in the theater parking lot, a lone, very nervous sheriff's deputy got out his car and approached the van with his revolver drawn. Peering inside, he shouted: "I want to see everybody's hands. And I want each of you to leave—one by one— from the front door. I want to see your hands at all times."

At gunpoint, everybody very slowly exited the van.

Within minutes, two other patrol cars arrived. Deputies had weapons drawn as we were being lined up against the side of the theater and searched. I tried explaining to the cop: "We don't really have a gun. Our roadie just held up his hand to simulate a pistol, like playing cowboys and Indians. The asshole in the Jensen just panicked."

Glancing towards the box office, I saw about 50 fans lined up to buy tickets for the evening's performance. Great! This was their introduction to the band playing here tonight, spread-eagled against the wall by a bunch of cops.

Unable to find a weapon after their rigorous search, the police cut us loose. As their patrol cars disappeared, The Push popped out of the bushes. "Willie, Willie." He shook his head. "You're always gettin' us in trouble. You gotta clean up your act." I think he meant it.

We couldn't help laughing the next morning when we spotted the headline on the Garberville newspaper: "Canned Heat Contained."

On the verge of our second tour with The Push, he impulsively— and optimistically—decided to spend thousands of dollars buying a 20-year-old bus, which he customized so the band could live in it while we toured.

This was not your grandfather's Winnebago. This was an old bus with wooden bunks and strange plumbing put together by his outlaw cyclist buddies. Ken Kesey would understand. I used to call it "The Dr. Zhivago bus" because it reminded me of the infamous train the movie hero took through the Urals during the Russian revolution.

The Push also hired "Weird Wayne" a jobless outlaw cyclist as the driver. I asked if the outlaw had all the proper licenses, training and experience to chauffeur the band on our upcoming tour. "Oh, fuck yes," The Push said. "He knows all that shit."

Climbing the grade out of L.A. on our way to the first gig in

Denver, the bus came to a wheezing halt. After repeated tries to get the old diesel started, Weird Wayne ran down the battery. He ordered us off: "It ain't happenin'. I'm gonna roll-start it in reverse."

Poised at the top of the pass on Interstate 10, the bus hurtled blindly backwards down the hill into the oncoming traffic.

Suddenly, he popped the clutch. BAM! The engine exploded in a blast of oil and parts, and the bus slowed to a halt beside the road. The driver got out, glaring at the black smoke pouring out of the engine compartment: "Well, shee-it...it works with Harleys."

Dana, our assigned tour manager and The Push's partner, pulled out a wad of cash the size of a baseball: "Here, you guys. Take a plane."

Another gig that stands out in my memory was the one The Push booked in the San Francisco area. It attracted Canned Heat's normal entourage of bikers, hippies and misfits. It wasn't a packed house, but our hardcore fans were there to show support. Several club owners were in the audience to audition us for future gigs, which made Push anxious because earlier in the day Henry was already pretty drunk. By the time we were getting ready to perform, he still seemed a little bombed. There's always a lot of pre-show tension in a dressing room and the last thing you need is a fucked up band member. It's bad enough to have someone fucked up while we're playing or after we've played, but before we play is total lunacy.

To this day, I don't remember where I got them or who gave them to me, but I could feel a couple of pills in my left pocket. I was sure they were uppers—Benzedrine or speed—so I passed them to Henry hoping they would sober him up a little.

Our performance resembled a Cheech and Chong comedy. Henry was swerving all over the place and eventually fell...Whamp!..right onto the left side of my drums. It turned out I gave him the wrong drug, a downer called Thorazine, a really strong anti-psychotic and muscle relaxer. He blamed me for getting him all fucked up and ruining the set. Thank God, the audience was a San Francisco kind of crowd. They were ready for Canned Heat; they knew something like that could happen. They didn't laugh then, but I'm sure they must have later. At the time, we didn't laugh either. Now, when we think about it, we just crack up.

Meanwhile in Mexico City, our former band member Tony de la Barreda has become a record executive for RCA Victor and got the company interested in our album that was produced for Cream Records but never released in the United States. He promoted it as a tribute to Bear, under the title: "In Memory of Bob Hite: 1943-1981."

Ironically, it was the one Canned Heat record The Bear hadn't liked.

To coincide with its release, we booked a performance with John Lee Hooker in Mexico City on July 11, 1981 at La Sala de Armas in the Magdalena Mixuca section of town. This was The Boogie Man's first visit to the Mexican capital, and as expected, it turned into a gigantic *reventon.* The venue was a huge building that had been used for the 1968 Olympic Games. Earlier that day, the government tried to prevent havoc by deploying two platoons of fully equipped *granaderos*, the riot police, but the crowd was so big and there were so many gate-crashers that when the *granaderos* tried to station themselves at the front doors, the mass of hungry blues rockers overwhelmed them like a panzer attack, breaking down their line and crashing through the wooden gates.

By the time we arrived with Hooker, almost 20,000 people were crammed inside and the show had been on for several hours featuring new local bands. The *banda,* or crowd, already out of control, was roaring: *"Orale, orale, orale cabrones."*

The building's solid concrete walls were about five stories high with rectangular openings at the top for ventilation. From the balcony of the dressing room area above the stage, I could see people periodically slipping through the openings. Our die-hard fans were scaling the outside walls to storm the bastion, using belts lashed together as makeshift ropes.

Hooker, already in his mid-60s, was horrified by the crowd and its reaction. "Fito, you tell the guys in the band to stay right next to me on the stage. I'm afraid of these crazy motherfuckers." Clutching the microphone, he shouted: "Why don't you act like civilized human beings?" This was pretty funny, considering most of them didn't understand a word of English. Then, he grabbed his guitar and started with the slow blues tune "I'm in the Mood." The song was like a sedative, helping us regain control and continue the show. Once again, demonstrating the power of music.

Our south of the border extravaganza had a very sad postscript.

Tony was suddenly stricken by a mysterious illness that made him a quadriplegic. After a series of treatments, he recovered the use of his upper body, but to this day, he is a paraplegic confined to a wheelchair. We still stay in touch and he has become very religious, praying for the salvation of his old rock n' roll buddies.

Back in the U.S., a revolution was taking place in the world of rock: a thing called music videos. With his usual enthusiasm, The Push decided to produce a video called "Boogie Assault," featuring Canned Heat and co-starring his biker friends, including members of the San Fernando Chapter of the Hells Angels. The project was financed by a mixed bag of investors that included a number of unsuspecting yuppies who must have been recruited while partying with The Push. The plot was a surrealistic melange of drug smugglers, commando musician frogmen, and outlaw motorcyclists dressed in monk's robes brandishing automatic weapons while riding choppers.

One afternoon while we were filming at the ranch of the owner of "Easyriders" magazine, the director (who was a straight arrow, Hollywood type) remarked that the crew would need weapons for the scenes to be filmed the next day. Expecting neutralized Hollywood prop guns, he was astonished when the cyclist cast appeared toting an arsenal of loaded semi-autos, full autos, M16s and machine guns, followed by two guys with real grenade launchers and another one who opened a box of grenades. The real topper though was the guy lugging a duffel bag; he pulled out his prized possession. "Can we use this? This is a real fuckin' bazooka. We could have a scene where I waste a semi or something."

The director never really zeroed in on the bikers' wavelength. Towards the end of the shoot, when we were filming in a warehouse, he distractedly shouted to nobody in particular: "Kill that light in the corner."

The place suddenly sounded like East LA. "Bam. Bam. Bam." An Angel with an Uzi killed the light. Permanently.

The director phrased his requests more carefully after that.

While we launched into the video—one of the first ever—Henry's wild lifestyle and drinking got him kicked out of the band again. On our way to a gig at the Lone Star Cafe in New York City, Henry was drunk and obnoxious. Big Ernie, who was always a nice guy, finally lost his patience and slugged him, knocking out one of his teeth. In silence, we drove Henry back to the hotel where we left him. We were angry, frustrated and just plain tired of his alcoholic bullshit.

In L.A., we replaced him with Walter Trout, a young, gifted guitar player we discovered at the legendary California jazz-blues club The Light House in Hermosa Beach.

Work on the video dragged on and on, month after month, far longer than any of us expected. The Push was as determined as any Cimino or NYU film school student to complete his vision. We started calling him and Sonny "Dino de Laurentis and Cecil B. DeMille."

They really got into it, whipping out script rewrites, debating plot twists and motivations, driving the project deeper and deeper into re-shoots and using up more and more production money.

The Push, who was not a man of mild enthusiasms, had become lost in the mania of the avant-garde film maker, roaming the West on his chopper to search for scenic backgrounds, convinced he had finally found his true role in life. Every time he saw some special effect or camera angle he liked on TV or in a movie, he tried to work it into the script.

Unfortunately, while The Push was re-creating "Apocalypse Now" on Harleys, Canned Heat was not working. He was too busy directing to even book us into the usual punch-and-stab biker bars.

We got a brief boost from British blues veteran John Mayall, who asked us to join him for a month-long tour of the United States. It was good to have some money in our pockets, even though the job was double work because we had to play our own set and then back John in his. When Mayall went home to England, we were back to waiting around while The Push worked on script rewrites with a couple of outlaw buddies. In the next 10 months, we only played three gigs, bringing on a full-scale insurrection.

Mike, Walter and Ernie called me in San Marcos.

"Fito," said Mike, "there isn't going to be any band left unless we fire The Push. He's had over three years to make things happen and we're still sitting around going broke while he and his biker friends are flipping out, thinking up new plots for that stupid video. We have to play to live. We have families to feed. If we can't do it with Canned Heat, we'll have to leave."

291

I had to agree. Because we're a working band, it's not just a question of money. Not being able to perform affects us psychologically, we lose our chops. Much as I had come to love The Push, it was clear Canned Heat wouldn't survive "Boogie Assault."

"Mike, I'm down here in San Marcos. Why don't you take care of it?"

"It's your band, Fito, you have to do it."

"Great. Now, it's my band. During the past two years, you guys have been doing all kinds of shit without even consulting me. Now, it's my band. I'll be in town Friday. We'll go see him then."

"I don't think I can make it Friday."

"So when can you make it?"

"I think, like, never, man. I mean, this is your job."

I didn't have to say what we were both thinking. The Push was a huge guy who knew no limits, a guy with some truly dangerous friends who aren't famous for tolerating fuckups. These were people nobody double crossed. And by this time, they had sunk a fortune, suitcases full of hundred dollar bills, into the video that they expected us to complete and make successful. I asked for volunteers among the other band members but nobody would come with me.

I had a cold lump in my gut as I drove alone to the new production office they had just opened above a hot dog stand in North Hollywood. The office turned out to be a cubicle with a biker mama loaded on speed stationed outside the door as a receptionist.

The Push and Sonny were sitting at a large table they used for a desk; two huge biker buddies stood on both sides like centurions. I knew The Push could simply break all my bones with his bare hands right then and there. I figured that whatever was going to happen was going to happen and there was no point in wasting time.

I just laid it on him, right at the start: "Push, we know your heart's in the right place, but we haven't worked for close to a year because of the video. We just can't keep you as our manager any more."

The Push looked like he'd been punched in the stomach. The color drained from his face. I was squeezed simultaneously between terror and pity.

"Fito, what are you saying?"

"You're fired."

It was out. I waited.

There was no roar, no fury, no engineer boot in my face. I was almost ashamed of my fears. He was simply hurt and dismayed. By now, his sense of self had become strongly meshed with his role as our manager and the producer/director of our video.

He and Sonny tried to talk me into continuing the relationship. Sonny even grabbed a briefcase and threw it open to show me bundles of bills. "Come on, Fito, look at that cash. Look at all that money, all of that is money we're willing to invest in you guys."

"It's not just a question of money. The band's morale has collapsed because of the lack of work."

It was very difficult, but I knew I had to hang tough. I told him that much as he loved Canned Heat and we loved him, we had to have a new manager.

Sonny said: "Well, we have to give you credit for having the balls to handle it face to face."

I had been saved by the code of the outlaw biker, the part that says that a righteous brother settles differences up front, man to man, no bullshit.

Once he accepted it as done, The Push was back in form. "I guess they left it to the biggest guy. Tell the others that I think they're a bunch of back-stabbing, pussy motherfuckers." He was especially mad at Ernie, who he put in the band as his inside man; he should have tipped him off that he was about to be fired.

"I know you have obligations on the video," I said. "No matter what else happens, I promise the band will complete it."

"Promise, bullshit," thundered The Push. "If one of your guys don't show up for a shooting session, or one of you is late, I'll personally waste him in front of everybody. I don't give a fuck if I go to jail. I'll fucking tear your head off."

On this note, we parted friends, and we still are.

And I made good on my promise to finish "Boogie Assault."

Every time I look at the video, it strikes me as a monument to an era, a legacy of bubblingly creative minds and an unusual friendship. Unfortunately, the plot and the camera work aren't very good and the sound is muddy. All the passion The Push poured into it wasn't enough. Along came MTV with slickly-produced videos that zoomed right past Canned Heat and our outlaw biker auteurs.

But it was a pioneer effort, one of the first music videos, a form that took off from there. Not many people ever saw "Boogie Assault," but The Push had the right vision. His dreams were too big for even him to wrestle to the ground. But like Hemingway's old fisherman, he gave it a hell of a try. And I'm still not sure I ever knew his real name.

Even though Push wasn't our manager any more, we were still on good terms with the Angels and all the other biker clubs, so Mike contacted a well-known Beverly Hills attorney named Jerome Cohen to help us negotiate an Australian tour promoted by the Aussie chapter of the Hells Angels. We did five really tough, but successful, weeks of one nighters with the club members taking care of everything. It was during this trip that we developed close and lasting friendships with "Vinnie," "Macka," "Animal," "Ball Bearing," "Guitar," "Stiff," "Lumberjack," "Pog," and "Aggy."

Australia, with its natural beauty and great highways that go on forever, is a motorcyclist's dream. And its history, where many of the pioneers were convicts, makes it fertile ground for an outlaw mentality that's expressed by the many different biker clubs scattered throughout the island continent. Besides the Hells Angels, a few of the other clubs are the Nomads, Bandidos, Coffin Cheaters, Vietnam Vets MC, Rebels, and Comancheros.

We wrapped up the tour at the notorious Broadford Biker Festival, a three day carnival on a 20-hectare property owned by the Hells Angels 70 kilometers north of Melbourne. Because the Angels police the scene themselves, there's no trouble, no busts, and no bad vibes. But to get in or out, you have to run a gauntlet of police blockades where they search you for weapons and drugs and make you take a breath test.

Along with the strippers, skydivers, naked boob competitions and rock and roll, weddings are performed, sex acts consummated both on and off the stage, plus the obligatory raffle of a Harley-Davidson at the end of the festival. As usual, we were the closing act. Before we went on, the bros got us all wired on speed. While bare-breasted Aussie mamas danced around us and Angels got their dicks sucked in the wings, we played with blood-shot eyes until dawn arrived. That's what they wanted from us and that's they what they got: The Real Boogie Assault.

Over the years, we've continued to maintain our relationship with the bros. Canned Heat has played more biker gigs than any other band in history. Clubs all over the world consider it a matter of prestige to feature Canned Heat at their festivals. From Sturgis to Switzerland, from Canada to the UK and from Germany to Australia, it's a never-ending link. Our boogie music and their motorcycles. It's our culture.

Easyriders, the number one biker magazine, once wrote: "If the music industry ever decides to award a Grammy for guts, heart, pride and sheer determination, that award should go to Canned Heat hands down."

When the Hells Angels celebrated the 40th anniversary of its founding at a nightclub outside San Bernardino, there were only two kinds of non-Angels on hand: Canned Heat, playing inside and ring upon ring of police in patrol cars outside. At the other end of the social spectrum, we performed in Milwaukee at Harley-Davidson's 90th birthday bash, a showcase for RUBs (rich urban bikers) wearing silk bandanna headbands and riding $20,000+ machines.

That Canned Heat became a sort of show-biz subsidiary of the Hells Angels and other outlaw clubs may sound strange, but the stereotype of bikers as a bunch of brutes is inaccurate and unfair. Many of them are shrewd, intelligent businessmen who know how to listen and have certain rules that they live by.

In a way, I relate to those principles better than I relate to the so-called straight world. I've been ripped off and fucked over by a lot of promoters and lying, thieving record company executives, but never by an outlaw biker. They have an organization with rules and their own ethics. In my experience, doing business with them has always been hassle-free.

When I got home after the Australian tour, I realized that San Marcos, which I originally fled to as a peaceful haven, was really very boring. It was time to go back to the city. Like Canned Heat, L.A. was a deadly insanity I just couldn't walk away from.

It wasn't long before I was back in the grind. One afternoon while rehearsing in a recording studio at my friend Steve Terlizzi's house, a raucous laugh from the control booth caught my attention. I was surprised to discover this boisterous sound coming from a beautiful, delicate, fine-featured, Audrey Hepburn-like young woman named Sheri Riley. It was love at first sight. She reawakened in me the wonderful feeling of oneness with someone else, a partner in life. It had been years since I experienced such an emotion. Within weeks, she moved into my house and soon after we were married.

The rehearsals at Steve's were for a rhythm and blues EP (extended play) called "The Heat Brothers," which turned out to be the beginning of the end of The Mouth Band. Mike, who was coproducing with me, was a good singer but not a traditional blues man; his roots were mainly rock n' roll and we disagreed on which direction the band should take.

I also discovered that Mike and the other guys were using the band as a vehicle for their own personal gain. They didn't appreciate what Canned Heat was truly about. Without letting me know, they secretly booked gigs in crummy joints in South L.A. as the Heat Brothers and the Canned Heat Band. They didn't tell me because they knew I wouldn't play for the kind of money they were getting. I didn't want to cheapen the name and sell out like a lot of other musicians do out of necessity. It was, and still is, very important for me to keep some kind of dignity and position in the industry. Mike and the guys were so horny to play, they let it interfere with their judgment, so I dissolved The Mouth Band.

After almost three years of letting other people do just about anything they wanted with the band, I returned to L.A. I had a new wife and I realized that it was time to take proper care of Canned Heat. That once again, if anyone was going to do it, it had to be me.

It was almost three years since Bear had turned to me outside the Palomino and said "I'm leaving." It was over five since Pam had gone raging into the night. The scars were there, but the wounds had healed.

"The Mouth Band" L to R - Walter Trout, Rick Kellog,
Fito de la Parra, Mike Halby, Ernie Rodriguez

296

With "my children" Ray & Haakie touring in Europe...Pass the pipe!

A present from our East German fans...WOW!

Bob Hite

298

Henry Vestine

Alan Wilson

Larry Taylor

Me

Me with dancers at Australian biker festival

Me with "cop" dancers at biker festival

Me checking out even more birds down under

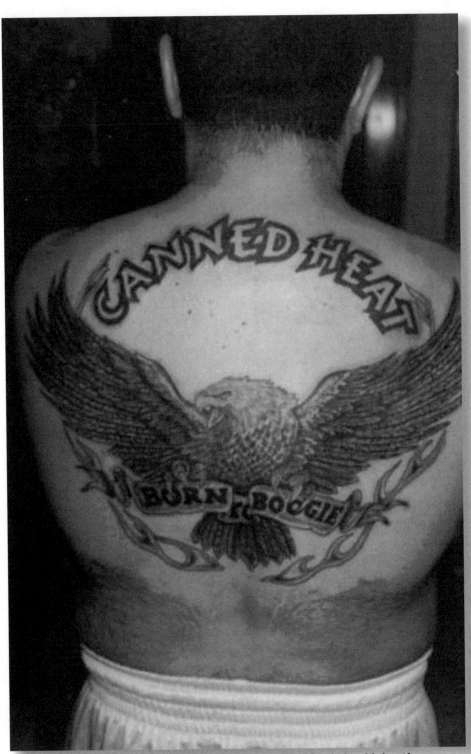

There are fans, and then there are FANS! John Valentino displaying his tattoo.

WE ARE NOT A ROYALTY COMPANY

Royalty: A share paid to an author or composer out of the proceeds resulting from the sale or performance of his/her work.
The American Heritage Dictionary

We should be rich. Lots of people I meet simply presume I *am* rich.

I have played on three gold singles, four gold albums, a platinum album and hell, a *triple platinum* album. You can hear our music on commercials for Pepsi Cola, General Motors, Levis, 7-Up, Amtrak and Miller Beer. When the big corporate advertising suits want to evoke the 60s, just the magic side of that Jekyll-and-Hyde era, what do they play? Probably "Goin' Up the Country" or "On the Road Again."

I have played on more than 50 albums, been on radio and TV more times than I can count.

In America, entertainment success like that means big money. Even the fringes of success means big money.

The *Los Angeles Times* runs a Sunday column focusing on the real estate deals of celebrities, semi-celebrities, pseudo-celebrities and who-the-fuck-is-that? I see guys in there all the time who have less of a track record in this business than I do, selling their $2.5 million mansion in Montecito to buy a $4 million estate in Newport Beach.

The Bear died in poverty, desperately trying to scratch up enough money to get his electricity turned back on. The only money Henry had was what he kept in his wallet.

And I'm not rich. Not even close. We love to play for the people and all, but money is certainly one reason I'm out banging drums in blues clubs at my age.

No, I'm not poor either. A lot of credit goes to my father for stubbornly but wisely confiscating and investing my earnings when we were on top of the heap. Some goes to me for buying some real estate and staying out of the hard drug sinkhole that ate up so many people close to me.

But rich? like Mick Fleetwood or Santana or Sir Paul McCartney? Nope. I'm a working man, a musician stuck on the road till the sticks fall from my hands.

The story of what happened to our money is typically Canned Heat. We played the music, we had the hits, we delighted the people and the money rolled in. But not to us. It went to somebody else. A whole lot of somebody elses. And it still does.

First of all, you have to know how we get paid, the royalty merry-go-round. It works—or is supposed to work—this way:

Writer/Publisher/Mechanical Royalties: This is the money the author of the song is supposed to get each time anyone performs the song or buys a copy of the sheet music so they can learn the song to perform it, or the song is played on the radio, TV or used in a film.

These royalties are usually divided between the author and the publisher. The percentage varies, but it's typically 50-50 between the writer and the publisher (the owner of the copyright).

Artists Sales Royalties: This is the share those of us who played and sang the music get from the retail price you pay for a record or tape or CD. These royalties provide what sounds like a fortune when the recording is a hit, but are still a miserable percentage of the total amount you, the fan, pays out. When you buy a CD costing, say $12, the guys playing on that CD split about $1.

In our best days, when we were headlining at Woodstock and jamming big arenas, we got a nickel of every dollar that fans spent on our albums. And we split that five ways—a penny per dollar came to each of us.

In many cases, the royalties are split. For example, when Canned Heat recorded "Let's Work Together" by Wilbert Harrison, the writer's royalties—called "publishing"—went to Wilbert and his publisher, while the Artists royalties went to Canned Heat.

When Canned Heat was formed in 1966, the band members decided to split all income from all sources on an equal basis, share and share alike. This included all artist, publisher and writer royalties, live performance money and any income from any source.

This was all written down in a proper and very business-like contract that we all signed.

Years passed. We led harum-scarum lives. As an administrator, the Bear was not what the guys at Harvard Business School have in mind. A house burned down. Another one was flooded repeatedly. Our manager ended up in prison on drug charges.

With all that, the original contract is long gone. We have many other documents however that confirm this was indeed our arrangement, including tax records, and affidavits from past accountants and business managers as well as individual financial records and testimony from all living members of the group.

This is important when discussing writer's royalties. Usually, only one or two writers are listed on the original writer/publisher contracts—and the credits on the recordings themselves—rather than all five band members. But regardless of who was credited, we were all supposed to share in the money because we all wrote these songs in jam sessions together, throwing in inspirations and criticism.

Trying to pry apart some percentage of who contributed what would be impossible. Anyone who even imagines that's possible never wrote a song the way Canned Heat does.

Then there was the biggie, the financial H-bomb—the famous Denver marijuana bust, where we lost the remainder of our publishing royalties.

In its original contract with Liberty Records, the band gave the label half the future income from its publishing royalties, a really nasty practice that was common at the time. Before a year was out, they were all arrested on that phony Denver charge, all but me. I wasn't in the band yet.

For an event I wasn't even present at, the Denver bust certainly had a lifelong impact on me.

Skip Taylor needed $10,000 for bail and defense lawyers. Without the cash, the band would be no-shows at key gigs. The rest of the guys would be going to prison just as we were about to become stars. The only source of money like that was Liberty Records and the label's executives drove a devil's bargain. They would turn over the cash only in return for the remaining half of the band's future publishing royalties.

So, in exchange for $10,000—which went directly to an attorney to spring the boys—we were left with no publishing royalties on the band's most famous songs and albums.

Now the sad tale of how we also lost our artists' royalties as well: In 1973, after Alan's death, Canned Heat was in the red approximately $30,000 in unearned advances—a not uncommon situation for recording artists—to what had become Liberty/United Artists.

Skip made a deal with the record company's president that allowed Canned Heat to leave United Artists to sign with Atlantic Records for a new start.

The understanding was that the continued sales of all the 1966-1973 Canned Heat albums and tapes, which United Artists still owned, would pay off the debt after we left.

At the time, it seemed like a good deal. Who knew, back then, that down the road a few years there would be a new recording format called compact discs? Who knew that our old albums would be re-issued in this new format, in some cases selling more heavily than the original vinyl records did? Who knew that all the hard work we had put into those albums would never make us another cent, even while they sold more and more copies. They still sell.

Who knew? Certainly not us.

Fucked again.

And we didn't even know what had happened. Like the Denver Bust, the true measure of what had been done to us took years to become clear.

The $30,000 was repaid decades ago but to this day, EMI—which took over United Artists—pays not a cent to us for the continuing sale of those early albums. We figure EMI has made enough money on those CDs that even if we still got only our miserable 5 percent share, we'd have about $1 million coming to us.

There's worse to come.

In 1969-70, Canned Heat appeared on both Woodstock soundtrack albums, put out by Atlantic Records. Even though our contract with Liberty (now EMI) allowed us to make separate deals on movie and soundtrack royalties, EMI convinced Atlantic (now Warners), in a sweetheart deal between the two conglomerates, to send all our Woodstock album royalties to them, rather than pay Canned Heat.

Both Woodstock albums are now platinum several times over, and our share, conservatively estimated, would be about $300,000. But except for an initial $10,000, we have seen not a dime from the recording of our best known performance, a highlight of our careers.

I meet fans who presume I'm rich because I played on those fantastically lucrative Woodstock albums and film.

I got less than $2,000 for that.

Alan's death brought more complications, which still haunt us.

For a while after he died, we followed our old system. Artists sales royalty checks went to Skip's office, he took off a commission and divvied up the rest in five equal shares.

When Skip left the band in 1978, Howard Wolf took over. He had to get a court order to compel the record company to continue paying him Alan's share of the royalties—instead of sending them all to Alan's family—so he could continue the practice of equal sharing among all band members.

Many of our biggest hits, of course, had Alan's name on them as writer. Sometime in the 1980s, after Wolf had left us, Alan's family got a court order that his royalties be paid to them. They stopped sharing the royalties with the others in the band, ignoring the sharing agreement which was Alan's idea in the first place because he thought of the band as a brotherhood.

Because we can't produce our long-ago contract, and blues-band traditions have piss-poor legal clout versus slick attorneys, EMI felt obligated to pay the royalties on songs credited exclusively to Alan only to his family, the people whose letters Alan ignored and threw away unread.

As this is written, we are still pleading, battling and negotiating over these things with EMI and Alan's family, still hoping that someday there will be a just settlement. Skip Taylor wrote to the CEO of EMI in the mid-1990s outlining just these complaints, desperately trying to make him aware of the situation and maybe even touch his heart.

To date, EMI's answer has amounted to: If you don't like it, tough. So sue us.

Woodstock and the Denver Bust and Alan's death. Such ancient history for most people. But those of us who went on with Canned Heat live with these ghosts every day. They haunt our bank accounts.

And let's not forget the pirates, who in my opinion should be executed, especially in Europe where tiny principalities facilitate illegal reproductions without enforcing international copyright laws. Canned Heat has been devastated by these guys.

The best example is "Live at Topanga Corral," released by Scepter Records, a company that ceased to exist over 20 years ago. European pirates got their hands on the masters and have issued more reproductions than I can count. In 1996, my friend and Number One Canned Heat Fan Walter De Paduwa, AKA Dr. Boogie, sent me at least 18 different covers of CDs with 18 different titles, *all* of them simply containing the same music from the Scepter record.

Of course, we've never collected a cent from these people and we never will, although I would love to track down one of these bastards some day and introduce him to some of my Hells Angels friends. In an alley. Late at night.

These pirated albums are ruinous to us, flooding the market with really old material that swindles buyers who think it is new and eating into the sales of our new releases, which we do control.

I fought a two-year legal battle with Australian record company executive Peter Noble over his refusal to pay royalties on three CDs, finally winning a legal settlement worth about $15,000. Guess what my legal fees were?

Yeah, $15,000.

As you read this, I'm most likely on the road, maybe in Europe, autographing pirated CDs. At virtually every show, fans show up holding out these pirated works for me to sign—discs they bought in good faith. With tears of rage in my eyes, I force myself to smile and sign and thank them for being at our shows. What else can I do?

International copyright conventions be damned. From my experience, piracy is out of control.

While a lot of this may sound unrelentingly negative, there are exceptions. I've found decent, music-loving people in the business, executives of integrity who actually pay royalties, like those at Takoma Records, as well as some of the Europeans I've dealt with, especially Bernhard Roessle and Thomas Ruf, based in Germany.

Many record companies do all they can to avoid paying royalties. If you want to get paid, you're forced to beg, scream and fight. Most of the time it's only the lawyers who get rich.

In the mid-60s in Mexico, a friend of mine had a hit record. Months went by and he received no royalties. But he was persistent and managed to get an appointment with the president of the record company.

"Royalties?" snapped the pompous CEO. "We are not a royalty company. This is a record company. Now, get out of here before I have the security guards throw you out."

In my dealings with record companies all over the world, I can't help but remember that callous answer, because no matter what language they speak, the message is the same: "We are not a royalty company.".

For the record, out of more than 35 Canned Heat CDs on the market, these are the only titles legally pressed and distributed, and on which the band members can expect to be paid royalties:

1. "Boogie Up the Country," Inakustic-Germany
2. "Canned Heat In Concert," King Biscuit Flower Hour Records/BMG
3. "Gambling Woman," King Biscuit/BMG
4. "Internal Combustion," sold by me personally at concerts and via The Web page cannedheatmusic.com
5. "Reheated," sold by me personally and via the Web
6. "Canned Heat Blues Band," Ruf Records and via the Web
7. "Boogie 2000," Ruf Records, worldwide
8. "The Boogie House Tapes," Ruf Records, worldwide

FULL CIRCLE

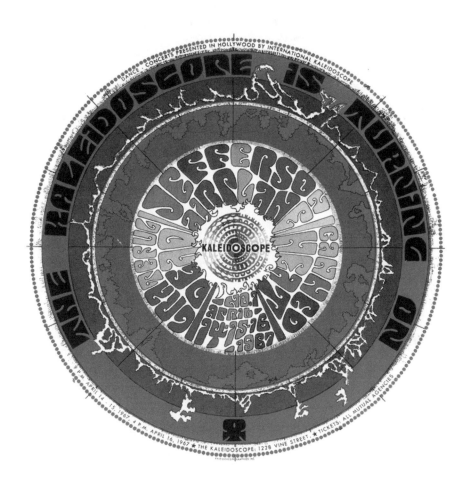

Within a few days after the Mouth Band was officially dissolved in mid-1985, I contacted Henry, who was living in Eugene, Oregon. He told me about this great singer/guitar/harmonica player called James Thornbury, who he'd worked with occasionally. I asked for a cassette so I could consider him for Canned Heat and I was very impressed with the quality of his voice. I was also told he was very good-looking, clean and sober, and a nice person. Wow! I couldn't believe such a musician existed and was available too!!

With help from my loyal friend/roadie Joey Orozco and without hesitation, I arranged for them to come to Los Angeles to start rehearsals. Since we still needed a bass player, they offered to bring along their friend Skip Jones, another accomplished musician. They also brought a very smart, friendly school teacher named Mari Nomack, who was their manager. With the exception of Henry, all of them were into organic food—a dramatic change from the boozing, drug-taking bands of the past, which is why we dubbed this unit the "Nuts and Berries" band.

Although we worked well together and did a couple of U.S. tours, this only lasted a few months. When Larry found out I had dissolved the Mouth Band and was forming a new lineup, he called me offering to rejoin, because the Hollywood Fats Band didn't have that many gigs. More importantly, Larry, like me, always believed in Canned Heat's greatness.

To make the band even stronger, we decided to bring Ronnie Barron back on board. Once again, we had an outstanding musical force, but—as usual—it brought with it all the personality clashes and never-ending problems that result when you combine all these talented characters and their idiosyncrasies.

We started Canned Heat's 20th Anniversary Boogie Tour with three months of grueling gigs throughout Australia promoted by Peter Nobel. Luckily, on this tour we met Ray Axisa, who made up for all the short-comings of his boss. A Maltese Australian, biker bro, party animal and excellent sound engineer, Axisa took extraordinary care of us and this developed into a great friendship. In fact, we like the way he mixes our sound so much that every time it's possible we fly him in to tour and party with us all over the world.

During this Australian tour, Ronnie again—in spite of his great talent—could not function socially and gave us all kinds of problems to the point where two weeks before the tour was to end he just decided to return to LA. Fortunately, we were able to perform as a

**1986 Line-up. L-R Larry Taylor, James Thornbury,
Henry Vestine, me, Ronnie Baron**

four piece band without a keyboard player and do well—sometimes even better.

By now you must wonder why I would continue to hire people like this. Number one, regardless of their fuck ups, they're friends. And secondarily, they are such superb, world-class musicians that there are very few people can do what they do.

Back in the States, we played a few gigs but Larry, true to his pattern of always searching for perfection, was becoming unhappy with the band again. He started lobbying to kick Henry out without a valid reason, other than a dislike for his personal style. Even though Henry was drinking again, he promised me that he would only consume beer when we were working. This time, he kept his word and was doing okay, but Larry's power was too overwhelming and I was forced to fire Henry. This is the only time I felt Henry was let go without good cause.

In the '80s there was a new generation of blues players, a few years younger than us, who turned their backs on the trends of the '70s and started the new blues awareness that has swept America and the world. Premier examples of this school of music were brothers Jimmie and Stevie Ray Vaughan, Hollywood Fats and Junior Watson. Henry called this generation of blues players "Would-Bes" because of their insistence on imitating the early black blues masters, note by note, mood by mood.

At Larry's suggestion, we brought in blues guitar player Junior Watson to replace Henry as lead guitar. Originally from San Jose, California, Junior had been co-founder of the well-regarded blues band "The Mighty Flyers" for 11 years; he'd also played with John Lee Hooker, Charlie Musselwhite and Big Mama Thornton. His credentials were excellent and he was ready for a change to a band with a harder edge than the swing-oriented Mighty Flyers. Henry labeled this lineup the "Would-Bes."

During this time, I was also involved in a business venture. I opened a paint and body shop specializing in European and high performance cars called EuroBody in the San Fernando Valley. Again, I didn't want to depend solely on Canned Heat for my livelihood, so I took the risk and invested time and money into the business hoping It would succeed. Unfortunately, during the

With Sheri on our wedding day, Aug. 23 1986 "The happy times"

absences caused by being on the road, my wife Sheri, who I loved very much, disappointed me deeply.

Sensing her change in attitude towards me, I connected a tape recorder to the telephone before I left for a short tour. When I got home, my worst fears were confirmed. Our five year relationship tragically came to an end. This was one of the worst things that had ever happened to me. Once again, it was like the "nail that separates from the flesh."

In the midst of this personal tragedy, Larry and I co-produced "Reheated" to reflect the quality of our music at the time with absolutely no consideration given to commercial appeal. We knew better than to try to commercialize Canned Heat. We had tried it earlier with Cream Records and it didn't work. It just wasn't us.

The sessions were challenging. We decided to record some of the songs with only one microphone in the center of the room, a technique reminiscent of the very first blues and rock records made in the 1950s, using room sound and no over dubbing. The songs were played live, direct to a two-track machine.

As the project went on, James T's and Junior Watson's talents blossomed, making this CD an artistic achievement we're all very proud of. As always, Larry and I provided a kick-ass rhythm section, which was surprising to me, considering the emotional turmoil I was going through at the time. There were days when the pain of losing Sheri seemed to be the only thing that dominated my mind. I was playing almost like a zombie.

While in Europe, I negotiated the release of "Reheated," receiving an advance that covered our initial investment and even gave us a little profit. What a triumph.

For the U.S. distribution of "Reheated," our manager Eugene negotiated a 17% licensing deal with Chameleon Music Group formed by Stephen Powers, a former executive with Capitol Records. This was the same label that originally released John Lee Hooker's mega-hit "Healer." (The famous recording sessions we did for $150 dollars and no royalties to help John Lee Hooker revive his career.) We had great hopes for "Reheated" and it got excellent reviews. But only a few months after its release, bad luck struck again. Stephen Powers had a disagreement with his business partners at Chameleon triggering the dissolution of the record company. As a consequence, "Reheated" is available only in Europe and now through our Web site. One more example of artists placing their hope in a company and then the plug gets pulled with absolutely no consideration given to the effect this will have on the careers of the musicians.

It was during this period that I got another heartbreaking phone call. This time from Larry. "Fito, sit down. Hollywood Fats just died. He overdosed at some friend's house shooting cocaine and heroin."

I felt terrible, but I wasn't surprised. Fats, after all, was the Bear's Burger Brother. He followed Bob's steps in life as well as death. They both loved the blues, overeating, carrying-on and getting loaded to the max. And they both paid with their lives. Like Bob, it was a great loss to all of us who love and appreciate good music. His brilliance has yet to be repeated or surpassed by anyone, when it comes to traditional blues guitar playing.

Coinciding with the release of "Reheated" in the late '80s, Europe became Canned Heat's main market—more important than the United States, Latin America or even Australia—with the band touring there two or three times a year. The Europeans, ironically, have a deeper appreciation of blues and jazz-based music than Americans. They've always loved Canned Heat.

By now, under my command we had outgrown the excesses of the '60s. Even Henry was placed under certain (but occasionally ignored) controls and despite all the adversity that rained down on us through the years, we put on a series of successful concerts.

One night stands out vividly in my mind. We were in the middle of a particularly long tour and had just finished a good two hour-plus show at the Grosse Freiheit in Hamburg, Germany. In the dressing room afterward, everyone knew it had been a kick-ass performance that really got through to the audience. We had a definite sense of accomplishment. There was a wonderful feeling of brotherly love and camaraderie. Everyone was caught up in the rapture of the moment. We were cracking jokes non-stop and actually enjoying each others company in spite of the grueling schedule.

The feeling that night was one of absolute purity. It had nothing to do with fame or fortune, but everything to do with the powerful vibration that flowed from us to the audience and from the audience back to us. It was a feeling so strong that it enveloped us in a special aura. It was a feeling that was even better than sex and better than drugs.

When I got back to my hotel room, that pleasurable sense of accomplishment still lingered. Laying down before I faded into sleep, the thoughts of my dear father who had passed away only the year before hit me and brought me to tears. Good tears. "Dad, I've really done something you'd be proud of. I wish you were here to share it with me." Maybe he was. This brought a smile to my face and a sense of peace.

Drifting off, I reflected on the fact that in spite of the loss of our two best known members and all the trials and tribulations we've endured, Canned Heat can still cut it by delivering a good quality show, giving me credibility as the leader of the band. That's where the band failed in the past, the drunkenness...the rowdiness. I don't mean we aren't drunk and stoned and rowdy anymore. It's just that now, we aren't drunk, stoned and rowdy ALL the time.

Respect for Canned Heat continues to grow in Europe. In fact, we've acquired such a strong following that Walter de Paduwa, a.k.a. "Dr. Boogie," a Belgian record company executive and a successful radio personality, has named his home "The Boogie House," decorating the walls with the covers of every Canned Heat record ever released. Walter's place has become a haven for us whenever we hit the continent and we've developed a very close friendship.

Over the years, I've often been asked what my most important accomplishment has been in terms of the band. The answer: What our music has done to the fans we've played for. The feelings we've caused them to experience. I don't think there is anything more important or gratifying than playing a good show and knowing that you did it.

After our disappointment with the record company that released our "Reheated" CD, we worked steadily with back to back tours that were utterly exhausting and where we made some money but weren't really advancing our careers. As a result, Junior Watson took off on his own and I made a deal with an exhausted Larry so he would only have to play gigs that were worth it financially and easy to get to. Those events caused the "Would-be" lineup to dissolve in the early '90s.

Coincidentally, Harvey Mandel called me from Florida that same week offering his services. I immediately hired him and Ron Shumake, a talented bass player that I met when we played together with Ronnie Barron at a couple of after-hours jam sessions at Homer and Eddie's Bistro in West Los Angeles. This lineup, which still included James T., did several tours in Europe, Australia, the U.S. and Mexico.

Even though we lacked a deal with a record company, my "fixedness of purpose," combined with the enthusiastic support of our manager Eugene, inspired me to produce a new album called "Internal Combustion," the title reflecting my interest in motorcycles and the approaching close of the 20th Century. Unfortunately, while we were working on this project, Harvey became weary of the

EANNED HEAT

Would-be line-up-L-R Larry Taylor, Me, James T, Junior Watson
grueling pace and decided to quit, moving to San Francisco to play mostly local gigs.

During this period, I received phone calls from Steve Fodor, a well-known piano player on the LA blues scene, and Lee Magid, an established manager/producer, also from LA. Both wanted me to check out this impressive "hot" female guitar player/singer named Becky Barksdale, who was from Port Arthur, Texas, the same hometown as Janis Joplin.

I was in the middle of producing the "Internal Combustion" CD, and needed a guitar player, so I skeptically went to see her perform at a small, funky, pool table-filled beer joint. In my mind, I couldn't imagine a woman being part of Canned Heat. We're too testosterone-driven and biker-oriented for the average chick. However, Becky was not average and that night she impressed me with her stage presence. A pretty, petite brunette, she had gorgeous

James Thornbury

legs, a strong voice and good rapport with her audience. I offered her the gig with Canned Heat, which she immediately accepted, with the understanding that she was under contract with Magid. He didn't object, knowing this would be a good career move for her financially and she really needed it.

My reason for hiring her was based on Fleetwood Mac. Like Canned Heat, it was a group that started as a blues band in the '60s, lost a key member, Peter Green, and almost faded into obscurity until it hired a couple of women and gained greater fame than it ever had before. I didn't expect this move to turn us into another Fleetwood Mac, but I thought it was worth a try.

I booked a long European tour mainly in France and Germany. Larry agreed to come along, and adding Becky worked well, since most of our fans are men anyway; they loved her. The trip was very successful—better than I ever expected.

This was followed up with well-received performances in Hawaii and the U.S. Now, it was time for Becky to formally commit to the band and to finish "Internal Combustion." Unfortunately, she too diminished Canned Heat's greatness and thought she could do better on her own. Her judgment was also affected by outsiders and wannabe managers constantly telling her how great she was and how she could do better on her own. I tried a couple of times to get her to commit to being a full-fledge member of the band, at least for another year, but she kept stalling. She was obviously not born to play with Canned Heat.

After a couple of frustrating conversations, I sadly fired her. By now, I had grown fond of her, but more importantly, we were on a successful roll that she interrupted with her indecision and insecurity.

With Becky gone, Larry suggested we hire Smokey Hormel, a lead guitar player who made a name for himself around LA with group's like "The Blasters." Similar to Hollywood Fats, Smokey came from a wealthy family, but his life was his music, which means little or no money. For a real artist, that's immaterial.

We rehearsed a couple of times and then played a gig at the Strand in Orange County, where we were off-balance and knew it. Larry and I even had an argument on stage. The performance that night simply wasn't up to Canned Heat standards.

The next day Larry and I talked on the phone and ended up having a major fight; we couldn't agree on anything. It got so bad I was physically sick. It wasn't only Larry and his unreasonable demands (he wanted us to stop playing our hit records), but I felt overwhelmed by a sense of futility and sadness, dealing with Canned Heat had become a constant uphill battle.

With Walter DePaduwa, "Dr. Boogie" alongside a tank in Bastogne, Belgium, site of the Battle of the Bulge.

As I pulled up on my motorcycle in front of the photo lab to have new pictures made of yet another lineup, I reflected on how many times I had to go through the same bullshit because of constant personnel problems, many of then triggered by Larry's search for perfection, requiring me to fire and hire people to comply with his demands. New pictures, new bios, more name changes, more struggle for credibility, more work for Fito without the other band members even realizing it or appreciating it.

At precisely that moment, I decided I'd had enough. I tucked the negatives back inside my motorcycle jacket, slammed the bike into gear, and tore out of the parking lot at full speed (something one should never do on a motorcycle when you're under stress).

I stormed into my house and called Eugene, ready to let Canned Heat die. "I hear you, Fito," Eugene said, trying to calm me. "I know you're going through some heavy changes and Larry's attitude is clearly not helping. If you want to continue on your own, I'll call him and fire him."

I hung up with a sense of anguish. I didn't want to lose Larry's friendship over this, but I just knew we could not go on together. Sadly, Larry and I stopped talking to each other for nearly two years. But after all, I was the band leader; he simply had to go in order for

326

Fito on "Dr. Boogie's" Canned Heat Harley.

me to be able to remake Canned Heat.

The next day I received a message from Smokey saying that if Larry was not in the band, he wasn't interested in continuing. For the record, Hormel only played one gig with us.

It is very difficult to work with musicians who want control, but won't accept any responsibility. More than once, I've offered to relinquish the leadership of the band. It's very easy for the sidemen to complain and create friction among each other and try to take control on stage. But when it comes time to be responsible, like taking care of business: phone calls, faxes, airline tickets, dealing with promoters and record company executives, they vanish. Most musicians like to nag but don't know—and don't want to know— how to function in the real business world.

I thought the breakup with Larry and Smokey would finally be the end of Canned Heat, but with Eugene's encouragement, I somehow gathered the energy to carry on. Of course, with Larry out of the picture, my first phone call was to Henry. I also called Junior Watson. The idea of having these two great lead guitar players together for the first time was killer and became the foundation of the band until late '97. I wonder why I never thought of it before. The combination of Junior's traditional playing with Henry's rock approach was what one of our fans dubbed "baad-d and devastating" (in the best sense of the words).

After a few rehearsals, we hit the road. We were all happy with the results of the new lineup, which I called the "Heavy Artillery" band. It still included James T., Ron Shumake and myself, plus the two killer guitar players, Henry and Junior.

In 1992, I recruited Ira Ingber, a talented LA songwriter/guitar player/producer to work on "Internal Combustion," because I wanted the CD to have a contemporary feel. His songs and his contribution to all aspects of the production helped achieve that goal. The result was a very good, hip product, which we finished in 1994, after several personnel changes that made the sounds on the CD even more multi-colored. In addition to the core unit of James T., Ira and myself, the CD features the most important Canned Heat members still alive: Larry Taylor, Henry Vestine, and Harvey Mandel.

Coincidentally, Skip Taylor popped unexpectedly back into our lives. After an absence of almost 20 years, I got a call one day. "Hi, Fito, I heard through the grapevine that you just finished a great Canned Heat CD. I'm in the process of starting a new record company with the backing of some very rich and influential people here in Minneapolis. I'm very interested in listening to it. How soon can I expect a copy?"

That afternoon I Fed-Xed a complete promo package to Skip, who was remarried and living in Minnesota where his new wife was from. I had invested over $40,000 of my own money in this CD, making it the most expensive production I'd ever done, so I was delighted at the prospect of recovering my investment and releasing the new CD, even if I didn't make a profit on it.

Skip and his partners in River Road Records liked the project and made me a decent offer that I immediately accepted. It was good to have Skip and his company backing us. It was reminiscent of "The Golden Age" when we felt a sense of security and optimism for our future. We even did a video with a song I sing called "Remember Woodstock" with a lyric written by Skip to coincide with the 25th anniversary of the famous festival.

Becky Barksdale Boogieing with The Heat

Photo: Mareike Strum

Once again, that dark cloud that hovers over Canned Heat cast its ominous shadow. Skip had a falling out with the partners of River Road and within a few months of the release of "Internal Combustion," the record company ceased to exist.

Again, a project that started to take off and got good reviews, faded into obscurity due to a misunderstanding between powerful business people who didn't give a fuck about the repercussions their actions would have on the artists and their careers. It's hard to believe that such a fucked-up thing could happen twice in a row. First with "Reheated," now with "Internal Combustion."

During an Orange County Blues Festival held in Dana Point, I had my driver Pepe pick up Ronnie Barron, who had just suffered two strokes and undergone a life-saving heart transplant. Poor Ronnie. Even though he'd lost the use of his left arm and leg, and was living on borrowed time thanks to the new heart, his songwriting ability and his virtuosity with his right hand were still great. We featured him on the "Internal Combustion" CD on the song written by him entitled, "I Used to Be Bad." In the middle of our performance, I invited him to sit in. It was so gratifying to see him smile and play the piano with only one hand. It had been years since that infamous Montreal gig where he walked off the stage in the middle of a performance and then proceeded to attack each one of us with his "I'm better than you" insult.

In the dressing room after the Festival, we were passing the after-set joint, when Ronnie unexpectedly looked around the room and nodded to each band member. With an apologetic smile on his face, he said: "You're better than me, you're better than me, you're better than me." This was the new Ronnie Barron. He was rectifying some of his earlier mistakes when he "used to be bad."

But the new heart couldn't stop the inevitable. Ronnie's health declined, along with his desire to live. What else could be expected from a great artist, once his mobility deteriorates to the point of near paralysis? During his last months, he was confined to a wheelchair and his mind also started to weaken. Ronnie passed away in March of 1997.

Another tour of Australia was arranged and James gave me notice, so I would have plenty of time to find a suitable replacement for him, which was not easy. In addition to singing, James plays the harmonica, the flute, and both standard-tuning and open-tuning guitar. But after "serving" 10 years in the band, and going through many campaigns with me, this great singer and truly decent guy finally found true love and decided to marry and settle down with a lovely young Australian called Molly from New South Wales, one of the most beautiful areas of the world.

How typical of James to be so thoughtful. I've always believed that it's not only the talent, but the person, who is important. As time goes by, I believe this even more. I'd rather play with someone who may not be that good of a musician, but is a person you can live with. It's very difficult to work with a bunch of prima donnas, who think the world owes them something because they play an instrument well. It's important to evaluate people not only for their talent and their history, but also for the attitude they're going to bring to their work.

When we got back in the States, I contacted another singer/multi-instrumentalist named Robert Lucas, who I'd met about a year before in Denmark at a blues festival. He sat in with us and sounded good. After Becky left, Larry and I discussed adding Robert to the band, but as long as James was with us, there wasn't a need. Now, with James happily married Down Under, we hired Lucas in 1995, making this late-'90s lineup one of the strongest since the beginning of the band.

Long Beach-born Lucas has been devoted to the blues since he was 15. Interestingly, one of the first LPs he bought was a copy of Canned Heat's very first album. Robert cultivated his passion for the blues for 15 more years, developing seven CDs of his own, which resulted is his being nominated for a W.C. Handy Award before joining us. With his boisterous stage presence, typical for a blues shouter, and his physical appearance reminiscent of a baby Bear, Alan and Bob couldn't have hoped for anyone better-suited to sing, play and party with Canned Heat. Around the same time I hired and lost two bass players before giving the job to Greg Kage, a talented multi-instrumentalist who'd been working as our roadie for over a year. An easygoing guy, he fit right in. He's been with us ever since.

In 1996, we did three successful European tours and two extensive tours of the U.S., playing in several festivals along with a wide range of nightclubs, including The House of Blues in LA and New Orleans. Towards the end of the year, the band was tight, mean and kickin' ass. We alternated with ZZ Top in Austria, The Fabulous Thunderbirds and Robert Cray in Norway and received the most favorable reviews. This gave me the incentive to make another "big push," World War I-style.

I knew it was important to record the band while we were still hot and tight from the hundred plus shows we'd recently played. I also knew that as the year came to an end, everything would slow down. I wanted to capture the energy we had before our chops went down from lack of activity throughout the winter. So I summoned all the energy I could, and using money earned from the tours that year, I decided to produce another CD entitled "The Canned Heat Blues Band."

Fortunately, by then, Larry and I had reconciled and our friendship was stronger than ever, so I asked him to be a part of the project because he is, without question, the best bluesman in the world when it comes to playing the acoustic bass. He agreed and also recommended using a two-inch 16-track format, reminiscent of the late '60s that provides a very rich, fat sound. He also suggested hiring Paul Dugre, a gifted engineer with an impressive background. Paul built a studio at home and installed old, traditional equipment to capture the richness of tone that seems to be lost now with modern digital technology. A real technical whiz who worked for Ampex, Paul even incorporated tube-powered equipment into his system, which delivered exactly the sound we wanted.

Because we were tight, our approach to the sessions was very efficient. We managed to finish the entire album in less than 40 hours, following our tradition of putting down the songs on first or second takes. We didn't spend endless hours picking at the tracks, like many other groups do, sometimes ending up with something worse than what they started with. Larry summed it up best when he showed up to record with us: "Once we have a sound, we lay down the song...'no stupid shit'." These became words to live by.

We're very proud of the CD because it reflects the strength and soul of that lineup, while at the same time, it keeps the Canned Heat tradition alive. Our close friends and fans who've heard the material agree.

As the band that many critics said "made the blues palatable for mainstream audiences," our dream of seeing blues music accepted all over the world, especially the United States, finally came true, although we still don't get the recognition we deserve. Worldwide, the blues in the late '90s is bigger than it's ever been. There are blues societies, clubs, record companies and magazines specializing in the blues on almost every continent. Most of them ignore Canned Heat due to ignorance and a heavily politicized scene. And now with its increasing popularity, there are thousands of blues bands, which has actually created over saturation and confusion in the marketplace. As a result, the year 1997 began slowly, with hardly any bookings, until we managed to land tours in Australia and Europe, even though today's band is actually much better than in the mid- '70s when we were a marquee name with recording contracts.

Our traditional audiences still keep coming. The bikers, the hippies, the Vietnam vets. These are our people. The Woodstock nation became more conservative than their parents; they betrayed themselves. But the kids are learning. For a teenager, attending a Canned Heat gig is an act of rebellion. In fact, we're attracting a whole new generation of fans. At a recent concert, a pretty young girl recently told me: "My parents found Jesus so they couldn't come, but they said you were their favorite band before they were saved so they sent me to see you."

Although our most desperate days are behind us, the road isn't a rolling party any more. It's a battle, a losing battle with cramped airline seats, lonely nights in crummy hotel rooms, long days on the highway, and roadside diner food. The only time we enjoy ourselves is when we're on the stage. There are thousands of fans who still treasure us, and we love to please them. So "the music is free, but we charge to get there." I really believe this.

After almost a lifetime of effort, I was weary, frustrated and angry. The years of lack of recognition, were finally grinding me down. We kept Canned Heat alive and playing. I met every threat to the band's existence, from death to personality clashes to irresponsible management, with some kind of effective response. But it was getting increasingly hard to ignore the steady stream of reports, mostly in the mainstream media, that we didn't exist. No matter how many times I told myself to ignore the ignorant reporters, the oblivious critics, it still hurt me, like a bayonet in the gut. I bleed every time I see some reference to Canned Heat that says it died years ago, or that it died with Alan, or with The Bear, or that it exists "in name only." It happens all the time. It's like waking up every morning knowing there's a Mafia contract on your life for no reason. You just wait for the pain of the next bullet. A big part of the problem is the Associated Press wire service, which got it wrong decades ago and never bothered to correct their sloppy, unprofessional files. Every time there's a Woodstock or Monterey or 1960s anniversary piece, a "where are they now?" retrospective, out comes the same totally false report, which other news outlets routinely pick up and use.

Another example is the book "The History of Rock and Roll" published by Rolling Stone. The bastards simply killed us off without making even the simplest effort to check the facts, make a quick phone call, listen to the output of music we've recorded, or talk to the thousands of fans who've been coming to our concerts over the years.

Our latest recordings were well reviewed in the specialized music trades, like DISCoveries, Goldmine and Blues Revue. It's only the general media that keeps reporting us dead. We didn't die. The day Skip found Alan in the underbrush in Topanga Canyon, we were on the stage, playing. We finished the gig with tears in our eyes, but we finished it. As Bear took his last breath in my van, while the roadies hammered on his chest trying desperately to revive him, I was on stage at the Palomino, drumming. And less than a month later, Canned Heat was back on the stage in Australia.

Alan and Bob were the founding fathers all right, but what they founded was a band that wouldn't quit, a band that went on playing while their bodies were still warm. Musicians joined, musicians left. Henry and Larry fought and left and rejoined and fought again. Weeks on the road, months on the road, years on the road. Rivers of money, trickles of money, no money at all. Big arenas, biker festivals, cut-and-shoot roadhouses. Failed loves, broken bodies, broken hearts. We played on. Living the blues, we paid the price.

Canned Heat has never stopped existing, never went under, as many other bands from our Golden Era did. Look at the band names on those old psychedelic festival and dance hall posters from the '60s. How many of them were drawing crowds in the 1990s? The Grateful Dead, the Rolling Stones, Santana and Canned Heat. Period.

We didn't disband and come together again for "reunions" years later, as so many other bands did. Nothing could kill us. I wouldn't let it. It was a sort of madness, but it took a hell of a lot of work and dedication. Some critics, delivered the most stinging insult of all: They would mention Henry or Larry, but not me. I guess they figured Frank Cook was the original drummer and I was just a replacement.

But there was no Golden Age until I joined. That's me on those old gold records, not Frank. I was just as central to the classic Canned Heat lineup, just as important to its sound and to its life, as Ringo Starr was to the Beatles. Nobody dismisses Ringo as just a replacement for Pete Best. But even Ringo didn't keep the Beatles playing for three decades. I tell myself not to give a damn, that it's the fans' opinions that count. To thousands of people, from Brussels to Brisbane to Boise, we're a legend, an American institution.

But it does hurt.

Sometimes it hurts a lot.

It was hard lining up the '97 Australian tour because Watson and Lucas, increasingly unhappy with the money we were making, kept taking outside jobs. But we eventually pulled it off in May, even though there wasn't much money. I was hoping a tour like this would boost the band's morale, especially Watson and Lucas. I wanted to make them feel part of the brotherhood again.

Two days before the end of the tour, in a hotel in Newcastle, I received a call from my agent Paul Barbarus. "Fito, I don't know how to tell you this. Your mother passed away two days ago. Sorry, man. It took me this long to track you down." Five minutes later I was on stage, singing "On the Road Again" with lyrics that were painful in a way Alan hadn't foreseen: "Oh, my dear mother left me, when I was quite young...." I tried to keep the tears out of my voice, remembering Bear used to say: "The worst thing you can do is bum trip the people. They're paying us to get the party going."

In September and October, we lined up a 26-day tour that included France, England, Holland and Belgium. And in spite of our bad luck not getting a recording contract in the States, the European tour was brightened by licensing deals for "Canned Heat Blues Band" with three small independent labels, England's Mystic Records, Belgium's Rowyna Records, and Germany's Viceroots. We received a modest advance and average royalties, raising hopes that both the tour and the CDs would do well.

My optimism quickly evaporated as I waited at the international terminal in Los Angeles for Henry to arrive from Eugene, Oregon, for our flight to France. Hobbling toward me was an old man, stooped and sunken-cheeked, with skin like white tissue paper. He was barely able to shuffle along.

"Hey, Fito," he waved.

I couldn't believe it was Henry. I was accustomed to him not aging well because the abuse he'd given his body would have killed most people many years ago. But this was a big change. He was worse than I'd ever seen him. He could hardly breathe. He scarcely managed to croak "Hello."

"Henry , you look terrible. What have you been doing?"

"I'm okay," he mumbled. "Stayed up too late last night."

"Henry, we have a tour, a big tour. This is going to be a lot of work. I told you for Christ's sake to take care of yourself."

"Don't hassle me, Fito. I'll be fine. I'll sleep on the plane. Don't worry. Everything will be okay."

It wasn't. When we arrived at Charles de Gaulle airport in Paris, Henry couldn't walk through the terminal. We had to get a wheelchair and push him to the van.

The tour went well. London. Paris. Brussels. We were really cooking on stage. And as long as he could stand, Henry was kicking ass, hitting the kind of solos only he could do. The fans were turned on and it was wonderful to feel that shower of enthusiasm we got on our best nights.

One evening in a small town in Bordeaux, while he was deep in the red wine that made the place famous, Henry turned to me. "We've gotta come back here more often. They'll always love us here." I was touched.

Unfortunately, the logistics on this trip were very poor. We would drive eight to 10 hours almost every day to get to the next gig. We were all sick with colds and flu, the usual curse of European tours in winter, and the long, chilly drives were making us sicker.

Henry was hit harder than anyone. Although he had trouble breathing, he was the same old Henry. He wouldn't quit smoking. He must have gone through two packs of Marlboros a day, which really made me worry. Then, I remembered that he'd gotten very sick on a tour of Germany two years before and I thought he was going to die, but his amazing constitution pulled him through.

We took the Eurotunnel from France to London and as we were checking into the hotel, Henry reached in his mouth and pulled out a tooth. It sat there, scarlet and white in his shaking palm.

"Don't look at me like that, Fito. They just fall out. I don't know how to stop 'em."

He could barely walk from the elevator to his room. He stopped partway and leaned against the wall to light up a Marlboro. Henry

Henry's arms and new teeth.

wouldn't see a doctor and he refused to go home. But he agreed to take it easier on stage. From then on, instead of performing the entire gig, which usually ran about an hour and a half, he played only four or five numbers. The rest of the time, he sat on the side of the stage, taking a cigarette break and drinking a beer.

By the third gig in England, I finally gave in and agreed to let him sit down while we performed. I had always refused before, telling him that "If you can't stand up on the stage, you have no business being on the stage. You should be home or in a hospital." I really wanted him to return home; I even offered to pay him for the five upcoming gigs, if he'd just go.

"Henry, you're out of gas. Go home. See your doctor and recover. I don't want you to die on the road. I told you that before. Don't die on the road, man."

For Henry, I didn't have to add—like too many guys do in this band.

"No way, Fito, don't do this to me. I want to finish the tour. C'mon man. I belong here."

Against my better judgment, I let him stay.

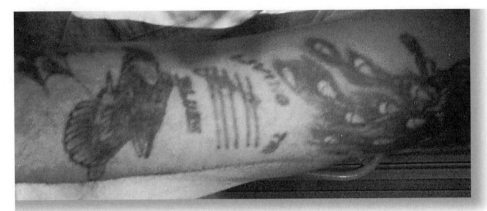

Living The Blues

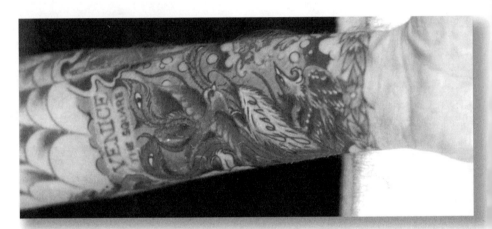

Venice/Jesse

Rebel

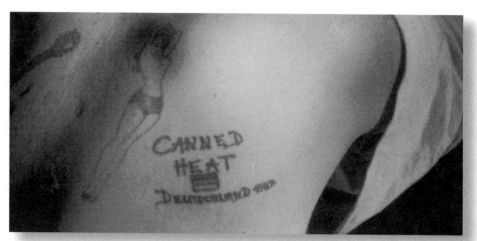

C.H. Deutschland 1982

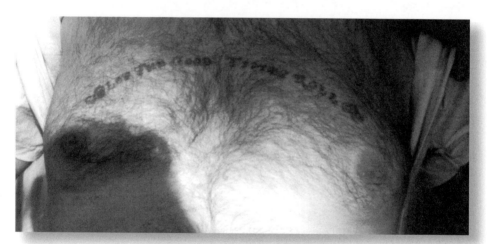

Let the good times roll

C.H. Australia 1985

In London, right before our performance at Shepherd's Bush Empire, we were in the dressing room when an old biker buddy offered Henry a line of cocaine: "Hey, Henry, want some?"

"No thanks, man. I ain't got the energy for that."

It was the first time in 30 years I'd heard Henry refuse a hit of any kind of drug whatsoever. Once that would have made me feel really hopeful. Under the circumstances, it worried me even more.

Henry went on stage that night and played one of the most brilliant performances of his career. The spark of genius that he searched for so diligently all his life, the inspiration that he prayed for at the altar of excess, came to him in full strength. We were all tired and sick but Henry set us on fire. We played a blistering set, as good or better than anything the band did in the old days. We had the fans in ecstasy.

We stumbled back into the dressing room, sweaty and exhausted but feeling fulfilled. "I've seen you guys play a lot of times, but this was the best I've ever seen Henry," said Paul Meredith our English tour manager.

"Yeah," I said quietly, looking at Henry sitting slumped in a corner, gasping for breath. "Like a nova."

"What?"

"A nova. A star that shines its brightest just before it explodes and vanishes."

I hope those who were there treasure the memory of Henry's playing that night. It was indeed his nova performance.

The following gigs were a true Calvary. We were all sick and exhausted, and Henry rarely played for more than a few minutes at a time. Morale was at its lowest. It was clear that despite the European success of the CD, the band would have one of its worst financial years ever. Lucas and Watson were in perpetual revolt.

We played the last three gigs in Belgium to full houses of adoring fans, but we were only going through the motions, hardly speaking to each other, just hoping that the goddamn tour would end. Our last performance was Saturday, October 18th at a lovely farmhouse turned into a blues club in the town of Gouvy close to Bastogne, site of a famous World War II battle. After the show, I said good-bye to everybody and shook Henry's hand.

"Take care, Henry. I really hope you get well. Please do all you can to recover and have a safe trip home."

"Thanks, Fito, you take care."

That night, I drove to Overijse to stay in a hotel close to Dr. Boogie, because he was doing a special on me and the band on his weekly radio show the next day.

The rest of the band was to leave the following morning for Paris to catch a plane home, but they overslept, missed the plane and had to get rooms at a hotel near the airport for a flight the following day. Ignoring the pleas of the other band members, Henry still refused to go to a hospital.

That Monday, October 20th at 9 A.M., Rick Young, the road manager, called everybody so they wouldn't oversleep. Henry asked for 10 minutes more. Down in the lobby, everyone waited. Twenty minutes passed.

"Hey, Rick, call Henry and see if he needs any help, so we can get the hell outta here," yelled Watson.

The phone rang. No answer. They looked at each other apprehensively. A chambermaid let Rick into the room. Henry was sitting on the edge of the bed, slumped forward, dead. When they eased his body back and laid him down, a puff of smoke floated out of his mouth.

The band headed home, leaving the body with the Paris police and ambulance crew. On their stopover at Heathrow airport near London, Rick called Dr. Boogie, because he knew where to find me. When Walter arrived at my hotel to tell me the bad news, I was chatting with Sherry Mossman, a Florida-based blues journalist who met up with us in Brussels. Poor Sherry. She thought she was going to be writing about a party-filled band tour. Instead, she wound up in the middle of another Canned Heat tragedy.

The next morning the three of us drove to Paris and located the funeral home where I was to officially identify Henry for the French authorities. Henry's body was stiff and cold on the slab, his eyes and mouth open. He was wearing a T-shirt from a biker festival in Paris. He insisted on coming on the tour, it turned out, with severe asthma, emphysema, cirrhosis of the liver and—unknown to us—lung cancer.

Walter, Sherry and I held each other and cried. I reached over and kissed Henry's forehead. A couple of my tears glistened on his face.

"Good-bye, my brother, I shall miss you."

I was half thinking of grabbing him by the shoulders, shaking him and screaming: "I told you not to die on the road, motherfucker. I told you so many times not to do this."

But I looked at Walter and Sherry. This was hard enough on them without me blowing my cool.

I looked out into the Paris street, at the passing traffic, and again at Henry's body. I thought back 26 years to Alan, so alone, so desperate, embracing death under the Topanga sky at the peak of our popularity. Alan, forever young in our minds, spared the long slide downhill that he wouldn't have minded at all.

I thought of Bear, stumbling into the van for his last ride, dying by his own foolishness in confused misery because he wasn't a star any more. Never to know that we were going to bounce back a bit, that some fans would never have left him, that he could have been the boogie king to the grandchildren of the Woodstock generation.

Henry was one up on them. Henry too, had been one of the founding fathers of Canned Heat. He too, helped set the tone for the band in its wild youth and its stubborn middle age. For all his self-destructive life, he never sought out death. He never wanted to die. He wanted more out of life, not less. He wanted intensity, but he wanted it on his terms, and he got it; 26 more years of it than Alan, 16 more years than Bear.

Henry was born to play with Canned Heat.

As were we all.

All the real life Blues Brothers.

A few days after I got back to Los Angeles, I organized a simple ceremony at Hinanos, one of Henry's favorite bars on Washington Avenue in Venice. I gathered some of his best friends in LA, current and former band members, bikers, and just plain buddies, and we all drank a beer and smoked a Marlboro in his memory.

When his ashes arrived from Paris, a major service was held in his hometown of Eugene, Oregon, where he's at peace. A trust fund was set up to collect money so that someday, when space travel is more accessible, his ashes can be scattered over the Vestine crater on the dark side of the moon, as he requested in his will.

Alan forever in the forests, the Bear blended forever into the Pacific Ocean and Henry on the moon. We should have put that in a song.

Although his death was very painful, it should have brought together the remaining members of Canned Heat, solidifying our determination to go on, to bring out the new CD and keep alive the legacy of this great, indestructible band. Henry leaving us had been a feature of life in Canned Heat since the Fillmore in the '60s. Even when he was in the band in the last few years, his health was so bad that we often played without him. Just because he wasn't coming back was no reason for the band not to go on.

If this was a Hollywood movie, that's what would have happened. The CD would be a big hit and I'd be there in the final scene, drumming like a madman while the crowd cheers. But Canned Heat has never been a Hollywood kind of story. Henry's death aggravated and accelerated the rancor within the band and a lot of it was focused on me.

I returned to my house on the central California coast to find a pile of letters and faxes from Europe, Australia and the States. They were all trying to book Canned Heat. We even had some offers from a couple of new places—I suppose they didn't realize Canned Heat was still around until Henry's obit got such big play in The Independent in the UK, and The New York Times and People magazine in the US. I sat down at my computer terminal and sent them all the same reply: "Thanks, but I'm not sure there is a Canned Heat any more." Then I dumped all the requests in a cardboard box and stuck it in the garage.

I starting thinking, maybe, finally, it was time to just pack it in. Alan dead. Bear dead. Henry dead. No record contract. No big hits. No money from the hits we did have. Night after night on the road, a lifetime jammed into vans, watching the highway roll under the tires in the dark, sleeping sitting up in planes and buses. Friends becoming enemies, friends falling apart, friends dying on the road. Reaching deep to give the blues the intensity of youth when youth has been burned away.

I hung around the house for a couple weeks, discouraged, trying to think of what I could do with my life now. More letters and faxes came in, trying to book the band. I dumped them with the others in the garage. I had never been so low.

After several days of high winds and winter rain, the sky cleared one morning. It was cool but bright when I got up at dawn. On a whim, I cranked up my latest BMW motorcycle, an R100R, the one

343

Henry 1994 in Australia. Photo Wolfgang Gonaus

the company made as a last gift for those of us who love the classic old German bikes before phasing out that engine. I took off down the coast and over the mountains. I figured I'd ride for an hour, maybe two. Just cruising around the mountains.

There's a road that winds over the Coast Range and far off into the empty plains to the east. It goes from a series of tight, kinked switchbacks into a long stretch of sweeping, high speed curves, mile after mile. Then there are long, arrow-straight stretches through a desert basin and then back into the mountains, winding upwards through the pine forest, followed by a long descent into sprawling LA, hundreds of miles south. As the morning went on, I just kept going, no plan, no goal, but drawn somehow south. I've ridden that road scores of times, sometimes on the way to LA and sometimes just for the hell of it on a long loop from my house and back. I know just about every curve now and I work at taking them a little more smoothly each time, going just a little faster, trying for just a little more

Henry's last performance in Gouvy, Belgium, Oct. 1997

control. It's an exercise you never do perfectly, just better or worse, a competition with yourself and the road.

That day, I was in some sort of groove. I swooped, I flew, I nailed the apexes, the engine note rose and fell seamlessly on the shifts. I was hitting well over 100 on the straights. It just felt so good to be alive and to be doing this thing I love. Doing it well.

By afternoon, I was into the northern edge of LA. I knew where I was going now. I pulled off the Simi Valley Freeway, and worked my way through the San Fernando Valley traffic into the still semi-rural curves of Topanga Canyon. Suddenly, I knew where I was headed. I'd soon be passing Bear's old house, the slope where Alan died, the vacant lot on a curve where The Topanga Corral once stood, where I first heard Canned Heat on that night in 1967 and where we built our sound in the hippie days.

I cruised slowly along with the rush hour traffic in the winding canyon. I suppose some would say I should have stopped at those places, paid a little respect to the Old Days, but I didn't. I've been there many times and probably will be again. I rode on past, with just a glance.

The Bear's house has been remodeled, with strangely curved outer walls, looking nothing at all like it did back then. The Corral's location is just a messy vacant lot on a sharp curve. Somebody has some heavy machinery stored there. I went on until I hit the beach and could go no farther.

I watched the sun go down on the Pacific Ocean and it occurred to me that this had been a perfect day. And it does not have to end here. I can go back and do it again.

I turned the bike around and headed north, knowing the mountains would be cold in the dark and it would be after midnight by the time I got home, hundreds of miles away. But I felt good, really good.

And as I went back past the Bear's old place, I thought: This was worth doing, just to get it right, just this once. And the band is like that too. The blues life can be heartbreaking, the money a dribble, the strain on our bodies enough to kill us. But there are high points like Henry's last good gig in London—when we get it right. We nailed the Canned Heat sound as well as we ever did with Alan and The Bear.

Reaching for those moments has been my life. Not always getting there, but trying because when it works, when it all comes together, the experience cannot be matched. Indeed, life can be good.

There are those, even those in the band, who say Canned Heat is dead. I say it isn't. Just as there was one more ride for me today, so there can be one more gig for Canned Heat tomorrow. There will come an end but it isn't here yet.

Maybe I'll have another night on stage as perfect as the ride I just finished. Maybe you'll have a night that perfect listening to us. So long as that hope lasts, we should go on.

As I passed through the canyon, with all its ghosts and memories, I had a sort of special conversation with Alan and Bear in my head:

"Okay guys, it was your band when I met you, and I've thought of it as my band for a long time now. But we've come full circle. It was always our band, ours and a lot of other people's, people who played in it, people who enjoyed it. Each of us had our job and mine was to keep the beat and keep the faith. And that still feels good."

I remembered a dream I've had every now and then, for years now. In the dream, I'm always beside a van, loaded with speakers and amps, helping the roadies unload behind a red-brick theater in some hard and rainy old city. Loping along toward us is The Bear, grinning and jiving. The Bear is back. It gives me a warm feeling.

The last time I had that dream, Henry was there too,

Henry at the Theaterfabrite, Munich Germany, 1987. Photo: Andreas Ruoff

autographing an album for a sweet young thing as he really did shortly before he died. I look over his shoulder at what he's writing: "I want to come on your tits."

I actually laughed in my helmet as I rode north, leaving the canyon behind me.

The 1998 line-up. L-R Greg Kage, Robert Lucas, Me, Larry Taylor

EPILOGUE

Larry Taylor returned to Canned Heat to replace Henry Vestine on lead guitar and Skip Taylor signed on again as manager and producer.

Under a new four-album deal in 1999 with Ruf Records, headed by German blues enthusiast Thomas Ruf, the band released "Boogie 2000," which reached the Top 20 on the charts in England. A double CD collection of vintage works, "The Boogie House Tapes," from the archives of arch-fan "Dr. Boogie," was readied for release in 2000.

Said *Blues On Stage* of the "Boogie 2000" CD: "Canned Heat remains as relevant to the blues today as they were thirty-something years ago... There's something indefinably wonderful about the guitar sound." The *Blues Connection* called the grouping "one of their strongest lineups ever." The *Chicago Music Hub* said: "Canned Heat is energized and playing boogie like there's no tomorrow."

In 1999, the band made five European tours and played close to 200 gigs, including a New Year's Eve appearance at the official Los Angeles City Millennium Celebration.

It was not time for the music to die.

At the Graz Orpheum , Austria 1996 Photo: Wolfgang Gonaus

At the Metropol, Vienna Austria 1994. Photo Wolfgang Gonaus

Fito in the 90's

Germany 1996. Photo Gunther Hille

351

France, 1997

Photo: Gérard Mayeur

At Rosarito Mexico, 1998 Photo: Kathleen McCann

CANNED HEAT DISCOGRAPHY

Albums listed in chronological order
as they were recorded

TITLE-RECORD CO.	BAND MEMBERS	RECORDING INFORMATION
VINTAGE CANNED HEAT JANUS JLS 3009	Bob Hite-vocals Alan Wilson- vocals/harmonica/slide guitar Henry Vistine-lead guitar Stuart Brotman-electric bass Drums-unknown	Produced by Johnny Otis Recorded in 1966 at El Dorado Studios, in Los Angeles, CA These recordings were released after the success with the Boogie Album and they have also been the main source of material for many pirate releases.***
CANNED HEAT LIBERTY LST-7526	Bob Hite-vocals Henry Vistine-lead guitar Larry Taylor-electric bass Frank Cook-drums Alan Wilson- vocals/harmonica/slide guitar	Produced by Cal Carter Recorded in 1967 in Los Angeles, CA at Liberty Studios I was introduced to Canned Heat with this record. I love it -****
BOOGIE WITH CANNED HEAT LIBERTY LST-7541	Bob Hite-vocals Alan Wilson- vocals/harmonica/slide guitar Henry Vistine-lead guitar Larry Taylor-electric bass Fito de la Parra-drums	Produced by Dallas Smith Engineered by Dino Lappas Recorded in the beginning of 1968 at Liberty Studios Horn arrangements and piano by Dr. John Creaux This is the all-time classic and the one that made the band world-wide famous.*****
LIVING THE BLUES LIBERTY LST-27200	same as Boogie With Canned Heat the "classic" line up	Produced by Canned Heat and Skip Taylor Engineered by Richard Moore with assistance from Ivan Fisher Sides 1 & 2 recorded at I.D. Sound Recorders, in Hollywood, CA Sides 3 & 4 recorded at The Kaleidscope, in Hollywood, CA Horn arrangements and piano on Boogie Music by Dr. John Horn arrangements on Sandy's Blues by Miles Grayson Piano on Sandy's Blues by Joe Sample Another classic recorded in 1969.*****
LIVE AT TOPANGA CORRAL WAND WDS 693	same as Boogie with Canned Heat	Produced by Skip Taylor and Canned Heat This record was actually made at the Kaleidoscope in 1969 since we were under contract with Liberty,Skip decided to sell the project to Scepter/Wand records telling them it was done at the Topanga Corral in ' 66 and ' 67 to avoid legal problems This one has also been a source for countless pirated releases and the band never received any money for this LP or CD.****
HALLELUJAH LIBERTY LST-7618	same as Boogie with Canned Heat	Produced by Skip Taylor and Canned Heat Engineered by Richard Moore Recorded at I.D. Sound Recorders, Hollywood, CA in May 1969 Another classic that also features Ernest Lane and Mark Naftalin

TITLE-RECORD CO.	BAND MEMBERS	RECORDING INFORMATION
		on piano, Elliot Ingber, and Javier Batiz on background vocals, and Mike Pacheco on bongos. Another favorite of mine, some consider it the most sophisticated album we made with several odd measure tunes.*****
CANNED HEAT COOKBOOK LIBERTY LN-10106	same as Boogie with Canned Heat	Released in 1970. It is a compilation of some of the most popular tunes recorded in the three first albums for Liberty. Also available on CD. Now a worldwide favorite.*****
FUTURE BLUES LIBERTY LST-11002	same as Boogie with Canned Heat except Henry Vestine, who was replaced by Harvey Mandel in August 1969	Produced by Skip Taylor and Canned Heat Engineered by Tommy Oliver Recorded early 1970 at Village Recorders in Los Angeles, CA Piano and horn arrangements by Dr. John Another classic with a heavy environmental message that included the american flag upside down on the cover and a write up by Alan Wilson about the destruction of the forest entitled "Grim Harvest". This LP was banned by several outlets because of it's subversive nature, now it is a very desirable collectors item that includes the hit "Let's Work Together".*****
CANNED HEAT '70 CONCERT LIVE IN EUROPE LIBERTY LBS-83333	same as Future Blues	Produced by Skip Taylor and Canned Heat Recorded in April 1970 mostly at the Albert Hall and other English halls. An unplanned release that in the beginning we were skeptical about, but it became popular anyway.****
HOOKER AND HEAT LIBERTY LST-35002	John Lee Hooker-guitar/vocals Alan Wilson harmonica/ piano/guitar Henry Vestine-lead guitar Fito de la Parra-drums Tony de la Barreda-electric bass	Produced by Skip Taylor and Bob Hite Engineered by Dino Lapis Recorded in May 1970 at Liberty Studios, Los Angeles, CA Mixed in London, England in September 1970 Our first project with John Lee, it was a memorable session that resulted in this timeless classic, also available on CD.*****
HISTORICAL FIGURES AND ANCIENT HEADS UNITED ARTISTS UAS-5557	Bob Hite-vocals Henry Vestine-lead guitar Fito de la Parra-drums/piano Tony de la Barreda-electric bass Joel Scott Hill-guitar/vocals	Produced by Skip Taylor and Jim Taylor Recorded at Village Recorder, Los Angeles, CA in 1971 Featuring Little Richard on piano and vocals, Clifford Solomon on saxophone, Charles Lloyd on flute and, Harvey Mandel on guitar.Our first without Alan in an attempt to keep our popular status and still rock on. High energy!****
MEMPHIS HEAT BLUE STAR (France) 80607	Memphis Slim-piano/vocals same as Historical Figures same as New Age	Produced by Philippe Rault Recorded in Paris in the summer of 1973 and 1974 in two different sessions. Also featuring The Memphis Horns.****

TITLE-RECORD CO.	BAND MEMBERS	RECORDING INFORMATION
GATE'S ON THE HEAT BLUE STAR 80603	Clarence Gatemouth Brownguitar/fiddle and vocals same as Historical Figures	Produced by Philippe Rault Recorded in Paris at the same time as the Memphis Slim sessions This record features Canned Heat and other unknown french musicians invited by Mr. Rault to complete the project we didn't finish.***
THE NEW AGE UNITED ARTISTS UA-LA 049	Bob Hite-vocals Henry Vestine-lead guitar Fito de la Parra-drums Richard Hite-bass James Shane-guitar Ed Bayer-piano	Produced by Skip Taylor Engineered by John Stronach Recorded at The Record Plant, Los Angeles, CA 1972 dedicated to the memory of Clara ward, it features her on "Looking for my Rainbow", her last recording.***
ONE MORE RIVER TO CROSS ATLANTIC HATS-421132	same as The New Age	Produced by Barry Beckett and Roger Hawkins Engineered by Jerry Masters and Steve Melton Recorded in 1973 at Muscle Shoals Sound, Muscle Shoals, AL Featuring the Muscle Shoals Horn ensemble, and Roger and Barry on some tunes. It was a lot of fun to do these sessions and learn from these great producers. But the tide was already against us with the disco music trend.****
THE TIES THAT BIND-CD ARCHIVE ACH-80002	tracks 1-10 same as The New Age track 11 Harvey Mandel on guitar tracks 12-14 add Tony de la Barreda on bass and Alan Wilson-guitar/harmonica	Produced by Tom Dowd and Fito de la Parra This CD is a compilation of three different sessions Tracks 1-10 done at Criteria Studios in Miami, FL during 1974 Track 11 Dirk Dalton Studios, Santa Monica, CA during 1977 Tracks 12-14 recorded by Fito de la Parra on a two track machine during rehearsal at The Veterans Hall, Hollywood,CA 1970.**** Released on CD in 1997.
CANNED HEAT HUMAN CONDITION TAKOMA TAK 7066	Bob Hite-vocals/harmonica Fito de la Parra-drums Richard Hite-bass Chris Morgan-guitar Mark Skyer-guitar/vocals	Produced by Canned Heat Recorded in 1977 at Takoma Studios, in Los Angeles, CA Featuring the Chambers Brothers, done in times of extreme adversity due to the popularity of disco music but the Heat is still hanging on!****
HOOKER N' HEAT LIVE AT THE FOX VENICE RHINO RECORDS RNLP-801	John Lee Hooker-guitar/vocals Bob Hite-vocals/harmonica Fito de la Parra-drums Richard Hite-bass Chris Morgan-guitar Mark Skyer-guitar/ vocals	Produced by Howard Wolf and Canned Heat Engineered by Gary Stauffer Recorded in 1978 live at the Fox Venice Theatre, Venice, CA Featuring Ronnie Barron on the piano and, the Chambers Brothers on vocals. Again boogie'n with the Hook on a memorable concert.****

TITLE-RECORD CO.	BAND MEMBERS	RECORDING INFORMATION
CANNED HEAT IN CONCERT CD KING BISCUIT 70710-88005-2	Bob Hite-vocals/harmonica Fito de la Parra-drums Larry Taylor-bass Hollywood Fats-lead guitar Jay Spell-piano/vocals	Produced by Fito de la Parra Recorded live in September of 1979at Brookhaven Long Island, NY on the tenth anniversary of Woodstock. Great recording, in my opinion this is the best live Canned Heat ever.***** available now on CD
KINGS OF THE BOOGIE DESTINY RECORDS DLA-1007	Bob Hite-vocals/harmonica Henry Vestine-lead guitar Fito de la Parra-drums Micheal Halby-guitar/vocals Rick Kellog-harp/vocals Ernie Rodriguez-bass/vocals	Produced and engineered by Jerry Barnes Recorded in 1981 at United Western Studios, Hollywood, CA this was Bob's last recording and some of the tracks are sung by Rick Kellog and Micheal Halby.****
IN MEMORY OF BOB "THE BEAR HITE" 1943- 1981 "DON'T FORGET TO BOOGIE RCA (Mexico) MILS-4529	Bob Hite-vocals Fito de la Parra-drums Larry Taylor-bass Henry Vestine-guitar Jay Spell-keyboards/vocal Hollywood Fats-guitar Mike Halby-guitar/vocals	Produced by Bob Tood Recorded in 1980 originally for Cream records but never released until Tony de la Barreda who was working for RCA-Mexico decided to release it after Bob's death in 1981.****
THE BOOGIE ASSAULT AIM 1003	Fito de la Parra-drums Mike Halby-guitar/vocals Ricky Kellogg-harmonica/vocals Ernie Rodriguez-bass/vocals Walter Trout-lead guitar/vocals	Produced by Peter Noble Recorded live in Australia during 1982 This was supposed to be a release for Australia and New Zealand only. But Mr. Noble licensed the record worldwide violating our agreement and causing all kinds of problems that culminated in a lawsuit I started against him. It is an unauthorized release and one of my least favorite Canned Heat.**
THE HEAT BROTHERS "84 ALA S1996	same as Boogie Assault with the exception of Rick Kellogg	Produced by Fito de la Parra and Mike Halby Engineered by Jimmy Mayweather Recorded in 1984 at Bijou Studios in Hollywood, CA Good rocking EP with four songs.****
BOOGIE UP THE COUNTRY inak 8804 CD	Fito de la Parra-drums Henry Vestine-lead guitar Larry Taylor-bass/vocals James T-guitar/vocals/harmonica	Produced Bernhard Roessle Engineered by Peter Heuberger Recorded live in Kassel, Germany October 1987 Nice live record introducing James T and, with Henry and Larry together again after 17 years.****
2.BLUES FESTIVAL LIVE IN BONN HALF MOON RECORDS-CD 8851	same as Boogie Up The Country	Recorded live at the Biskuithalle September 27, 1987 The recording engineer Gerd Rautenbach Together with british bands Dr. Feelgood, Stan Webb's Chicken Shack and Man. Fun concert. Available on LP or CD.****
REHEATED AVAILABLE THRU OUR WEBSITE www.cannedheatmusic.com VARESE VINTAGE 3020661092	Fito de la Parra-drums Larry Taylor-bass James Thornburyharmonica/guitar/ vocals Junior Watson-lead guitar	Produced by Fito de la Parra and Larry Taylor Engineered by Marvin "The Blade"McNeil Recorded at Lyon Studios in Newport Beach, CA in July 1988 With a completely new line-up and new outlook on the band's direction we produced this blues album that is now considered a classic. Available on LP or CD.****
THE HEALER CHAMELEON/SILVERTONE D1-74808	John Lee Hooker-guitar/vocals Fito de la Parra-drums Larry Taylor-bass Henry Vestine-lead guitar	Produced by Roy Rogers Engineered by Sam Lehmer Recorded at Russian Hills Studio in San Franscisco CA, in 1989 John's most popular album, featuring many other artists. More details about this session on the "Hooker n Heat" chapter

357

TITLE-RECORD CO.	BAND MEMBERS	RECORDING INFORMATION
CANNED HEAT BURNIN' AVAILABLE THRU OUR WEBSITE www.cannedheatmusic.com GERMANY SPV084-08572	same as Reheated	Produced by Fito de la Parra Engineered by Keith Walker Recorded live in Australia during April 1990 Available on LP or CD.****
INTERNAL COMBUSTION AVAILABLE THRU OUR WEBSITE www.cannedheatmusic.com	Fito de la Parra-drums/vocals James Thornburyharmonica/guitar/ vocals Henry Vestine-lead guitar tracks 2 & 3 Larry Taylor-bass tracks 6, 7, 8, 9, & 11 Harvey Mandel-lead guitar tracks 5, 6, 7, 8, 9, and 11 Junior Watson-guitar on tracks 1, 2, 4,10 Ron Shumake-upright bass on tracks 1, 10 electric bass on tracks 2, 3, & 4 Ronnie Barron-piano on tracks 1 & 2 Ira Ingber-guitar on tracks 3, 4, 5, 6, 7, 8, 9 & 11	Produced by Fito de la Parra and Ira Ingber Engineered by Marvin "The Blade" McNeil Recorded at Studio 56, Hollywood, CA 1991 & 1992 This CD is a celebration of 25 years of survival with all the living members of Canned Heat and other fellow musicians.*****
UNCANNED!-THE BEST OF CANNED HEAT EMI CD 7243 8 29165 2 9	same as Canned Heat (first album) and Boogie with Canned Heat	Produced by Canned Heat Executive Producer-Bruce Harris EMI This is a compilation of some previously unreleased tracks, some single 45 releases and a combination of other songs from our first 4 albums. Available as a double CD.*****
CANNED HEAT BLUES BAND AVAILABLE THRU OUR WEBSITE www.cannedheatmusic.com RUF RECORDS GmbH worldwide	Fito de la Parra-drums Henry Vestine-lead guitar Larry Taylor-acoustic bass Robert Lucas- vocals/guitar/harmonica Junior Watson-lead guitar Gregg Kage-electric bass	Produced by Fito de la Parra Co-Producer-Robert Lucas Engineered by Paul Dugre Recorded at Paul and Mike's Recording Studio in Burbank, CA October/November of 1996. Our latest with a very strong line-up and Henry's last appearance. Available on CD.*****
GAMBLIN' WOMAN MAUSOLEUM CLASSIX BMG 71278-60026-2	same as Reheated & Internal Combustion	Produced by Fito de la Parra/Ira Ingber/Larry Taylor Compilation of material from Internal Combustion & Reheated.*****

Released as single 45's not included in LP's

CHIPMUNK SONG/CHRISTMAS BLUES LIBERTY 56079	same as Boogie with Canned Heat	Produced by Skip Taylor and Canned Heat in 1969 Great idea to join with the Chipmunks and boogie, Fito plays piano on Christmas Blues. An all time classic.*****
LOW DOWN/TIME WAS LIBERTY 9046B	same as Boogie with Canned Heat	Produced by Skip Taylor and Canned Heat in 1969 Time was same as Hallelujah side A—side B utilizing same rhythm track of Chipmunk song adding stinging lead guitar and lyrics.*****
WOOLY BULLY/MY TIME AINT LONG LIBERTY 56217	same as Historical Figures (side A) same as Future Blues (side B)	Produced by Skip Taylor and Canned Heat in 1970/71 Side A a funny idea to do that famous song and maybe get a hit. Side B same as Hallelujah.
POOR MOON/SIC 'EM PIGS LIBERTY 56127	same as Hallelujah	Produced by Skip Taylor in 1970 Alan moaning about the idea of dumping earth's waste on the moon. Side B same as Hallelujah

TITLE-RECORD CO.	BAND MEMBERS	RECORDING INFORMATION
THE HARDER THEY COME/SIDE B ? ATLANTIC	same as One More River to Cross	Produced by Skip Taylor in 1973 We went to see Jimmy Cliff's movie together and fell in love with the song theme, so we decided to record it. Very rare.

The following is a list of bootleg/pirate releases that I include in this discography for a historical perspectiveonly. I ask the general public not to buy them since they have only harmed Canned Heat's career.

THE OWL UNDER THE MOON-CD	same as Boogie with Canned Heat Historical Figures and Ancient Heads and Canned Heat	Different sessions from Monterey Pop Festival to 1971
LIVE AT TURKU ROCK FESTIVAL	same as Historical Figures and Ancient Heads	Recorded live at the Turku Festival in Finland in August 1971. This is an unauthorized release of a tape sold by Richard Hite to Bear Tracks. Discontinued after I contacted the label.
CANNED HEAT LIVE AT THE TEXAS INTERNATIONAL POP FESTIVAL	same as Future Blues	Recorded live in 1969, 2 weeks after Woodstock
HOT BOOGIE CANNERY-CD	same as The New Age	Live from Montreux, Switzerland 1974
JAMMIN' WITH KALEIDOSCOPE	same as Boogie with Canned Heat	Recorded at the Boston Tea Party in 1969
REAL FUTURE BLUES-LP	same as Hooker and Heat, but without John Lee Hooker and add vocals by Bob	Recorded live at Kickapoo Creek Festival during July 1970
LET'S WORK TOGETHER-LP	same as Boogie with Canned Heat and Vintage Canned Heat	Recorded live at Montreux in 1970
ONE STEP BEHIND THE BLUES		
STRAIGHT AHEAD		
THE GREAT CANNED HEAT ROLLING AND TUMBLING THE MAGIC COLLECTION DUST MY BROOM ON THE ROAD AGAIN BIG ROAD BLUES ROLLIN' GUITAR		These unauthorized releases have been flooding the market for some time now. They all have basically the same songs, taken from Vintage Canned Heat LP and Live at Topanga Corral LP. The band never received any money or communication from the record companies that produced these bootlegs.

1999/2000 Releases

BOOGIE 2000 RUF RECORDS RUF 1041	Fito de la Parra-drums Larry Taylor-rhythm/lead guitar Robert Lucas-Vocals/harmonica/ slide guitar Gregg Kage-Bass/vocals	Produced by Skip Taylor & Fito de la Parra Recorded April/May 1999 at Rock's Cool Records Van Nuys, CA Engineered by Willie Basse With guests Javier Batiz, Cannibal & The Headhunters, Michael Finnigan, Rob Rio, and Dave Woodford End of Millennium CD-Boogie on!*****
THE BOOGIE HOUSE TAPES RUF RECORDS RUF GmbH	1967-1976 various line-ups from the band during those times, specifics on CD	Produced by Fito de la Parra/Walter De Paduwa Vintage collection assembled & remastered from Dr. Boogie's & Fito's tape collections. Double CD to be released in 2000. Mastered at Digital Sound Lab. Zedelgem, Belgium

www.cannedheatmusic.com

INDEX

Fito's co-authors, Terry and Marlane McGarry, shown here attending a dinner at the Imperial War Museum in London. They've been Fito's motorcycling companions since his youth in Mexico City, where Marlane was a rock music writer for the Mexico City Daily News and Terry was a correspondent for an American wire service. At an encounter at Wolf's, a grungy biker hangout deep in the forest (the one with the dollar bills on the walls and the shooting range out back), Marlane said, "Fito, you should write your autobiography." "I'd really like to. I'd love to tell the real CANNED HEAT story, but I can't do it alone, I'll need help." After a handshake, continuing encouragement and four years of hard work, Fito's stories and pictures have become a book.

Steve LaVere — Photographer

Most of the early photographs in *Living The Blues* are by the renowned blues historian Stephen C. LaVere. Steve LaVere took more photographs of Canned Heat than anybody during their early years. Steve met Alan Wilson at the 1964 Newport Folk Festival when Alan was accompanist to Son House. He met Bob Hite in 1965 at the Jazz Man Record Shop in Los Angeles when both attended, and occasionally participated in, the Saturday afternoon jam sessions. That was a year before "Canned Heat" was even a gleam in anybody's eye. When the band made its first major appearance at the Monterey International Pop Festival in the Summer of 1967, LaVere borrowed a camera and photographed their performance. It was the beginning of Steve's professional photography career and he continued to photograph Canned Heat whenever he could. Steve took the first pictures of Fito as a member of the band, as well as the widely published shot of the band on motorcycles which was used to promote the band's first hit single, "On The Road Again." One of his last assignments was to collect all the band's baby pictures and set up the shoot for the Canned Heat family portraits, one of which appeared as the inside spread of the album "Canned Heat Cookbook." Many of Steve's pictures remain unpublished, but we thank him for sharing his art with us and allowing us to use a portion of his wonderful work within these pages.

CANNED HEAT
MERCHANDISE ORDER FORM

NAME:

ADDRESS:

CITY, STATE & ZIP:

ITEM:	QUANTITY:	AMOUNT:
"LIVING THE BLUES" BOOK, $19.95 each		
"BOOGIE 2000" CD, $9.95		
"CANNED HEAT BLUES BAND" CD, $9.95		
"INTERNAL COMBUSTION" CD, $9.95		
"CANNED HEAT IN CONCERT" CD, $12.95		
"REHEATED" CD, $9.95		
"BOOGIE HOUSE TAPES" DOUBLE CD, $12.95		
CANNED HEAT T-SHIRT, MED. $19.95		
T-SHIRT, LRG. $19.95		
T-SHIRT, X-LRG. $19.95		
	TAX:	
	SHIPPING:	
	TOTAL:	

SALES TAX: California Residents please add 8.25% Sales Tax to total purchase price

SHIPPING &
HANDLING:
For Cd's, Tapes & T-Shirts add:
U.S.A/Mexico/Canada—$3.50 (Two Units, $4.50)
Europe—$5.50 (Two Units, $10.00)
Australia—$6.00 (Two Units, $8.00)

For "Living The Blues" Book add:
U.S.A—$5.00
Mexico & Canada—$7.00
Europe—$12.00
Australia—$15.00

CHECKS &
MONEY ORDERS: Please send Order Form with Payment to:

CANNED HEAT
P.O. BOX 52
NIPOMO, CA 93444
U.S.A.

CREDIT CARDS: Please see our Website (www.cannedheatmusic.com)

THANK YOU FOR YOUR ORDER!
DON'T FORGET TO BOOGIE!